# A NEW LOOK AT FIELD INSTRUCTION

## PUBLICATIONS OF THE COMMUNITY ORGANIZATION CURRICULUM DEVELOPMENT PROJECT

*Community Organization Curriculum in Graduate Social Work Education: Report and Recommendations,* Arnold Gurin, published by CSWE. 1970.

*Community Organization and Social Planning,* Arnold Gurin and Robert Perlman, co-published by CSWE and John Wiley & Sons, Inc. 1971.

*Community Organizers and Social Planners: A Casebook,* Joan Ecklein and Armand Lauffer, co-published by CSWE and John Wiley & Sons, Inc. 1971.

*A New Look at Field Instruction: Education for Application of Practice Skills in Community Organization and Social Planning,* Jack Rothman and Wyatt Jones, co-published by CSWE and Association Press. 1971.

*Students in Schools of Social Work: A Study of Characteristics and Factors Affecting Career Choice and Practice Concentration,* Deborah Golden, Arnulf Pins, and Wyatt Jones, published by CSWE. 1970.

# A NEW LOOK AT
# FIELD INSTRUCTION

*EDUCATION FOR APPLICATION*

*OF PRACTICE SKILLS*

*IN COMMUNITY ORGANIZATION*

*AND SOCIAL PLANNING*

## Jack Rothman and Wyatt C. Jones

**ASSOCIATION PRESS**

*published in cooperation with*
Council on Social Work Education
NEW YORK

DEDICATED TO OUR STUDENTS
. . . and to *their* students

A NEW LOOK AT FIELD INSTRUCTION

361.8
R846n

# Contents

26241

# Contents

# Foreword

This book, along with several other publications, is the product of a three-year comprehensive study of the community organization curriculum in graduate social work education sponsored by the Council on Social Work Education (CSWE).

This volume, entitled *A New Look at Field Instruction,* includes an overview of the historical antecedents of field instruction and, from data compiled from many sources, a picture of the patterns of field instruction now existing and presently emerging at many schools of social work offering concentrations in community organization. Field instruction, in this volume, is seen in a broad perspective as "professional application"—a view which provides a new base for class and field activities, and which encourages new developments within the social work curriculum. Various suggestions for new patterns and methods for field teaching are provided. The authors have also included much new and useful information on simulation games and programmed instruction.

Other publications resulting from the project include a report, *Community Organization Curriculum in Graduate Social Work Education: Report and Recommendations,* by Arnold Gurin; a textbook, *Community Organization and Social Planning,* by Arnold Gurin and Robert Perlman (co-published by CSWE and John Wiley and Sons); *Community Organizers and Social Planners: A Casebook,* by Joan Ecklein and Armand Lauffer (co-published by CSWE and John Wiley and Sons); and *Students in Schools of Social Work: A Study of Characteristics and Factors Affecting Career Choice and Practice Concentration,* by Deborah Golden, Arnulf M. Pins, and Wyatt C. Jones (published by CSWE).

Publication of the findings of the community organization curriculum development project occurs at a significant time. Major

social problems facing our nation underscore the critical need for
personnel with competence in community organization and social
planning. The changes in the curriculum in schools of social work
and other institutions of higher education at this time and in the
foreseeable future are greater than ever before.

The findings, recommendations, and new resources provided by
the Community Organization Curriculum Development Project and
this volume on application of practice skills should be of value to
faculty, students and practitioners of social work and other disciplines.

The Council on Social Work Education and the field of community organization and social planning owe a debt of gratitude to
Jack Rothman and Wyatt Jones for preparing this valuable and
important document, to Arnold Gurin for his able and creative
leadership of the total community-organization curriculum development project, and to the rest of the project staff and to the advisory committee for their many contributions.

Our thanks go also to the Office of Juvenile Delinquency and
Youth Development, Social and Rehabilitation Service of the U. S.
Department of Health, Education, and Welfare, whose grant made
possible this project, and to the J. Aron Charitable Foundation,
Inc., whose grant assisted in the publication of the monograph.

ARNULF M. PINS
Executive Director
Council on Social Work Education

# Introduction

The Community Organization Curriculum Development Project of the Council on Social Work Education was initiated in June, 1965, with a grant from the Office of Juvenile Delinquency and Youth Development, Department of Health, Education and Welfare. Its purpose was to contribute to the development of a systematic, comprehensive curriculum to prepare social workers to perform professional roles in community organization and social-planning programs. The term "community organization" or the abbreviation "C.O." is used throughout this volume to refer to practice in community settings involving organizing and planning functions.

Three significant developments lent urgency to the Project and set the framework of its study: (1) The growth of governmental programs and grass-roots activity in the 1960's requiring personnel with expertness in urban social problems, community organization, and social planning. The Office of Juvenile Delinquency, as the first of the community-action programs and the precursor of antipoverty programs, was particularly concerned about the inadequacy of existing personnel, both quantitatively and qualitatively. (2) The development of community organization as a method concentration in a growing number of schools of social work, its acceptance as a concentration on a parity with casework and group work in the Curriculum Policy Statement of 1962, and the desire of faculty teaching community organization to improve and strengthen the curriculum. (3) The large growth in the numbers of social-work students who wished to concentrate in community organization and to work in action and planning programs.

The curriculum recommendations prepared by the Project Staff are detailed in its final report entitled "Community Organization Curriculum in Graduate Social Work Education: Report and

Recommendations" and published by the Council on Social Work Education. This volume supplements and expands that report. The other publications of the Project are listed in the Foreword.


A significant part of the overall curriculum proposals consists of "methods" or "practice" courses in community organization and social planning. Experiences provided for students in developing community-organization competency are offered in both classroom situations and field placements. McGlothlin (84) has suggested the generic term "application" to refer to the totality of these learning experiences having to do with the acquisition of operational practice skills. In his usage, professional application includes what social workers have customarily referred to as "field work" but also implies skills exercises, observation of practice, role playing, laboratory experience, simulation games, programmed instruction, and similar activities. "Application," in this sense, is a broader term than "field instruction" and includes the arts, skills, and techniques of practice activity wherever taught and however learned. Its wider scope provides a new conceptual basis for viewing field instruction as well as a new mandate for the coordination of class and field and for the integration of the student's educational experiences. Accordingly, it is hoped that this volume may be useful in resolving some of the problems of field instruction in social work generally and may offer some insights into the still broader question of education for the development of application skills in professional education regardless of discipline.

In arriving at this perspective and keeping it constantly in focus, the Project staff has benefited immeasurably from the insights afforded by three relatively recent volumes dealing comparatively with education for practice among the professions. These are: *Education for the Professions,* The Sixty-First Yearbook of the National Society for the Study of Education (42), and two seminal books by William J. McGlothlin, *Patterns of Professional Education* (83) and *The Professional Schools* (84). These works have informed our general approach and are referred to recurrently. Other works on professions and professional education that have been useful are: Lloyd Blanch, *Education for Professions* (12); Elliot Dunlap Smith, ed., *Education for Professional Responsibility* (130); Kenneth S. Lynn, ed., "The Professions," *Daedalus*

(76), and A. M. Carr-Saunders and P. A. Wilson, *The Professions* (19).

In the preparation of this volume, a variety of sources of information were freely utilized. The Project staff had the benefit of regular consultation with the Advisory Committee of the Curriculum Development Project, and with the professional staff of the Council on Social Work Education, and its committees. In addition, staff obtained considerable information and the basis for informed impressions by means of conversations with a cross section of community-organization faculty and students through a series of visits to schools, projects, and training centers throughout the country. Selected schools of social work furnished the Project with detailed reports on innovative practices being employed or contemplated in their curricula.

A thorough review was made of the published literature on field instruction in social work and on education for application in other professions. The resulting bibliography of items is printed at the end of this volume.

The Project itself made several collections of relevant data. These included a survey of all accredited schools of social work to determine their enrollment, the numbers of students in community-organization sequences, the duration of their concentration, numbers of students in field placements, and the types of agencies used for field instruction. In the spring of 1966 and again in 1967, community-organization students, field instructors, and C.O. sequence chairmen were administered questionnaires designed to collect detailed information on the nature of their field placements and some assessment of the success of their experiences. An independent survey was also conducted of ten professional schools and interdisciplinary programs in several universities in the Boston area to explore, among other subjects, their use of field instruction. In addition, profitable use was made of the suggestions that came from the discussions of several papers presented by the staff at Annual Program Meetings of the Council on Social Work Education and at special meetings at the National Conference on Social Welfare.

From these data, the Project Staff reconstructed the historical antecedents of field instruction and developed a composite picture of the existing and emerging patterns of field instruction employed at a majority of the schools of social work having community-organization sequences. This provided the raw data for assessment and for the design of recommendations.

The Community Organization Curriculum Development Project was under the general direction of Dr. Arnold Gurin and (in 1969) Dr. Robert Perlman, the Heller Graduate School for Advanced Studies in Social Welfare, Brandeis University. Dr. Arnulf M. Pins, Council on Social Work Education, served as associate director. The field instruction project was under the overall direction of Dr. Jack Rothman, School of Social Work, the University of Michigan, who collaborated with Dr. Wyatt C. Jones, the Heller Graduate School, Brandeis University. Dr. Jones took major responsibility for the surveys reported in Chapter 1 and for the editorial composition of the volume. Other staff personnel of the Project and of the Council on Social Work Education and the members of the advisory committee provided advice and ideas throughout the course of the preparation of the manuscript.

# 1  The Current Scene: A Survey

Early in its history, the Project recognized the need to identify the principal issues in the professional education of social workers preparing for careers in community organization. A high priority was given to the collection of data that would make possible objective generalizations about the current status of instruction for community-organization practice.

In the fall of 1965, the Project initiated an informal survey of all schools of social work in order to obtain information concerning their concentrations in community organization. In 1966, an unstructured questionnaire was administered to the C.O. students and field instructors in seven of the larger schools with older, more established programs. On the basis of these replies and a critical review of the results by a group of C.O. faculty, the questionnaires for students and field instructors were revised and a new schedule to be completed by C.O. department chairmen was prepared. (See Appendix A.) The questionnaires were circulated in the spring of 1967 to all twenty-three schools identified as having two-year sequences in community organization.

The responses from these informants, together with the leads obtained from answers to open-ended questions on the previous survey, gave the Project staff the most objective information available about the current scene. For purposes of comparison, the data obtained from all students entering schools of social work in 1966 as reported by Golden (51) and the parallel study of casework, group work, and C.O. students undertaken by Lauffer (70) are also used where appropriate.

## C.O. Students

Of the seventy accredited schools of social work in the United States and Canada in 1967, forty-three had organized curricula in community organization, although five of these schools had no students in this sequence at that time. The 789 C.O. students in these schools represented 8 per cent of the total enrollment (10,131). The twenty-three schools having two-year concentrations had 562 students or 71.2 per cent of all C.O. students. Completed questionnaires were returned by 422 students in twenty-one of these schools for an overall response rate of 75.1 per cent. The coverage was very good for most schools but variable: three schools were complete, three had one questionnaire missing; eleven had three to nine missing; and four had approximately half reporting.

The 422 respondents were about evenly divided between first- and second-year students: 223 to 199. Their sex ratio, 60 per cent male to 40 per cent female, is the reverse of the proportions for all social work students in the 1966 entering class, indicating a preponderance of men in C.O. concentrations. About a third are twenty-one to twenty-four years of age and entered graduate school directly from college. An equal number are twenty-five to twenty-nine years of age and had a one- to five-year hiatus between college and social-work school. About 20 per cent are in their thirties and have had from five to fifteen years post-college experience. Some 10 per cent are in their forties and 3 per cent are in their fifties. For the latter groups, this may represent a new career or at least a new specialization within their chosen profession. About half of the students are married, and 5 per cent are widowed, separated, or divorced. Of those who have been married, 45 per cent have no children and another 26 per cent have only one child.

Prior to entering social-work school, more than half had full-time work experience in the social-service field, and almost all of the others engaged in part-time, summer, volunteer, or other work. This work experience reveals a strong commitment to the newer types of community action and service: thirty-seven have been in the Peace Corps, seventeen have served with VISTA, eighty-three have work in Community Action Programs, and fifty-two in other OEO programs. Civil-rights organizations have attracted 111 and other community programs ninety-four of these students. In all, 70 per cent of the students report some experience in one of these areas, and almost a fourth have worked in more than one of them.

Thus, while students tend to be young, they come with community experience and exhibit social idealism.

About 20 per cent have a grade-point average of A in their graduate academic work and 33 per cent have A's in field work. Only 5 per cent have C's in academic work, and a similiar proportion made C's in field work. While no comparable data are available for students in other concentrations, these grades seem relatively high for graduate work, and the differential between academic and field work supports the general impression that students do better in the latter, or perhaps that grading criteria are different.

## Field Placements

In assessing the nature of the student's field placement and his evaluation of the experience, the questionnaire provided for responses related to more than one field placement. This additional series of questions was answered by 184 (43.6 per cent) of the students who indicate a secondary, satellite, or short-term assignment in a different agency or one that involves another type of activity. The primary fields of service or problem areas represented in these principal and secondary placements are shown in Table I.

TABLE I: C.O. STUDENT PLACEMENTS BY FIELDS OF SERVICE (1967)

| Field or Problem Area | Principal Placement | | Secondary Placement | | Total | |
|---|---|---|---|---|---|---|
| | N | % | N | % | N | % |
| Neighborhood development, grass-roots organization | 117 | 27.2 | 35 | 19.0 | 152 | 25.1 |
| Coordination and planning, health and welfare council | 72 | 17.1 | 28 | 15.2 | 100 | 16.5 |
| Housing and urban renewal | 32 | 7.6 | 33 | 17.9 | 65 | 10.8 |
| Psychiatric services, mental health, retardation | 40 | 9.5 | 8 | 4.4 | 48 | 7.9 |
| Youth, group, recreation | 27 | 6.4 | 15 | 8.2 | 42 | 6.9 |
| Intergroup relations, civil rights, labor unions | 24 | 5.7 | 10 | 5.4 | 34 | 5.6 |
| Schools, education | 15 | 3.6 | 12 | 6.5 | 27 | 4.5 |
| Child and family service | 14 | 3.3 | 7 | 3.8 | 21 | 3.5 |
| Employment, vocational training | 14 | 3.3 | 6 | 3.3 | 20 | 3.3 |
| Public assistance, welfare | 16 | 3.8 | 3 | 1.6 | 19 | 3.1 |
| Medical, public health | 11 | 2.5 | 8 | 4.4 | 19 | 3.1 |
| Corrections, courts | 5 | 1.2 | 3 | 1.6 | 8 | 1.3 |
| Other | 35 | 8.3 | 16 | 8.7 | 51 | 8.4 |
| TOTAL | 422 | 100.0 | 184 | 100.0 | 606 | 100.0 |

While 45 per cent of the principal placements are in neighbor-hood-development or coordinating and planning agencies, the numbers of assignments in housing and urban renewal suggest a rising demand for workers in this area. The use of C.O. students in agencies dominated by casework and group work may also be a new or rising trend. The thirty-four assignments in specialized areas such as intergroup relations, civil rights, and labor unions may represent the opening or expanding of employment opportunities in these fields—or at least a trend in student and faculty interest.

## Activities and Settings

The questionnaire identified three major types of activities in which students might be engaged: (1) organizing people, (2) working with client groups, and (3) working with staff and personnel. These were further detailed to specify the settings and tasks involved. The students responded for both their principal and secondary placements. (See Table II.) Not only do these placements indicate something of the breadth and scope of C.O. practice, they are also remarkably diversified, and almost every students has at least some of his assignments in each of the three categories.

In general, the level of responsibility permitted by the placement or allowed by the instructor is perceived by the student as somewhat limiting. Somewhat less than 6 per cent of the respondents report that they operate as "free agents with few limitations." A little more than a third describe their situation as somewhat less free—broad policies are set, but the student plans and carries out his own assignments. Some 45 per cent say that they and the instructor agree on tasks and then the student works on his own. However, in 13 per cent of the principal placements and 17 per cent of the secondary placements, the student reports that he receives detailed assignments that are closely monitored by the field instructor. This response might not be expected from a group with prior experience, of whom one half will be graduating as full-fledged professional in less than a month.

Another question sought to explore the significance of the assignment for both the student and the agency. The import of the question was to ask if the assignment contributed to his total educational experience and if his work constituted a significant input for his placement agency. With respect to the principal placements, 47 per cent of the students report that it is "plus for me, plus for

TABLE II: C.O. STUDENT PLACEMENTS BY ACTIVITY AND SETTING (1967)

|  | Total | |
|---|---|---|
| *Types* | N | % |
| **1. Organizing people in** | | |
| (a) Urban neighborhood, community-based | 319 | 63.5 |
| (b) Rural U.S. areas | 8 | 1.6 |
| (c) Citizens' interest group (city-wide) | 86 | 17.1 |
| (d) Social action group (not geographically limited) | 25 | 5.0 |
| (e) Other nongeographic areas of interest | 64 | 12.8 |
| TOTAL | 502 | 100.0 |
| **2. Working with client groups to** | | |
| (a) Redefine goals, formulate objectives for existing groups under agency sponsorship | 161 | 31.1 |
| (b) Engage in self-help activities with independently organized neighborhood (grass-roots) groups | 164 | 31.7 |
| (c) Obtain needed goods and services for unorganized categories of clients | 141 | 27.2 |
| (d) Carry out other tasks with community groups | 52 | 10.0 |
| TOTAL | 518 | 100.0 |
| **3. Working with staff and personnel in** | | |
| (a) Planning, developing new programs | 246 | 45.4 |
| (b) Implementing, staffing existing programs | 93 | 17.2 |
| (c) Research, data collection, analysis | 56 | 10.3 |
| (d) Publicity or public relations | 25 | 4.6 |
| (e) Activities with board members, volunteers | 51 | 9.4 |
| (f) Interagency coordination | 49 | 9.0 |
| (g) Budgeting | 3 | 0.6 |
| (h) Other activities | 19 | 3.5 |
| TOTAL | 542 | 100.0 |

the agency." About a third think it "plus for me but minus for the agency." Some 12 per cent report "minus for me but plus for the agency" and 6 per cent judge it "minus for me and minus for the agency." Thus, 80 per cent of the students think their assignment a plus for themselves (i.e., educationally meaningful) while only 60 per cent think it a plus for the agency (i.e., a significant contribution). Placement agencies may view this difference as a measure of their contribution to social-work education. Surprisingly, the assessments of secondary placements are somewhat more negative (25 per cent minus for student, 44 per cent minus for agency) when, hypothetically, the extra assignments might be viewed as an opportunity to maximize the significance of the total field experience for both parties. These data would suggest that secondary placements are remedial, i.e., they attempt to give the student a needed or missing experience, and are therefore valuable whether or not the student recognizes their significance.

In response to the question "Was your placement satisfactory?" the students' overall satisfaction with their principal placements seem relatively high: 65 per cent say it is satisfactory, 25 per cent say "Yes and no," while fewer than 10 per cent say "No." They are a little less complimentary of their secondary placements, indicated by a shift of five percentage points for "Yes" to "Yes and no."

Campus observers have noted that students frequently judge their field experience to contribute more to their total learning experience than does their formal academic instruction. Another question sought to identify the factors responsible for the level of satisfaction reported by the student. Was it the nature of the field experience, the character of the field instructor, or a combination of these influences? Almost half of the students think that the field instructor and the nature of the experience are both about equally responsible for their satisfaction. Another 36 per cent think it is the nature of the experience, while 17 per cent credit it to the field instructor alone. Again there is a shift with respect to the secondary placements, of about 5 percentage points from field instructor to nature of the experience. It is important here to note the significance placed on the nature of the experience itself in the student's evaluation of field learning.

The level of satisfaction expressed by the students is not strongly related to the field of service in which they have their placements. More than 80 per cent of the students in child and family services and medical, public health, and retardation services expressed satisfaction; more than 70 per cent in schools and education, corrections and courts, neighborhood development and grass-roots organization, intergroup relations, civil rights, and labor unions expressed satisfaction. On the other hand, highest levels of dissatisfaction were expressed by students in youth, group, and recreation services (33 per cent), public assistance and welfare (22 per cent), and medical, public health, and retardation (20 per cent). Satisfaction does not seem to be directly linked to whether community organization is a primary or second function of the agency.

## Supervision

Several questions sought to explore the students' perceptions of the supervisory and educational contribution of their field instructors. Community-organization professionals today are often busy, pressured, harassed people, and demands on their time produce a lengthy and irregular work week. For this reason, time for field instruction and supervision of students may be severely restricted. More than 40 per cent of the students report that they had field instruction conferences only once a month or less often; however, 57 per cent report that they were able to maintain regular weekly conferences. Half of the students report that they participate to some degree in group supervision, seventy-nine frequently, sixty-seven sometimes, and sixty rarely.

The problem of time for supervision may be more acute in community organization, but it affects other areas of social-work practice as well. Two recent conferences concerned with the problems of field instruction called forth the following questions from mixed groups of practitioners.

A second source of concern with respect to the price that agencies pay for their share in the educational partnership centered around the schools' expectation that experienced supervisors be assigned to field teaching. How realistic is this expectation in view of the short supply of experienced persons and the growing pressures on agencies to provide organized programs of continuing education for staff workers? (31)

It was frankly asked whether this kind of (conceptual) teaching can take place in the light of all the other demands on instructors and students in the field. How much responsibility can the field instructor carry for teaching—in addition to the use of method—knowledge, attitudes, values and philosophies that grow out of particular situations? (112)

## Recording

Recording in community organization has remained indeterminate, problematic, and/or neglected through the years. Because of the variability of the work unit, it has been difficult to standardize the recording procedures. The relatively unsuccessful efforts to produce logs, diaries, or protocols that might be analogous to process recording in casework and group work has contributed to the problem. Recording requirements appropriate for a committee meeting, a project report, or a social problem analysis may differ markedly. The complexity and multiplicity of C.O. assignments, problems, and actors militate against simple recording procedures that can capture the depth and subtlety of the interactions that comprise the processes encountered by C.O. students. The community-organization practitioner must be able to execute a great variety of written reports in the course of his practice: minutes, annual reports, narrative reports, summaries of activities, news releases, public letters, memoranda, grant proposals, study designs, research findings, policy recommendations, etc. The training situation necessitates the development of skills in these forms of writing as well as in the more typical analytical-introspective document. Elsewhere, Dunham (39) has described these various forms of recording in community organization.

The frequency of use of student recording was reported in the survey as follows: seventy-three always, eighty-nine usually, 148 sometimes, and 111 never. Thus, student recording is used with any regularity in supervisory conferences in only about 40 per cent of the cases. In some instances, records may also be used by classroom teachers, by faculty advisers, by students as a personal check on progress, or employed by the agency for administrative or research purposes. However, this minimal use probably explains the relative lack of importance attached to this activity by students: only sixty-four think it very important, 129 fairly important, 112 of little importance, eighty-five of no importance; thirty-two register at least their lack of interest in the subject by not bothering to reply to the question at all.

Schools are experimenting with a variety of different approaches to recording, but a definitive format is still to be developed (9).

### Content in Supervision

A previous survey had asked the students to list the topics discussed in supervisory conferences and to judge their relative importance. The second questionnaire presented a structured list of the topics mentioned in the earlier survey and asked the student to rank them with respect to their frequency and importance. The first, second, and third topic as ranked by the student was given a weight of 3, 2, and 1, respectively. The scores were totaled and the topics ranked from 1 to 6 for frequency of discussion and relative importance to the student, as shown in Table III.

TABLE.III: C.O. STUDENT ASSESSMENT OF CONFERENCE TOPICS

| Topic | Frequency discussed | | Relative importance | |
|---|---|---|---|---|
| | Rank | Score | Rank | Score |
| Specific job-related matters | 1 | 540 | 3 | 421 |
| C.O. methods and practice (strategies, processes) | 2 | 505 | 1 | 567 |
| Interpersonal influence | 3 | 375 | 2 | 485 |
| Agency setting | 4 | 347 | 6 | 157 |
| Professional growth (self-awareness, use of self) | 5 | 321 | 4 | 387 |
| Community resources and organizations | 6 | 292 | 5 | 371 |

Four of the topics maintain their relative places in these two rankings. However, in relative importance for the student, "Specific job-related matters" falls from first to third and "Agency setting" falls from fourth to sixth. It is interesting to note that students rank as important the more professionally substantive matters dealing with C.O. method and interpersonal influence and see as less important the concrete, on-the-job, and agency-informational matters. The frequency with which the latter topics are discussed in conferences is highly related to the exigencies of the job, and their relative importance is appropriately judged by the student to be lower as he moves away from this particular experience. The similarity of these two rankings does not support the criticism sometimes made that supervisory conferences are judged by students to be largely irrelevant.

## Class and Field Coordination

Several questions were included to explore the students' responses to the efforts now being generally made to integrate field and classroom learning experiences. The students are, if anything, more generous in their judgments of these efforts at coordination than are the C.O. department chairmen, reported later. Almost one fourth of the students (99) recognize that serious efforts are being made and that field and class reinforce each other very well. Almost a third (128) note that some efforts are being made, but not too successfully. However, 37 per cent (154) report no efforts being made, but see no serious conflicts. Only 8 per cent (33) think field and class are often contradictory with resulting gaps and confusions from their point of view.

In an effort to identify the areas of coordinaton or conflict, specific questions were asked about the degree of integration of field experience with social-behavioral science courses, with courses in the welfare-policy sequence, and with C.O. methods courses.

TABLE IV: C.O. STUDENT ASSESSMENT OF INTEGRATION

| Integration of Class and Field | Social Behavior | | Welfare-Policy | | C.O. Methods | |
|---|---|---|---|---|---|---|
| | N | % | N | % | N | % |
| Serious effort; successfully made | 44 | 10.5 | 57 | 13.9 | 153 | 36.4 |
| Some effort with some success | 153 | 36.4 | 127 | 30.8 | 157 | 37.5 |
| Some gaps; student makes his own synthesis | 136 | 32.5 | 96 | 23.3 | 63 | 15.1 |
| Little relationship between the two | 86 | 20.6 | 132 | 32.0 | 46 | 11.0 |

It is immediately evident from Table IV that the most efforts at integration and the most successful results have been achieved with C.O. methods courses. Almost three fourths of the students report a measure of success in this area. Less success is achieved with social-behavioral science courses, where fewer than half of the students see some success. However, students seem better able to make their own synthesis in this area. The effectiveness of efforts to achieve integration in the welfare-policy courses is mixed. About the same level of effort is reported as in the social-behavior sequence, but where this has not been done with any degree of success, the students are unable to make the synthesis themselves and more than half are left with some gaps or see little relationship between class and field. Obviously, a few schools that have tried have succeeded quite well, but a sizable number of schools have made little progress in effecting a meaningful coordination of class and field in this area.

## Students' Postgraduation Plans

A final series of questions were related to the future plans of the students with respect to employment and continued education. The fields of service they plan to enter upon graduation are shown in Table V.

TABLE V: C.O. STUDENTS' EMPLOYMENT PLANS

| Field or Area of Service | N | % |
|---|---|---|
| Neighborhood development, grass-roots organization | 62 | 20.9 |
| Coordination and planning, councils, federations | 59 | 19.9 |
| Public assistance, welfare department | 47 | 15.8 |
| Intergroup relations, civil rights, labor unions | 38 | 12.8 |
| Housing and urban renewal | 20 | 6.8 |
| Psychiatric, mental health, retardation | 19 | 6.4 |
| Child and family service | 14 | 4.7 |
| Medical, public health, handicapped | 11 | 3.7 |
| Schools, education, literacy, Head Start | 11 | 3.7 |
| Youth services, group, recreation | 9 | 3.0 |
| Corrections, courts, probation, parole | 6 | 2.0 |
| Employment, vocational training | 1 | 0.3 |

The largest proportions of students plan to work in neighborhood development, grass-roots organizations, and in coordination and planning councils or federations. These represent the more traditional areas of C.O. practice. The next largest group intends to go into public assistance, this representing for many a condition of their financial aid and may or may not correspond to their final career choice. The numbers of students desiring to enter the intergroup relations and civil-rights fields represent a potentially enlarged if not entirely new source of employment for professional social workers. To an extent, the same might be said for the fields of housing and urban renewal. For the treatment-oriented fields of social-work endeavor, the numbers of C.O. students desiring employment may reflect the growing recognition by direct-service agencies of the importance of their relationships to the community and to client groups.

Whether by accident or by design, very few students are currently located in placements in the fields of service that they plan to enter upon graduation. Only forty-eight second-year students are so matched. The field with the largest number of matches is coordination and planning, accounting for sixteen of the matches. In the light of rapid changes in the field and the probable fluidity in the career patterns of practitioners, this level of matching may be entirely appropriate.

While 30 per cent of the students have not made a firm decision about the field of their first employment, most of the second-year students are already committed: seventy-six have accepted jobs, forty-five are limited by the terms of a grant to a period of service within a specific agency, and nine others report that their plans are definite. Among the first-year students who have reached a decision, seven have jobs waiting for them, forty-nine are committed by the terms of a grant, and sixteen are definite about their plans. Only twenty-five of the students who have accepted positions or have definite plans are now serving in placements in the field of service in which they plan to work. Only four of the students on grants are now placed in the fields in which they will work. This lack of concordance between placements and future plans may be viewed, on the one hand, as capricious and may account for some of the dissatisfaction expressed by students. On the other hand, it may represent a conscious effort to broaden the scope of the student's training by exposing him to a setting other than the one in which he may already have had some experience or in which he plans to take his first job.

An unexpected finding was that 134 students have postgraduate-study plans. These include four second-year and eleven first-year students who plan to continue in a third-year program, twenty-eight second-year and twenty-one first-year students who will go on to the D.S.W. or Ph.D. in social work, and forty-three second-year and twenty-seven first-year students who intend to take an M.A. or Ph.D. in an academic discipline. While these plans may be delayed and some of them never realized, it is significant that more than a third of the students express a strong interest in postgraduate education. In the absence of any data about the plans of students in casework and group work, we can only speculate as to what these ambitions mean for students in community organization. To what extent it represents a loss to practice or a gain to teaching could only be ascertained by a longitudinal study of the careers of these students. There may be a tension in many students between a commitment to immerse themselves in the solution of social problems and a desire for advanced academic studies.

The high aspirations and ambitions of this group are further reflected in the level of practice they expect to enter upon graduation and to achieve at the peak of their careers. These ambitions are detailed in Table VI.

TABLE VI: C.O. STUDENTS' GRADUATION AND CAREER PLANS

| Level of Practice | At Graduation | | At Career Peak | |
|---|---|---|---|---|
| | N | % | N | % |
| Direct practice | 264 | 62.6 | 37 | 8.8 |
| Supervision | 27 | 6.4 | 16 | 3.8 |
| Consultation | 20 | 4.7 | 56 | 13.3 |
| Administration | 54 | 12.8 | 131 | 31.0 |
| Teaching | 7 | 1.7 | 59 | 14.0 |
| Research | 14 | 3.3 | 15 | 3.5 |
| Undecided | 36 | 8.5 | 108 | 25.6 |

In sharp contrast with other social-work methods in which almost all graduates begin their professional careers in direct practice, almost a third of the C.O. students expect to begin their careers as administrators (13 per cent), supervisors (7 per cent), consultants (5 per cent), researchers (3 per cent), or teachers (2 per cent). In the minds of the students, there may be some overlap between administration and direct practice in community organization. This ambiguity would account for some part of these findings. Whereas most caseworkers and group workers may aspire to become supervisors at the peak of their careers, the proportion of C.O. students expecting to practice at this level is reduced by almost a half. This helps to explain something of the youthfulness and relative inexperience of the field instructors now active in C.O.: they are the only ones available.

While some 25 per cent of the students are undecided about their maximum career goals, of those who reported firm decisions, more than 40 per cent (131 students) expect to become administrators at the peak of their careers. Consultation (fifty-six students) and teaching (fifty-nine students) are the ultimate goals of another 40 per cent. Only 5 per cent expect to remain in supervision and 12 per cent in direct practice. The researchers are a stable lot with only one late recruit.

## Field Agencies and Instructors

Responses to the questionnaires were received covering 270 agencies and 291 field instructors. When these are matched with the responses of their students, they represent 327 field placements serving 422 C.O. students. Half of these agencies (163) are under private, nonsectarian sponsorship; almost a third (93) are public, forty-seven are private sectarian, and twenty-four are quasi-public or mixed sponsorship. The geographical scope of the agencies varies similarly: more than half (175) cover a city or metropolitan area; about a third (98) serve an urban neighborhood; forty-eight are state or regional; four are national or international; and two are rural.

The majority of the placement agencies indicates that their primary function is coordination and planning (136 are exclusively occupied with this function and twenty-six others indicate this in combination with other functions). The next function most frequently mentioned is direct service (eighty-eight exclusively, plus thirty-five in combination with other functions). Grass-roots organization or social action is the exclusive function of fifty-seven agencies and in combination with other functions of twenty-nine additional agencies. Eight agencies indicate that they fulfill all three of these basic functions.

The fields of service represented by these agencies are as broad as social work, including both traditional C.O. placements, direct service agencies, and the newer grass-roots and poverty settings. (See Table VII.)

TABLE VII: C.O. PLACEMENT AGENCIES BY FIELDS OF SERVICE

| Fields of Service | Primary | | Secondary | | Total | |
|---|---|---|---|---|---|---|
| | N | % | N | % | N | % |
| Neighborhood development, grass-roots organization | 63 | 20.6 | 20 | 27.8 | 83 | 22.0 |
| Coordination and planning, councils, federations | 73 | 23.9 | 15 | 20.8 | 88 | 23.3 |
| Housing and urban renewal | 11 | 3.6 | 10 | 13.9 | 21 | 5.6 |
| Psychiatric, mental health, retardation | 39 | 12.7 | 2 | 2.8 | 41 | 10.7 |
| Youth services, group, recreation | 40 | 13.1 | 2 | 2.8 | 42 | 11.1 |
| Intergroup relations, civil rights, labor unions | 20 | 6.5 | 7 | 9.7 | 27 | 7.1 |
| Schools, education, literacy, Head Start | 5 | 1.6 | 6 | 8.3 | 11 | 2.9 |
| Child and family services | 10 | 3.3 | 7 | 9.7 | 17 | 4.5 |
| Employment, vocational training | 15 | 4.9 | 2 | 2.8 | 17 | 4.5 |
| Public assistance, welfare department | 15 | 4.9 | — | — | 15 | 4.0 |
| Medical, public health, handicapped | 11 | 3.6 | 1 | 1.4 | 12 | 3.2 |
| Corrections, courts, probation, parole | 4 | 1.3 | — | — | 4 | 1.1 |

More than half of the agencies are engaged in neighborhood and grass-roots organization or coordination and planning. In the latter category, traditional placements in health and welfare councils or federations are outweighed by agencies representing the newer emphasis on comprehensive poverty programs. The next most frequent types are youth services and psychiatric services. These represent the thrust of juvenile-delinquency-prevention programs and the current interest in community psychiatry and mental health. The sizable numbers of agencies in intergroup relations, civil rights, labor unions, in housing and urban renewal, and in employment indicate the importance of these settings, many of which are relatively new to social work. The new or increased demand for community-organization functions in more traditional social-work settings is reflected in placements in public welfare, child and family services, medical, and school agencies. The few placements in corrections may be indicative of a trend toward an extension of such services to courts and prisons. The fields of service represented by the secondary placements account for the increased proportions of students who have experiences in child and family services, schools and educational programs, housing and urban renewal, and intergroup relations and civil rights.

Eveline M. Burns, a prominent social-work educator with a long-standing social-change orientation, has urged social-work schools to make a more vigorous effort to train for broader practice roles:

The social work profession is making only a minor contribution to meeting social need in the area of planning. Regrettably, social workers do not play any prominent role in broad social planning. . . . Social work has, of course, a contribution to make. But unless its educational system is changed, its contribution will remain a modest one. The profession must choose whether to confine itself to rendering of direct services to individuals (alone or in groups) or to participate in the major thrust of our time, which is directed toward change in our social institutions (17).

The community-organization programs at a number of schools are involving themselves in the thrust suggested by Professor Burns. They are, however, experiencing the attendant problems of lack of available field instructors who are experienced or social-work trained, inadequate academic support for the field instructor, and uncoordinated administrative procedures as between school and field. One of the key strategies for dealing with some of these problems, as we shall elaborate later, is the assumption of greater responsibility on the part of the school for field instruction. McGloth-

lin, again, places these developments in a more general framework
and provides a measure of outside independent support for this
development. He states:

As the professional school searches for and helps its students search
for new knowledge in the field, for new methods of preventing or reducing the problems with which the professions deal, and for ways of
extending the services of the profession to places where they are lack-
ing, it is helping students to become instruments of social progress as
well as practitioners of professions. A profession must lead as well as
serve (84).

The department chairmen were asked to rate the adequacy of
each agency as a placement for C.O. students. They judge eighty-
five agencies to be "good for all students," 142 "good for special
purposes," seventy-one only "so-so," and twenty-eight as "not one
of our better agencies." While these ratings are predominantly positive, they are by no means universally so. Almost half of the agencies are seen by the C.O. chairmen as specialized in some sense and
useful only for selected students, and almost another fourth are
viewed somewhat negatively.

The chairmen were further asked to indicate what features of the
placement are responsible for their judgments, whether favorable or
unfavorable. Only forty think it is due to the field instructor alone;
133 think it is primarily the nature of the experience, and 150 think
both of these elements are about equally responsible.

While the great majority (294) of the placements involve one
student to an agency or instructor, twenty units under school supervision include two or more students, six other units under agency
supervision have two or more students, and five units are classified
as group placements. Almost half of the agencies involved have
more than one student in placement, and sixteen have between six
and 10 students assigned to them. These data document the extent
to which group placements in field units have grown in favor in
many schools. About eighty of the agencies use more than one
field instructor, and fifteen have as many as five instructors.

Almost three fourths of the field instructors are male. About one
half are under thirty years of age, and another third are under fifty.
Some 86 per cent of the field instructors are agency employed but
14 per cent are school employed, and two work on a cooperative
arrangement between agency and school. Only twenty field instructors do not have advanced or professional degrees, and in addition

to those with M.S.W., twenty-two have M.S. or Ph.D. in a discipline other than social work. About 83 per cent of the field instructors, therefore, have an M.S.W. or higher social-work degree. However, only 35 per cent of the field instructors specialized in community organization. About 60 per cent of the professionally trained field instructors majored in another method in school: about 30 per cent in casework, 27 per cent in group work, and 3 per cent in administration or research. The years of different kinds of experience reported by this cadre of field instructors are detailed in Table VIII.

TABLE VIII: C.O. FIELD INSTRUCTORS' YEARS OF EXPERIENCE

| Years of Service | Kinds of Experience | | | | | |
|---|---|---|---|---|---|---|
| | Professional Experience | | Employed in C.O. | | Service as Instructor | |
| | N | % | N | % | N | % |
| 1 year or less | — | — | 4 | 1.3 | 103 | 37.9 |
| 1–2 | 6 | 2.1 | 31 | 10.1 | 58 | 21.3 |
| 3–5 | 40 | 13.9 | 93 | 30.4 | 75 | 27.6 |
| 6–9 | 61 | 21.2 | 53 | 17.3 | 24 | 3.7 |
| 10–14 | 57 | 19.9 | 51 | 16.6 | 10 | 3.7 |
| 15–19 | 58 | 20.2 | 24 | 7.8 | 2 | 0.7 |
| 20+ | 65 | 22.7 | 20 | 6.5 | — | — |
| TOTAL | 287 | 100.0 | 276 | 100.0 | 272 | 100.0 |

Considering the "youthfulness" of the C.O. concentration in social work, there are a considerable number of experienced field instructors. More than 60 per cent have had ten or more years professional experience (the median is about twelve years); more than 40 per cent have been employed in C.O. or related work for more than ten years (median about seven years). The fact that this is the first field-instruction experience for almost 40 per cent of the group (median about one year) is evidence of the rapid expansion of this concentration, both within schools and in the number of schools offering a C.O. concentration. It also shows that many field instructors are novices in the educational enterprise and signals the need for more academic supports.

The adequacy of each instructor was judged by the C.O. chairmen, and the results were that 141 (45.6 per cent) are rated "above average," 128 (41.4 per cent) are rated "about average," and 40 (12.9 per cent) are rated "below average." While this question was skipped on eighteen questionnaires, the high proportion (84 per cent) rated as "average or above average" by the chairmen is a measure of their favorable view of the present situation. (Statisticians are at liberty to ponder what "average" means to these respondents.)

The majority (66 per cent) of the instructors have only one student assigned to them. Almost 20 per cent have two students; 8 per cent have three to five students; and 5 per cent have six or seven students. Any trend to be observed here would indicate the probability of an increased use of multistudent placements under group supervision.

## School and Agency

Eighteen of the C.O. department chairmen completed the school questionnaire. The three missing schools have about eighty students, of whom thirty-nine completed their questionnaires. While several of the reporting schools have had one-year sequences in C.O. that go back some twenty-five years, more than half have had two-year sequences only during the past one to three years. The newness of the concentration is strikingly illustrated by the fact that only two of the present programs have been in existence as long as eight years. About half of the schools (7) follow a planned sequence for first- and second-year placement of students that involves a progression from simple to complex assignments. This means neighborhood to city to state and region to national and even international settings. The content of instruction is also usually structured in a progression from grass-roots organization to planning and coordination. Seven schools, however, do not follow a standardized plan, and the other four use a variety of schemes to sequence their placements.

The school questionnaire sought to identify any special features of the field-instruction program now in operation or planned for the immediate future. In addition to traditional concurrent placement, the six techniques most frequently mentioned are detailed in Table IX.

Almost all chairmen are aware of these techniques and have considered the use of some or all of them in their programs. The two most often selected as good future possibilities are teaching centers and summer block placements.

Patterns of support and in-service training for field instructors are varied. Periodic meetings during each term are held by fifteen schools; intensive workshops or institutes are conducted by eleven

TABLE IX: SPECIAL FIELD INSTRUCTION TECHNIQUES

| Programs | Used at Present | Included in Class Teaching | Planned For Next Year |
|---|---|---|---|
| Laboratory | 6 | 1 | 1 |
| Teaching center | 5 | 0 | 4 |
| Satellite or short-term placement | 6 | 0 | 1 |
| Block placement during school year | 0 | 0 | 1 |
| Summer block placement | 3 | 0 | 1 |
| Group teaching | 1 | 0 | 0 |

schools; annual or semiannual meetings are also used by five schools. School contact with field instructors is made about once a month in thirteen schools; one has more frequent contact and four less frequent.

Extensive efforts are made in every school to coordinate class and field experiences. Just the number of such reported efforts is impressive: five schools list one or two, nine schools indicate three or four, and four schools identify five or six different ideas. The efforts most frequently mentioned include coordination built into both class and field assignments by interpretation of objectives, exchange of materials, and synchronization of experiences (reported by thirteen schools), regular meetings of field staff and classroom teachers (eight schools), class assignments incorporate field experiences for reports, papers, and classroom discussion (eight schools), student seminars (six schools), conferences with students using their records (six schools), assignment of one instructor as class-field liaison (five schools).

With respect to the effectiveness of these many efforts, only one chairman thought they were working very well, six report that some questions still remained unanswered, six indicate high hopes for new plans for coordination now being considered, and five confess that no solution to the problems could be seen at this time. This tenuous evaluation of integration efforts differs from the student opinion expressed in the structured questionnaire, but concurs with the opinions offered by students in the earlier, open-ended, informal instrument.

## Summary

This survey of community-organization field placements during the 1966–67 academic year serves to highlight characteristics of

C.O. students, their field-placement agencies and instructors, and the school programs in which they received their training.

*C.O. Students.* While these respondents are relatively young in comparison with all social-work students, about half are married, and most have had service experience in community projects or civil-rights work. About 60 per cent are male. Their student placements cover a wide range of agencies with 45 per cent in neighborhood development and coordination and planning—the more traditional settings in the field. A goodly number, however, are in newer settings—O.E.O. and C.A.P. agencies, civil rights, unions, and a surprisingly large number are also in direct-service agencies, mental health, employment, and public assistance. Most students (about 65 per cent) are satisfied with their placements, and almost one half think that both the field instructor and the nature of the experience contribute to their satisfaction. Supervision and recording are viewed somewhat more critically. The level of integration of field and class is high in C.O. methods courses, less adequate in the social-behavior and welfare-policy sequences. The employment plans of students follow closely the distribution of their placements except for larger numbers committed by grants to public assistance and to newer fields represented by intergroup relations, civil rights, and labor unions. More than one third express interest in postgraduate education, and about the same number expect to be in administration at the peak of their careers.

*Field Placement Agencies and Instructors.* The fields of service represented by these placement agencies are as broad as social work, including traditional coordinating and planning bodies, direct-service agencies, and the newer grass-roots and poverty settings. As community-organization programs become involved in social progress and institutional change, the schools are taking more responsibility for field instruction. Almost one half of the agencies are seen by the chairmen as specialized and useful only for selected students and another one fourth are viewed somewhat negatively. The newer trends revealed by this survey are toward group placements and multistudent units under school supervision. Almost three fourths of the field instructors are male, and half are under thirty years of age. Almost all have advanced or professional degrees and 60 per cent have ten or more years of professional experience, but only a third specialized in community organization. Only 13 per cent were judged by the chairmen to be "below average."

*School and Agency.* The "youthfulness" of the C.O. concentration is illustrated by the fact that more than one half of these schools have had two-year sequences for only one to three years, and only two have had programs as long as eight years. Special field-instruction techniques, such as laboratory, teaching center, satellite, and block placements, are presently used or planned for in most schools. Patterns of school support and in-service training for field instructors are varied, and efforts to coordinate class and field experiences are extensive. Only one chairman is satisfied with the effectiveness of these efforts, and five confess that no solution to these problems could be seen at the present time; the others were more or less optimistic about their new plans and the future in general.

# 2 Trends, Developments, and Problems

Our assessment of the current scene does not rely wholly on the results of the survey we have reported. It is distilled also from a careful review of the literature, extended consultation with informants in both schools and agencies, and an informed estimate by the Project staff based on experience, observation, and discussions with colleagues. The resulting overview of the problems and developments in the teaching of community-organization practice is summarized in this chapter.

## Change and Growth

We are examining a phenomenon at a fixed point in time, but it is one that is characterized by dramatic change. There has been rapid growth in the number of students in community organization, the number of schools offering community-organization concentrations, and the number of placement agencies utilized in field instruction. There has of necessity also been a sizable increase in classroom faculty, field instructors, scholarships, and other sources of support.

The increased demands for community-organization personnel have come not only from traditional agencies such as welfare councils, united funds, and settlement houses, but also from an impressive array of newer programs and agencies that have taken a social-planning or neighborhood-organization approach to their work, such as OEO, Model Cities, comprehensive programs in health, mental health, mental retardation, rehabilitation, and employment, delinquency-control projects, Peace Corps, VISTA, etc.

These developments may be seen as part of a more general movement in the professions. McGlothlin (83) states:

*Society's demands for professionally educated persons will continue to increase*. . . . Each profession we have studied assumes that demands for its services will continue and will probably increase, as population grows, prosperity expands, and the work-week shortens. Some professions, like engineering, teaching, social work, and nursing, face critical shortages now, without waiting for population growth. Most professional educators, in whatever field, can tell plaintive stories about how greatly the number of requests they receive for graduates each spring exceed the number of graduates.

## New Knowledge and School-Field Strains

There has been a knowledge explosion in the social sciences and the professions that are associated with community organization—sociology, political science, social psychology, planning, etc. A much greater potential knowledge base exists to inform practice than has been the case heretofore. To varying degrees this material is being incorporated into contemporary curricula.

Schools have sought to develop and expand the intellectual underpinning of community organization through strengthening the academic program. Social-science concepts and theories have been introduced, borrowed largely from sociology and political science, and more rigorous ways of analyzing practice have been employed. New and younger men and women of academic bent have been brought onto faculties either with doctoral training or familiarity with the social-science disciplines or both. Concepts and perspectives of allied professions such as city planning and public health are being increasingly called upon.

Agency field instructors in large measure have lagged behind the schools in these developments. Only a small number have had contemporary preparation in a specialized community-organization program or a substantive social-science background. Many field instructors have gone into community-organization practice without formal preparation. Only 35 per cent of the instructors in our sample had a graduate-school specialization in community organization, the others having taken the previously established route of initial preparation and experience in casework or group work. Berry (9) has described this phenomenon as follows:

Few community organization workers have time for training courses. Their daily tasks militate against deep conceptualized thinking. Many community organization co-workers come from other specializations and

their fame of reference is *that* specialization rather than community
organization. They may tend to be more comfortable when talking
about specific functions or specific skills rather than community organization process. . . .

Some school faculties, well versed in professional "lingo," tend to
frighten away the practitioner. . . . The chasm created by lack of common understanding and agreement on theoretical content of the community organization process, coupled with the difficulties of language,
may be hard to bridge. And I suspect the professor, in turn, may be
overwhelmed by the action-motivated community organization workers.

Actually, we are describing a situation that exists generally in
social work and is not limited to community organization. Costin
(29) drew a representative sample of faculty in schools of social
work and nonfaculty social workers from the NASW directory.
Among the nonfaculty, almost none held doctor's degrees; 88 per
cent held master's degrees and 12 per cent bachelor's degrees.
About half the faculty group were men; most of the nonfaculty
group were women. In the study, faculty rated significantly higher
than nonfaculty the importance of developing the student's comprehension of theoretical perspectives as contrasted with utilitarian
considerations.

Schubert (122) has graphically described the difference in theoretical training and outlook as between the newer faculty members
(particularly those in research) and the more practice-seasoned
field instructors. She states:

Field instructors have substantial experience in direct services to
clients and in supervision. . . . Their professional education was obtained twenty years ago or more, and most of them have not undertaken doctoral work. They are bound together by a common concept of
helping clients. For many of them, these bonds were formed at a time
when practice was dominated by women.

The research oriented faculty members come from what amounts to
a different culture. They obtained their MSW degree during the fifties
and, after a brief period of practice, undertook doctoral education
either in social work or in an allied field. They have an intense interest
in theory, are avid readers, and they communicate easily with the sociologists and psychologists. They are keenly aware of the gaps in social
work practice theory and have no hesitation in voicing their concern
about the profession's ignorance. Their orientation is that of the university, a society dominated by men.

This condition in social work, again, can be seen against the
broader canvas of developments in all professions. As new knowl-

edge builds up in volume and rapidity of development, specialists in producing, synthesizing, and applying knowledge for use will probably become more prevalent. These specialists will probably be located in the professional schools, as distinct from the world of practice. The schools will probably increasingly engage knowledge specialists with backgrounds and training in a variety of fields and disciplines to supply new information to the upcoming student group and to the already practicing professional group through programs of continuing education. McGlothlin, recognizing and applauding this development, states that "the curriculum cannot be allowed to become fixed and hallowed." (83)

1. *Role Strain.* In the turbulent situation in the world of community-organization practice, field instructors experience innumerable job pressures. Role strains develop between the production demands of the agency and the learning objectives of the school and student. For an agency practitioner in social work, service goals have a high saliency, and production requisites may become paramount. One is expected to exhibit a high or at least a moderate degree of loyalty to the goals of the organization, sympathy with the objectives of its program, and support for its modes of operation. As a field instructor, one is expected to have a critical, objective, relativistic stance regarding agency goals and methods, and to place a high premium on the educational needs of students. The practice-oriented person leans toward development of skill and technique, the education-oriented person toward enhancement of theory and knowledge. These competing claims may clash, especially in community organization where the agency's fundamental objectives may be implicated in the student's assignment. It may be more difficult in the social-issue-oriented context of community organization than in the clinically oriented treatment process to become immersed in personal and technical aspects of delimited tasks (123).

This dilemma has been observed in other studies and writings. Costin, in the study previously cited, indicates that her findings "reflect primarily the fact that faculty members, by virtue of their role in social work, are naturally more concerned with students and their development, whereas non-faculty social workers are more involved with clients and the problems involved in giving them service." Berelson (11) points out that a tension exists between a professional outlook or conception and an academic conception. The distinctions between the two he outlines as follows:

| *Professional Conception* | | *Academic Conceptions* |
|---|---|---|
| Training | as against | Education |
| Development of skills | as against | Development of wisdom |
| Development of depth | as against | Development of breadth |
| Specialist | as against | Cultivated man |
| Technical expert | as against | Scholar-teacher |

Teachers in professional schools face these divergent pulls all the time, but the interplay must be strongest in the operating field situation. Berelson's findings imply that teachers in the professional schools resolve the dilemma by coming down on the academic side.

Other professions that provide practice experiences for students find this tension existing in quite the same way that social work does. A specialist in medical education, for example, writes:

The scramble for interns that each year becomes more vigorous does not resemble the usual relationship between students and educational institutions. But the hard fact is that an intern is more than a student: he is a source of immensely important professional service to the institution fortunate enough to have him. Hospitals are established to render patient care, and the presence of interns substantially improves the quality of that care. . . . The internship has been designated primarily as an educational experience in the course of which a certain amount of patient care might be rendered by the intern. Today, there is a belief in many quarters that, despite the sincerity of intent, this order of priority has in many institutions been reversed. There is also a large body of opinion that the internship is an anachronism (100).

Some years previously, Edith Abbott came to a remarkably similar conclusion about the usual social-work field placement procedure:

"Farming out" . . . involved the assignment of students for a given number of hours a week to the office of a social agency. But most social agencies are short of workers and funds and they cannot and should not be expected to find the time for proper instruction in this important division of our work. . . . As educators we must, I think, acknowledge that field work has frequently, from an education point of view, been a wasteful use of the time of competent graduate students (1).

2. *Weak Tradition.* There is only a meager tradition of systematic thinking about field instruction in community organization—

thus compounding the problems of field instruction alluded to earlier. In the past, community-organization field instruction tended to be given passing attention. There were few students, often only one or two at a school, thus systematic development of field-instruction programs never evolved. There is almost a complete absence of a literature specifically on field instruction in community organization (an exception is the article by Mildred Berry (9) in the 1958 Council on Social Work Education Curriculum Study). Community-organization practitioners have been characterized in the past by a hard nosed, learn-by-the-seat-of-your-pants outlook. This is reflected in the paucity of case material and generalizable, analytical, theoretical writings. Lippitt (73), in compiling case materials for *The Dynamics of Planned Change,* commented on the special difficulties in obtaining documented case histories from the action-oriented community-practitioner group.

MacRae, at the time a distinguished agency practitioner himself, made note of the problem of proper field instruction:

> The provision of adequate field work experience for the community organization student must be a perplexing problem for the faculties of professional schools. Not only are opportunities limited in the direct-service agencies, but all too many community organization agencies are ill-prepared psychologically and professionally to undertake the supervision a student requires (78).

McNeil and Lefferts also comment on field-instruction deficiencies in community organization. They call for a student to be assigned actual operational responsibility in the agency under the direction of a responsible field instructor. They indicate the difficulty in accomplishing this:

> To place responsibility for such a piece of work with the field work student assumes that proper supervision is available. This presents a major problem since there is so little in the way of systematic knowledge regarding supervisory processes and methods in community organization. . . . To a considerable degree the supervisory process in community organization has been focussed on administrative matters and development of technical skills (92).

3. *High Risk.* Many agencies, particularly those above the neighborhood level and those involved in social planning, are reluctant to give students assignments involving social planning and a substantial amount of personal responsibility. Considerable fear exists

concerning the risk of failure. This is because, by their nature, community-organization activities are carried out in the public arena, involve relatively large numbers of people, and often include community influentials and elites. Failure on the part of a student is likely to have high public visibility and result in important and immediate repercussions for the community, the agency, the school, and the students. This risk probably accounts for the fact that many students in our survey report that they receive detailed assignments that are closely monitored. (See Berry (9) and Schwartz (123) for discussions of this issue.)

Berry suggests that the element of risk may be minimized through such techniques as rationally partialized assignments and phasing of the student's experience by starting with observation and working gradually to tasks involving greater degrees of responsibility. According to our survey data, some students are given trivial, routine, and busy-work assignments of the legman or messenger-boy variety. Other students, however, indicate that they are assigned significant, vital, and engaging tasks that challenge their initiative and stretch their capacities.

While the question of risk is salient in community organization, it has also received discussion in the direct-treatment methods. Bess Dana reports the following discussion at a conference of executives of national agencies:

> Question was raised in one group as to how much consideration had really been given to the cost to the client of field instruction centered on student, rather than client, need. Were sufficient safeguards provided to protect the clients against the trial and error characteristic of student learning? (31)

Educators attending this conference stated that steps were being taken to mitigate risk by delayed entrance into field instruction, observation prior to direct service, and better assessment of the student's capabilities before assignment (60a; 80a). The steps will be discussed later when Project recommendations are promulgated.

4. *Task Responsibility.* It is difficult to define a unit of work in community-organization practice. There are few delimited, easily encompassable categories, such as an individual client, a family, or a treatment group. Usually students are assigned to one or more projects, committees, councils, studies, social problems, staff members, etc., or they may be asked to observe and have limited participation in a wide range of agency programs and activities. There

is a problem of intensity versus extensity—participation in depth in a circumscribed set of tasks or broad participation in a wide range of tasks and events. The former usually entails a greater degree of personal responsibility for outcomes. In cases where a balance cannot be achieved, it is necessary to select one or the other of these emphases as it is not possible in the time schedule of students to accomplish both.

There has been but little consideration of this problem in the literature. One of the few discussions of the topic is by McNeil and Lefferts (92). They advocate definite personal responsibility in the placement, supplemented by a range of less responsible involvements that includes planned observation. "Through proper supervision, such observation can be meaningful because the student can be 'involved' in activities though he does not carry work responsibility." The team approach to student assignment, which avoids the hazards implicit in both the case and task approaches, has been suggested as a solution to this problem with respect to indigenous and other nonprofessional workers and might serve well a similar function with respect to student placements (8a).

5. *Time Schedule.* The time pressures and fluidity of most community-organization assignments make them difficult to confine in regularized two- or three-day-a-week schedule during an agency's program year. Students may not be on hand when events pop, situations ripen, committees meet, key community people wish to make an important contact, or special activities take place, such as meetings of the board of directors. Events race on between field days, and students complain that they must spend up to a half day catching up with what occurred since their last visit to the agency. The student may remain apart from or peripheral to the operations and the culture of the overall agency, which can be dysfunctional since it may be important for the student to experience the total agency structure and climate.

Community-organization tasks and projects vary greatly in the amount of time required for their development and completion. Some short-term projects may take a month or less, other projects may require three to five years (or longer) to carry through. Most placements in the community organization necessitate a considerable amount of time for orientation, socialization, and problem assessment. Students may require three months or a full semester to learn the agency, become acquainted with a target community, define a crucial social problem, and obtain relevant data, before they can commence to carry out sufficiently rationalized implemental strategies and tasks.

Both students and field instructors frequently complain of the difficulties they find in adhering to a segmented and broken weekly schedule while engaged in a community-organization field experience. A number of our respondents recommended block placement as a way of dealing with this problem.

The question of whether block or concurrent placements are most suitable for educational purposes has been a perennial issue in social-work education almost from the beginning. The concurrent class-field plan has been most prevalent. Still, there have been persuasive advocates of the block plan (125), successful experiences reported in its use (113), research suggesting that neither plan has a decisive advantage over the other (50), and comparative surveys that show mixed patterns of use of concurrent and block plans in various countries around the world (145). We will discuss this subject further at a later point. Here let us state only that one should not become ensnared in abstract advocacy of one or another structural form of placement. "Form follows function," and the function here is the maximization of community-organization professional education through the best temporal and substantive formulation of practice-skills learning.

## Class and Field

In the course of its investigations, the Project staff came to recognize that one of the major problems with respect to the teaching and learning of application skills is the discrepancy between what is learned in the classroom and what is learned in the field. Because of variations among settings and agencies, differences in backgrounds and orientation of field instructors, contrasting client groups, unequal stages in project development, and so forth, students have widely differing exposures in the field and consequently varied learnings. This variation in exposure makes integration with academic content problematical. Schools have little operational control over what is taught in the field and, in many instances, cannot state with even a modicum of exactness what students are actually learning. Recognizing the problems created by this lack of integration between the academic and applied components of the educational regimen, the Project staff directed a major portion of its attention to this issue.

In our visits and discussions, we found that students, faculty, and field instructors agree that there is considerable separation and discontinuity between what students are offered in the classroom and in field agencies. The results of the 1967 student survey, reported in Chapter 1, indicate less student concern about integration than we anticipated and less than was true of the 1966 sample where, in response to open-ended questions, they identified this as their most frequent and serious concern. However, in the 1967 survey, faculty members continued to view integration as a serious problem.

The nature of the stresses between the worlds of school and field is a principal concern of social-work educators. Field instructors report that they have insufficient information about academic subject matter, and classroom teachers are often skeptical of certain practices and learning experiences in the agencies. Some field instructors are critical of the amount and type of theory given in the classroom. Some students, while recognizing the deficiency, either ask that field experiences be better structured to test out theory or that areas of classroom content match more squarely the experiences and issues experienced in the field. Differences in intellectual backgrounds and outlook of academic faculty and field instructors account in part for different emphasis and lack of integration, but structural factors, such as physical distance between school and field, inadequate communication procedures between the two, and different functional demands in the two spheres of activity, also contribute to the gaps and confusions. In addition, faculty tend not to have recent experience in the newer programs and practices that are continually emerging.

The question of academic work and application skills, their relative weights and the interconnections between the two, is probably the crucial problem facing professional education. The following statement by G. Lester Anderson, a student of professional education, expresses well the dilemma involved:

Professional service rests on relative mastery of a relevant body of knowledge on the one hand and relative mastery of a professional craftmanship on the other. What is the appropriate balance for the study of these two facets of professionalism? Forces exist which would push professional education now one way, now the other. The forces in the educational environment, most frequently university forces, push for knowledge—knowledge which is derived from research and is rooted in and reinforced by theory. The forces emerging from practice push for craftmanship or skill—the "how we do it" which is practice. . . .

The dualisms of knowledge vs. skill, theory vs. practice, or basic vs. applied will probably be with us always. But these dualisms must be wrestled with continuously in professional education (4).

The commonly held assumption is that field work provides an opportunity to apply the theory learned in the classroom to actual situations and real problems. Logically there are four possible relationships between class and field:

1. *Class and field integrate.* The student has an opportunity to try out theory in practice in a direct and systematic way.

2. *Class and field supplement each other.* The two are different but they reinforce each other in providing what the student needs to engage in the practice of the profession. The classroom, for its domain, provides general theory, and the field, in its sphere, offers specific skills and develops professional self-discipline.

3. *Class and field are unrelated.* The two give different things to the student. One may concentrate on preparing the student to be a practitioner while the other may be irrelevant to that task. Thus the classroom may be providing theory that is so broad and general or so out of touch with the realities of the world of practice that it serves no purpose in educating students. Or the field situation may be so limited and restricted by the immediate problems, methods, or goals of specific agencies that it does not provide the grounding for emerging problems or methods that the student will encounter as he progresses in his professional career.

4. *Class and field are in conflict.* In this circumstance, not only does the student learn different things in class and field but these things are at odds with one another. Thus he might learn in the classroom that the "enabling" role is the only acceptable one and in the field that only an "advocate" role is appropriate for reaching a given agency objective. Or the reverse may be true—the classroom may project an activist role and the agency disavow it. The student is given discrepant information and antagonistic orientations.

Our general review of the field indicates that the community organization educational scene has included all four patterns, in differing proportions among different schools and agencies. Given the dominant field-instruction pattern currently followed by a majority of the schools, we would hypothesize that, of the various possible relationships detailed above, class and field in general supplement each other rather than integrate. Overt conflict or marked independence characterizes only a few limited situations. But the rhythm, tempo, logic, and flow of class and field are quite different, and this accounts for the difficulty of integration and for the limited success most schools report in achieving it.

We have indicated a number of trends and developments in C.O. field instruction. It is obvious that we are in a period of considerable flux; traditional methods and forms are being modified. A long-established model of field instruction has begun to loosen up as a result of new problems, personnel, and definitions of the practice world. As a summary of this section, we shall look at the historical antecedents and state conceptually the traditional model of field instruction. This will serve as a background for programs and approaches that are leading to its transformation.

## Historical Antecedents

The current pattern of field instruction originated early in the history of social-work education and has been retained with very little modification in essentials over the years. It would be well to view the conditions that led to the emergence of the particular pattern at that point in time and accordingly to assess its relevance for today.

One of the main features of social-work education is a heavy proportion of time spent by students in operating agencies throughout their professional educational career, upward of 60–70 per cent of the total school workload (56). There is probably more time spent in learning the application of practice skills in social work than in any other professional group. How account for it?

The impetus for social-work education came from practitioners in social agencies, and the earliest forms of education were rather informal discussions among practitioners themselves (144). Social agencies established the earliest schools of social work and favored a practical, applied, skill-producing bent. Mary Richmond conveyed this tendency in her admonishment that "it should never be forgotten that more emphasis should be put on practical work than on academic considerations." (115)

A heavy weighting was given to field experience quite early by schools, which were at the time independent, agency-run institutions, separate from universities (93). This was so not only because of the needs and mind-set of practitioners, but also because of the needs of social agencies to train their own personnel and maintain staff services at the same time. Kidneigh states in *The Encyclopedia of Social Work* (65) that "formal education for social work at first adhered very closely to the needs of voluntary agencies and differed little from the concept and content of apprenticeship training." In the interplay between the practice-oriented people that had dominated the schools and the academically oriented people brought onto faculties, such as economists and sociologists, the practical group won out (93). This is understandable, in that there was little at the time in the way of a well-formulated social-work theory, and hence prominence was given to a kind of apprenticeship in operating agencies with an emphasis on the development of concrete, practical skills (127). This training pattern became set and has been carried forward as a natural and desirable feature of social-work education. Marks (80) makes this point clearly: "Although field instruction developed out of the apprenticeship methods of the early years of social work education, it has come to be a central part of the teaching program."

We will add two general comments to the above that are by way of hypotheses:

1. Professions generally in their development and maturation move from a period when (a) education is controlled by practitioners and heavily emphasizes skill and apprenticeship, (b) to a period of independent professional schools, when skill and theory are given somewhat equal treatment, and finally (c) to a period when education is centered in the university under university control and intellectual concepts, and principles are given greatest emphasis.

Brubacher (16) in this study of the evolution of professions describes these three periods as follows:

At first there was a stage of apprenticeship, when training was quite *ad hoc* and empirical. Business, for instance, was learned on the job. . . .

Subsequently, apprenticeship gave way to an early form of school. Rensselaer Polytechnic Institute, founded in 1842, and the colleges of architecture and mechanical arts, established after the Morrill Act of 1842, were such schools for engineering . . .

Finally, there has been a struggle to merit true professional recognition—which implies university rank and affiliation and an "emphasis on theory" . . .

McGlothlin (83) summarizes this progression as follows: "In general, then, the trend of the curriculum in the various professional fields is to move toward greater emphasis on knowledge, concepts, and principals, with proportionately less emphasis on detailed instruction in the skills of practice or on special techniques."

Brubacher (16) maintains that old as well as new professions go through this process. "Training for the younger incipient professions—engineering, business, pedagogy, journalism, architecture, and the like—tended to pass through much the same stages of development as the older, more learned ones."

We would hypothesize that social work may be located in the middle stage because of a heavy and even disproportionate weighting in time and energy given to application considerations. Professional maturation would lie in shifting the *existing balance* of class and field to a *new balance,* which would also include class and field but with a heavier weighting on the academic-knowledge side.

2. We would hypothesize that the heavy field-work feature in social-work education has retained its original character largely because of a natural conservatism that prevails in all professions and a reluctance to modify old forms that are working at levels sufficient to maintain a suitable equilibrium in the professional system. Habit, past practices, professional pride all contrive to maintain the *status quo.* Anderson and Ertell make this point well:

> Undoubtedly the most powerful forces moulding professional education are those of history and tradition. One may well inquire why many things are as they are. Why does the basic study of law culminate with a baccalaureate degree, social work with a master's degree, and dentistry with a doctorate? There are, of course, historical justifications for past practices which continue present practices. But many such practices are often only the result of inertia (5).

McGlothlin (83) has described this tendency of professions to rigidity in meeting new demands placed on them, and Robert Merton (97) has related the phenomenon to more general sociological and organizational processes of ritualism. Closer to home, Mary Louis Somers and Paul Gitlin (132) have described ritualistic blockages to the creation of innovative practices in social-work field instruction and urged the profession to cross this barrier and to explore in a basic way new forms and arrangements in educating for application. Ripple (115a) has documented a number of these innovations.

## Characteristics of the Traditional Model

The pattern of education for application has remained fairly uniform and stable throughout the history of social work. In more recent years, schools have begun to experiment with variations. The pattern is described roughly in the summary that follows. This is a composite statement of the elements usually present in the established model. It is not an attempt to describe the situation at any one school or to characterize in detail even a group of schools. More detailed descriptions of the model may be found in Hale (56), Ryan and Bardill (121) and the United Nations survey of field instruction (144).

1. *Description of the Model.* The student enters the graduate training institution and is assigned immediately to a community social agency for field experience and instruction. Field experience essentially involves direct personal responsibility in actual practice, in order to give the student an opportunity to execute in action the concepts and theories learned in the classroom. Concurrent academic classroom attendance and field instruction in an agency (two or three days a week) occurs throughout the student's entire educational career. Basic supervision of practice (or field instruction) takes place in the agency under the direction of an agency employee who is assessed to possess practice competence and the ability to communicate it.

The major means of supervision is a weekly conference with this agency field instructor, the conference consisting of both educational and administrative components. The chief vehicle for producing the content of weekly conferences is lengthy and detailed process recording kept by the student of his performance in practice and his thoughts and emotional reactions related to his performance. These recordings are reviewed by the field instructor prior to conferences.

The student is ordinarily given a delimited assignment involving personal responsibility for practice, such as a certain number of cases, groups, or, in community organization, projects or committees. The student remains in a single placement agency on a regular weekly schedule for a nine-month academic year. In the second year a similar procedure is carried out in another agency, usually in a different field of practice (mental health, corrections, aging, etc.).

Agency field instructors are given assistance in their function by schools through orientation programs, conferences, workshops, and contacts through a faculty liaison person who is a regular member of the school faculty. Taking the role of a field instructor is ordinarily voluntary, carries no remuneration, and is honorific in the profession. The field instructor carries quasi-faculty status but may or may not be responsible for assigning a student a grade for his performance in the agency.

2. *Assumptions and Problems of the Model.* (a) *The student enters a community agency to engage in actual practice close to the outset of his graduate educational career.* This early entry into actual practice has some disadvantages for graduate professional education. In the first place, it is generally held in the professions that a knowledge base is required in order for there to be effective practice. A period of academic preparation is assumed by most professions to be necessary in order to acquire fundamental knowledge pertaining to practice. Secondly, practice fostered at too early a stage is likely to be of poor quality, even if supported by supervision, posing a risk to clients. The imperative to engage in practice under such circumstances discourages in students a responsible attitude toward clients or, for that matter, toward knowledge. If one can practice without knowledge, of what use or consequence is knowledge and how important are clients?

In addition, this early entry into practice may evoke intense or unnecessary anxiety in students, which can be a detriment to student learning. Recognizing that a moderate level of anxiety may enhance learning, one can ask whether for most students assignment of substantial practice responsibility at an early period evokes anxiety above the threshold useful for maximal learning. For further elaboration of some of these points see Aptekar (6), McGrath (86), Kindelsperger (66), and Towle (143).

(b) *Field experiences and learning of practice skills can best take place in an on-going social agency providing services in the community.* Agencies have long been viewed as ideal sites for field instruction for students because the situation is genuine—that is to say, agencies are close to actual problems and clients. At the same time there are certain inherent and recurring problems that are associated with training in a setting which is primarily service- and program-oriented. Experiences essentially grow out of operational problems and needs of the agency, with the result that it is difficult to control or sequence experiences to coincide with student learning needs or with the ordering of academic content. Often agency

functional needs, procedures, or rigidities may take precedence over
the requirements of maximal student learning. There is also a
danger that the student may have a narrow or limited exposure,
becoming inadvertently a captive of the particular agency outlook.
This inhibits his ability to look critically at a range of program-
matic, organizational or technological possibilities, or to engage in
intraorganizational manipulation to modify practice. For further
elaboration of some of these points see Dana (31) and Leyendecker (72).

(c) *Professional practitioners based in operating social agencies
make appropriate field instructors for students.* While agency practitioners have much to offer students, in the current situation there
are important considerations which militate against assigning the
bulk of field instruction to agency personnel.

Few agency practitioners currently have the knowledge foundation (social science and contemporary community-organization
theory) to instruct C.O. students adequately. This is probably true
also in casework as new knowledge accumulates and new knowledge areas are drawn upon—such as sociobehavioral theory. In
addition, agency personnel have heavy time and work pressures on
them which restrict their ability to provide instruction.

Agency personnel are apt to experience some degree of conflict
and role strain in performing the field-instructor function, as student learning needs and agency service requirements lead to con-
tradictions and cross pressures. For further elaboration of these
points see Costin (29), Miller (100), McRae (78), McNeil and
Lefferts (92).

(d) *The one-to-one conference method is the optimal means of
providing instruction to students in the field.* The intensity and care
available through personal tutorial arrangement gives attention to
the range of student learning needs and facilitates identification
with the profession through a close relationship with a practicing
social-work professional. At the same time, one-to-one field instruction, as the sole method, is a costly and even cumbersome means
of giving instruction. It may lead to overdependency and places
heavy responsibility for a wide range of learning needs on a single
individual.

A variety of instructional methods are necessary because different learning objectives may require different methods—individual
conferences may be appropriate for dealing with personality problems, informal group conferences for identification with the pro-

fession, formal seminars for transmission of information and techniques, simulation and programmed instruction for initial skill development, etc. Students can learn from and support one another if structured group interaction is provided. Advantages of group supervision and group learning are lost if one relies on one-to-one methods mainly or exclusively. See Williamson (150) for an elaboration of this point.

(e) *A meaningful educational experience can be devised on a regular weekly basis in an academic year in a single agency.* In community organization, tasks are often too fluid and episodic to be regularized in a work week. The length of the community-organization processes may encompass short-range projects of a month or two to long-range ones of two to five years or longer. Because of the importance of the total agency structure and milieu to community-organization practice, it may not be educationally sound to segment the student's experience in the agency during the work week. Flexible and variable time periods may be necessary for community-organization students, including possible use of a block plan, short-term delimited assignments, etc., as well as more sustained exposures. Two years in similar agencies using essentially identical training procedures absorbs a disproportionate amount of time in learning the mechanics of practice and acquiring basic skills as balanced against accumulating new knowledge or obtaining a broad and comparative overview of practices and programs. For further discussion see Berry (9), Schwartz (123), and McNeil and Lefferts (92).

## Some Emerging Approaches

A number of schools have been experimenting with significant variations from the traditional model. One strong trend is the use of prestructured, delimited field experiences, with a more explicit delineation of learning objectives and relevant teaching techniques. Two examples—one in casework and one in community organization—emphasize discrete tasks:

An experimental casework program at Chicago devised a sequence of steps for first-year students:

First Quarter: Become oriented to the base agency. Sit in on an intake interview. Visit resident in home for aged. Visit the family of child in treatment center and observe child in center. Observe a treatment interview. Participate in district-office intake process.

Second Quarter: Assume direct responsibility for three cases.

Use record to learn to write referral to another agency with home economist. Participate in district staff meeting. Visit vocational service agency.

Third Quarter: Take on one or more additional cases. Handle assigned intake interview. Write a psychiatric referral after attending consultation session. Discuss client transfer and termination with students and staff.

Using a variety of rather elaborate evaluative protocols, Schubert concluded that this experimental unit of students did at least as well as three groups of students in control units. However, the author concluded, "Interview observation is seen as an immediately useful teaching device that needs to be more fully understood and exploited." (122a) Success in placing students in predetermined assignments led to the finding that "for a substantial part of the entering class, a highly individualized placement process is not essential." (127)

A plan for all first-year C.O. students began operating at Berkeley in the fall of 1967 (110a) as a full-fledged policy and not as an experimental program. In general, the procedure involved the following sequence:

First Quarter: Observe and analyze the intake process in a community-action service center. Serve as a social broker for families and/or individuals located in the course of the intake process. Interview and observe the roles of selected professionals in major community institutions affecting neighborhood populations. Visit and observe at least one meeting of key organizations and associations in urban communities. Prepare a neighborhood profile and participate in a voter-registration campaign.

Second- and third-term assignments called for involvement of students in common experiences requiring a greater degree of personal responsibility. All students, working in teams, were assigned to organize tenants in public housing projects. Educational objectives focused on techniques of organizing low-income populations at the local level and the use of organizational structures and procedures such as committees and other task groups. Attention was to be given to cultural patterns of low-income populations.

Three other examples of innovative approaches that serve to structure community experiences for the social-work student are the community laboratory, satellite assignments, and the service and teaching center.

The University of Pittsburgh program revolves around the notion of a community laboratory (108) that provides a common experience for students in community organization as well as in the other methods the first eight weeks of school, prior to their assignment to an agency for actual practice.

The laboratory is organized into seven geographical sections with up to fifteen students in each. Each section has a faculty instructor and a local headquarters. In addition, there are some general sessions which students from all sections attend.

The laboratory is seen as giving students an opportunity to observe and analyze social-work practice and community processes. Situations are structurally planned so that students can meet area residents, talk with workers in antipoverty programs, and get to know the social agencies or other institutions in the community concerned with effecting change. Students are given interviewing and quasi-research assignments. They arrange to meet people from all the major social institutions in the community, are helped to focus on the gaps in services and to understand the network of complex interrelationships and social needs which develop in a neighborhood or community.

At Case-Western Reserve students are placed in an anchor agency for their primary educational experience and, in addition, are given a series of satellite assignments to supplement and round out their training. The satellite experiences are time-limited, specialized assignments that run concurrently with a regular on-going agency placement. The rationale assumes that, while continuing experience in an agency has merit, there is a limit to the range and variety of experiences that any single agency can provide for a student. The satellite program, then, compensates for whatever restrictions or limitations may prevail in the basic anchor agency, supplements and augments individual deficiencies in the student's experience, or permits the student to try out a new field or express a personal interest.

In recent years a number of schools of social work have established service and teaching centers (67) that fulfill a dual function: they are model social agencies serving their communities as well as excellent educational facilities for training students. The precise form for such centers is not of concern here. We wish merely to emphasize that these developments are consistent with the thesis of this monograph and reinforce the idea of a more controlled approach to education for application of practice skills which will be developed in the next chapter.

# 3 Some Guiding Principles and a Plan

The foregoing review has pointed out a number of critical and recurring problems and has indicated several avenues for strengthening field instruction. From this assessment, the Project staff has arrived at certain principles for guiding a field-instruction program, some suggested formats for such an integrated approach, and a scheme to implement these guiding principles. In addition, a number of suggestions are made for organizing the educational objectives and learning experiences.

## Some Guidelines

*Integration of classroom teaching and application teaching.* To the greatest degree possible there should be a systematic, planned, and structured interrelationship of academic and application components of social-work education. The key to the recommendations in this area is the notion that there should be no teaching of methods and skills courses without application experiences built into or closely correlated with the courses themselves and, conversely, that there should be no field assignment that does not include a teaching seminar. In other words, integration is to be achieved by looking at both the classroom work and the application of practice as courses, each designed to integrate knowledge and skills through experiences structured to provide specified learning outcomes.

*Diversification of teaching techniques and learning experiences.* For educational purposes there are limitations in depending upon a single agency over an entire academic year. Students may learn practice skills through artificially structured campus-based means —role playing, simulation games, programmed learning experiences, computerized community problem-solving exercises, and the like. On the other hand, real-life experiences can be partialized and delimited on a shorter- or longer-range basis in a variety of contexts, both in a specific agency and in the community but not centered in a particular agency, in order to teach different concepts and skills (conducting a survey, engaging in a fund-raising campaign, planning and running a voter-registration drive, etc.).

This approach frees the student from a restricted exposure in experience, philosophy, or method that is embodied in any one agency. The student receives a comparative perspective, one that enables him to examine agency practice critically rather than to accept the parochial orientation of a particular agency. This freedom from overinvolvement as a staff member in a single agency is especially important during the first year, when the student is getting an overview of the field. Later, it may be valuable for him to have the depth involvement that comes with total immersion in a particular agency.

Because this more diversified approach to teaching practice skills breaks loose from placement in a single agency over an academic year, we make use of McGlothlin's term "application" when referring to training in carrying out operationally the practice skills of the profession. "Application training" implies a broader teaching technology than has been typically associated with "field instruction" in social work.

*Greater direction and control by the school of the educational experience for teaching application skills.* This implies greater faculty involvement in teaching skills and relating such skills to conceptual and theoretical constructs. Classroom faculty should structure tasks and exercises, monitor them, conduct seminars and other educational experiences, and in other ways become more closely identified with the process of teaching application skills. Through greater faculty participation, integration may more readily be achieved and new knowledge relative to practice conveyed to students in a more direct way. In this way, faculty are also kept current with new developments in practice. Further, the essential responsibility of the school for the total education of the student, including practice skills, is made manifest in this proposition.

*Greater specificity of learning objectives by the school; explicating skills to be imparted and relevant tasks and experiences.* In place of a rather global and diffuse approach to field learning, we recommend that schools be much more rigorous and exacting in selecting from the vast array of all possible operations that practitioners may perform those delimited and defined sets of skills that they wish to inculcate in all students at various stages of their educational careers. In the recommendations in the following section, we will suggest laboratory sections attached to methods courses as one way of accomplishing this goal.

*Some rational and ordered sequencing of learning experiences according to a predetermined plan.* While the forms of progression may vary with different schools, agencies, and individual students, there are three main principles to be observed: (1) cumulative impact—as a student builds up to a given level of experience, all or part of the previous levels may be continued concurrently; (2) motivation must be maintained—experiences and tasks must be interesting, vital, and relevant to the student; (3) opportunities should be provided for variations in the plan based on individual backgrounds of students, such as exemptions or special advanced sections for more experienced students.

A representative series of cumulative sequential experiences might proceed as follows:

(a) Academic preparation, including an orientation to practice.

(b) Observation and discussion: visiting an agency; observing a practitioner engaged in specific tasks; attending certain community events, analyzing a meeting, etc.

(c) Simulated practice experiences and skills exercises: role-playing specific aspects of practice; carrying out computerized community problem-solving exercises; completing assigned practice tasks—preparing a proposal, writing a news release, conducting an interview.

(d) Limited structured experience in actual practice: community laboratory—neighborhod survey and plan of action; conducting of discrete short-term assignments in agencies.

(e) Actual practice in an agency with increasing scope and responsibility.

*Two areas of learning and related modes of training.* It is the view of the Project staff that there are two somewhat different (though related) kinds of learning that are necessary in order to develop competent practice skills. One has to do with the acquisition of specific skills, such as community diagnosis, staffing committee meetings, preparing budgets, influencing community elites, interviewing different kinds of community actors, etc. The other kind of learning is broader and not as easily defined or specified. It consists of two principal components: (a) The exposure of the student to a holistic experience in an agency—experiencing the agency as a total system; seeing the interconnections between one task and those of others in the agency; seeing the relationship of the agency and its program to other organizations and subsystems in the community; viewing the unfolding of multiple events and forces as they converge on the agency; experiencing time pressures, competing demands, and multiple role expectations in the course of performing on the job, etc. (b) The systematic development within the student of self-awareness and self-discipline in performing professionally. This means conscious attention to the use of the self as an instrument of change in a community context, under circumstances of multiple pressures. The realistic tensions experienced by the student require that he know his biases and limitations, be in control of his feelings and emotional responses, and attend consciously to his impact on others and to their effects on him in the performance of his professional responsibilities.

## Suggested Formats

One might envision a plan whereby the first year would include academic work, observation, discussion, simulated practice experiences, skills exercises, and delimited prestructured practice experiences in agencies or in the community at large. Experiences would be faculty planned, directed, and controlled. There would be a maximization of relationship between theory and practice, in that experiences would be expressly set to parallel specific academic content. The approach would represent full integration of class and field as anticipated in Chapter 2.

The second year would be more like the existing field-instruction pattern. It would involve a more holistic exposure of the "doing" of practice. It would be assumed that the relationship of class and field in this part of the training would be more *supplemental* than *integrative*—that is, relative emphasis in the field would be on such things as professional self-discipline, use of self, and practical aid in the carrying out of a multiplicity of practice tasks (learning about how agencies work and how one reacts to organizational structure, learning how to form relationships with different types of community actors, etc.). However, integration would be maintained to the greatest degree possible through a practicum seminar and other integrative features:

(a) Faculty-supervised field units in community social agencies.

(b) School-operated projects and agencies under faculty direction.

(c) Direct payment by schools to field instructors for their services—requiring specific tasks and continuing training.

(d) Other incentives and rewards (e.g., adjunct faculty appointments, tuition grants) to field instructors to assure level of performance and continuing training.

The Project is recommending that initially specific base-line skills be acquired through a laboratory experience established in conjunction with the methods courses. In accordance with the discussion in Chapter 4, class and field would essentially integrate. Thus, each methods courses would have associated with it a parallel laboratory comprising, on the one hand, practical tasks that would involve operationalizing the theories, concepts, and techniques taught in class and, on the other hand, an opportunity for systematic observational analysis of phenomena associated with the classroom teaching. The educational objectives regarding application skills should be derived at every point from what is being taught academically, primarily in the methods course, and thus should coincide with academic content. The analogue is the laboratory section of physical-science courses such as chemistry or physics, wherein the laboratory section gives the student a chance to become involved behaviorally with theoretical content taught within a parallel time period—observing demonstrations, conducting experiments, and engaging in practical operations. An important aspect of the laboratory would be the use of discrete, prestructural experiences in the communities. Let us here conceptualize this technique educationally.

If the objective, for example, is to help a student plan a meeting or prepare an agenda collaboratively with a committee chairman, he might observe a practitioner as he engages in his task, or he might assist the practitioner in a limited way, or he might be given this specific assignment to carry out independently for a practitioner under supervision. Instead of an ongoing agency field placement with all its richness, variability, and fluidity, this procedure would envision more short-range, specialized, and discrete observational and implemental experiences in the community and agency arena. The setting would be more real and alive, as compared to programmed learning or simulated approaches, but more arbitrary and, to an extent, artificial than would be reflected in continuing responsibility for a project in a field agency. The objective is to specify learning objectives in a concrete, defined manner and to structure a series of separate experiences in the community that will further these. The student is expected initially to develop understanding and skill with regard to a prescribed set of particularized practice activities, which he would later have an opportunity to put together in an ongoing agency placement.

These discrete experiences might be arranged through one or more established social agencies; they could be carried out in the community independently by students; the school itself might sponsor these activities on an *ad hoc* basis or through a service and training center, or sponsorship could be sought for certain activities through independent indigenous groups such as autonomous tenants' associations.

These tasks and experiences might cover a very wide range. Students could engage in a neighborhood survey independently or through an agency—learning such things as study design, questionnaire construction, interviewing, establishing rapport, analysis of data, as well as aspects of implementation of study recommendations. Practitioners in social work and in allied professions and disciplines might be observed in a wide variety of tasks. Interviews could be arranged with citizens, professionals, and public officials covering various institutional spheres and the entire spectrum of social class and power structures. The budgeting process could be observed in a United Way, and responsibility could be assigned for certain aspects of preparing a budget for an agency or independent citizen group. Students could be assigned delimited action tasks, such as preparing a legislative draft regarding a particular problem and getting it introduced into the city council or state legislature; they could organize and take part in a voter-registration drive, or draw up a grant proposal for an agency or independent group. They could prepare news releases or give public addresses in support of one or another program, cause, or event. By being released from the confines of a single agency and an ongoing responsibility, students could be freed to engage in a broad array of activities, under a variety of auspices, with an opportunity to be freely critical of professional and organizational practice. Such a

program would give assurance that all students are exposed to a
similar core of prestructured experiences incorporating consciously
prescribed educational objectives.

The use of discrete community and agency experiences is not new
in social-work education. What is new is the systematic and con-
certed use of this approach in designing application training curricula. And even in the latter capacity, several starts have been
made in schools around the country.

The approach being suggested here relies in part on the use of
observation. The position is taken that observation of effective
practice as conducted by a competent professional is a good prelude
for engaging in one's own practice (assuming an opportunity to
reflect on the experience and discuss the observations in an educationally meaningful way). A number of professional fields such
as medicine, dentistry, psychology, etc., build this into their training. This is at variance with a point of view which has been prevalent in social work for some time, which minimized the usefulness
of observation and stresses the value of John Dewey's dictum of
learning by doing. One learns best, according to this philosophy, by
engaging early in the stuff of practice and deriving learning from
one's mistakes as well as successes.

One of the few statements in the social-work literature that seriously examines observation as a potentially valid teaching method
was written by Alfred Kadushin (63). He deals with the observation of interviewing as a teaching device. Kadushin reports that
psychiatrists and clinical psychologists make extensive use of interview observation in training, while social workers make only sparse
use of it, mainly in public-welfare agencies with workers who have
had no previous social-work education or experience. The social-
work educators and administrators in Kadushin's study objected
to using observation on the basis of educational principles, casework theory, ethical considerations, and practical or administrative
factors. On the basis of comments from those few social workers
who had ventured to use this device. Kadushin reports, "Observation generally fulfilled its purpose without any apparent adverse
effects on the client, the worker, or the interview interaction." He
refers to the ease of direct observation as a training device, "since
it has flexibility, is readily available, and requires no special technical apparatus." Further support for the use of observation as a
technique can be found in the writings of the learning theorists,
where modeling is given high weighting as an educational tool.

Clearly, this process has gone on for a long time in C.O. whether acknowledged or not.

## Overview of a Scheme to Implement These Guiding Principles

The proposed approach to field instruction or application training incorporates a variety of methods and techniques geared to imparting professional skills. In general we are thinking of three sequential stages or emphases: (a) a laboratory-observatory, (b) a skill-development laboratory, and (c) a practicum. The first year will include (a) and (b) and the second will be comprised largely of (c).

(a) *The laboratory-observatory* (see Chapter 4) will be attached to the first-term methods course, which is a survey of community-organization practice. In the laboratory-observatory the student will be exposed to a wide range of practice contexts, programs, and skills. The focus is on obtaining an understanding of the nature and settings of practice rather than on learning practice skills. Students would be assigned to a particular focal agency for their own observation and limited participation but will also share observations and experiences with other students in common agencies or projects.

(b) *The skills-development laboratory* (see Chapter 5) is oriented toward teaching specific practice skills to students in consciously selected and controlled content areas. Schools would expect to determine a delimited range of skills that they judge important for students to acquire by the end of the first year and prior to entry into actual agency practice (practicum). The skills-development laboratory is similarly attached to an academic methods course where theory or conceptualization relevant to the application of skills is treated in a systematic way. Thus, if students in the laboratory are being trained in methods of decision making in planning, the methods course will cover various theories of and approaches to decision making. In the skills laboratory students would not be assigned to a given agency on a continuing basis but would engage in common experiences that might include simulation games, programmed instructional materials, community activities not connected with agencies, as well as tasks in selected agencies. Unlike the observatory, in the skills-development laboratory the students would be engaged in the actual "doing" of practice and the mastery of skills, but in a structured and controlled context.

The major implication of this laboratory strategy for further curriculum development would be an effort to design the academic content of courses in such a way that it would parallel the explicit skill-learning experiences and performance requirements being developed in the laboratory. This strategy has great potential for redressing the current lack of integration between class and field.

(c) *The practicum* will begin in the second year and is conceived of as a holistic and realistic agency experience where the student is expected to put the skills he has previously acquired into operation under circumstances approximating those the practitioner experiences on the job. Thus, the student is expected to apply his skills (and learn others) under conditions of reality which include temporal and political pressures, structural restraints, interpersonal complications, etc. The disciplined use of self and need to grapple more immediately with value dilemmas come to the fore in this phase.

The practicum resembles the approach to field instruction as currently employed in most schools. The holistic experience suggested might be realized either through a block placement or through concurrent placement depending on the student, school, community circumstances, etc. A faculty-run practice seminar would be established in association with the practicum, the purpose of which is to provide a measure of theoretical or conceptual coherence with regard to the relatively open-ended agency experience. While an agency field instructor serves this function in part, the school also has a responsibility systematically to tie the practice experience back into the academic program.

The second year thus entails the attachment of the student to a single ongoing agency or program for a period of time and the use of a practice seminar to reconceptualize and integrate the experience. It is therefore suggested that students be assigned a substantive project for which they carry primary responsibility over the course of the practicum. It might also be desirable to organize students into field units for purposes of the seminars.

It is useful to think of the summer period between the two years as a time for a bridging experience between the more particularized approach to practice in the first year and the more generalized approach in the second year. Thus, schools should suggest to students that they acquire a paid community practice job during the summer. The school might take a brokerage responsibility for seeking out positions and an educational responsibility at the end of the summer or the beginning of the fall terms to offer a modest workshop or seminar, the purpose of which would be to review the experience and place it in a theoretical and conceptual context. This should lead smoothly into the more educationally focused practicum.

A range of additional methods courses might be offered by any given school in the second year. These might or might not link with a student's practicum assignment—the main burden of integrating the field and class will fall on the practice seminar. These additional methods courses will serve to round out the academic program, provide additional intellectual content to students regarding practice methods, and give a particular character or emphasis to a school's curriculum in the area of community practice.

In the chapters to follow, we will draw upon three technologies that hold promise for an application training curriculum. These include (a) discrete, prestructured community and agency experience, including observation and *ad hoc* practice tasks, (b) simulations, including simulation games, and (c) programmed instruction. The latter two (see Chapters 6 and 7) embody elements of the new media, or emerging technologies, that are finding their way into educational programs of all types and at all levels. These new technologies are not relevant exclusively or even especially to application training. They are equally pertinent to more academic aspects of professional education. In this book, however, we will give emphasis to the utility of these new methods for the development of profession practice skills. These newer educational techniques have been introduced only haltingly and sparingly in social-work education. The idea of discrete community experiences has been used to a greater extent in social-work field instruction, but not always in a systematic way.

In laying out these techniques and the corresponding potential units of an application training program, we will not be specifying a particular field-instruction curriculum. Rather, an array of components of such a curriculum will be suggested. The way these components are combined and packaged to make up a curriculum will, of necessity, depend upon how a school defines its educational objectives and specifies its educational philosophy, and what it assesses to be the most effective way to attain these ends. Our intention is to provide schools with the building blocks of newer educational technologies that can then be molded particularistically into courses and syllabi according to the educational goals and strategies selected by the school. By way of further preliminary groundwork, we will specify several educational strategies around which application and training units may be grouped.

## Strategies for Organizing Objectives and Learning Experiences

The structuring of application training in social work becomes, to a degree, more problematical when a faculty-directed curriculum replaces one that is based in an agency. In the typical agency setting learning tends to be emergent and fluid, springing from the stuff of specific practice demands. Learning to influence a cooperative or recalcitrant committee chairman depends on whether one has an agreeable or disagreeable chairman, whether one was assigned to a committee at all, or whether the committee to which one was assigned actually materializes or doesn't disband. The experiences are real and compelling but unpredictable. A sequential and predictable ordering of learning experiences, on the other hand, necessitates an explicit rationale for each unit that is included and the temporal linkage between them. We will refer to such a rationale as an educational strategy, and several of those are listed below:

1. *Inventory of Typical Practitioner Tasks and Skills.* One approach to building an application-skills curriculum is to develop an inventory of typical practitioner tasks and skills. If one is training for practice, then one logically should build into that training the skills that practitioners are typically expected to execute in pursuing their professional responsibilities. Several listings of practitioner tasks and skills are in existence and could be utilized for curriculum design. One such listing, drawing on a number of studies, was compiled by the Project staff for use in the questionnaire for a pilot study of community-organization field instruction. It is reproduced below to suggest one type of inventory of practice tasks and skills.

    (a) Collecting information on a problem, services, etc.

    (b) Ascertaining attitudes and opinions of others.

    (c) Analyzing facts or opinions, interpreting data.

    (d) Recruiting people to join groups or organizations.

    (e) Trying to interest people in taking some action.

    (f) Identifying and referring individuals or families for specific services.

(g) Participating with agency staff in discussion and selection of goals.

(h) Participating with professionals from other agencies in discussion and selection of goals.

(i) Participating with citizens, residents, etc., in discussion and selection of goals.

(j) Writing position papers or reports.

(k) Disseminating and interpreting project by speaking at public meetings, committees, etc.

(l) Writing proposals for grants, agency consideration, etc.

(m) Making arrangements for meetings.

(n) Keeping minutes of meetings.

(o) Preparing agendas for meetings.

(p) Supervising other personnel in connection with project.

(q) Participating in the administration of the project.

Another study of activities of community organizers was conducted by Eva Rainman-Schindler (111) in the California area. A different type of study was completed by Arthur Dunham (40) focusing on tasks of community-development practitioners. An interview guide for the study of practice has been developed by the Project (see the Interview Guide reproduced in Appendix A). On a less-structured basis, faculty or experienced practitioners could be asked to list those skills they consider to be most relevant or important for practice.

A different manner of obtaining an inventory of skills to be taught is to ask students to indicate those skills they believe they lack or will need in the kind of practice in which they desire to engage. When this was done with the second-year class at the University of Michigan, the following inventory of skills was produced:

(a) Long-range planning to integrate antipoverty programs into ongoing local community social services.

(b) Work with the nonprofessionals (middle-class volunteers and lower-class indigenous leaders)—learning the various roles they can play; recruiting and training; meeting resistance; determining differences in relation to class and educational levels.

(c) Interpersonal influence skills—interviewing (giving and getting information or advice, influencing opinion/action); moderating conflict, handling anxiety, anger, affect; encouraging participation; clarifying function and roles.

(d) Committee technology and application of group dynamics skills—establishing a staff relationship (psychological problems);

planning agendas (the conscious use of agendas as strategies); handling minutes and reports (both as a routine and as a strategy); developing discussion-leadership skills and intervention skills for influencing a group's productivity and course of direction.

(e) Relationships among staff—working with differences: inter-group and interracial problems; professionally trained versus untrained and indigenous workers; mixed professional backgrounds; support for agency supervisors and executives vis-à-vis work for agency change.

(f) Training of indigenous committees.

(g) Promotional skills—fund raising; public relations; speaking.

(h) Acceptance of limitations—those imposed by employing agency, community, colleagues, etc.

(i) Administrative skills expected of entry worker—budgeting; supervision; staff selection, evaluation, termination; accountability; participation in staff meetings; working with board members and authoritative figures; understanding financial accountability and controls; preparing grant requests.

(j) Obtainment and maintenance of a job—interviewing the executive board; negotiating salary and conditions; supervisory supports.

(k) C.O. in specific settings—how are skills differently applied in public welfare, mental health, housing, urban planning, rural community development settings, etc.

(l) Life styles and language of the poor and minority groups—how to use appropriate language and to employ cultural elements to guide intervention.

To obtain an inventory or composite of practitioner activity, a school may use one of the existing compilations or do a new study of its own. Such a study might be strictly behavioral (observing practitioners on the job, asking practitioners to keep an accurate factual record of activities along the lines of a time study) or it might be an opinion type (interviewing practitioners to ask them what they do in a typical day, in a typical project, over the last week, etc.).

Having such an inventory is only a step on the way to a specfic curriculum design. Certain tasks or skills have to be singled out for training purposes. It is not possible during the two years of professional education to introduce the fledgling practitioner to all aspects of practice that will confront him throughout his practice career or even in the initial stages. A delimited number of circumscribed skills and tasks need to be extracted from the total range because of the impossibility of covering all or the superficiality of treatment involved in attempting to cover too many. Such a selection will, of course, be guided by the school's own definition of the nature and scope of C.O. which it has chosen to emphasize. Several criteria may be utilized in making such a selection, including:

(a) Frequency—those tasks and skills used most frequently by practitioners.

(b) Critical relevance—those tasks and skills that in the opinion of practitioner and/or faculty are most crucial for effective practice of a particular kind. While a given practitioner might spend a great deal of time engaged in filling out routine forms, this skill can be assumed to be learned automatically or through trial and error, as contrasted with the skill of preparing a legislative draft or conducting a survey of community needs and resources. In addition to using the judgment of experienced practitioners and teachers, it might be possible to conduct more empirical studies of critical relevance: Among more effective practitioners, what types of skills and activities receive emphasis? In successful as compared to unsuccessful projects, what were the significant differences in the types of activities in which practitioners engaged?

(c) Emerging role of the profession—those tasks and functions that will permit the profession to assume new functions and address new social problems in the society. This involves not only an assessment of current practice but an estimation of new roles to be assumed by the profession in a rapidly changing social situation. It implies placing the practitioner in settings and functions that will make an increasingly greater impact on social problems, as well as the utilization of new professional technologies as rapidly as they develop.

Assuming that a distinct set of practice skills and tasks has been identified, these still need to be ordered sequentially for purposes of education. Several possible principles for such an ordering include the following:

(a) Ordering tasks from more simple to more complex operations (writing a descriptive report of another practitioner's work, writing an insightful report of one's own practice).

(b) Ordering tasks with natural skill linkages (interviewing clients to obtain information, research activities involving more systematic interviewing).

(c) Ordering tasks according to the psychological and motivational set of students (beginning with skills that are of greater immediate interest of student, such as working with indigenous, low-income populations, and moving toward tasks that are of lesser immediate interest, such as how to work within bureaucratic organizations).

(d) Using units of aggregates at different social-system levels, and proceeding in either direction (working with individuals, small groups, organizations, communities, states, regions, or nations).

A series of practice-skill areas, identified by the Project staff from a number of studies, are listed in Chapter 5. These have been grouped into certain logical clusters that incorporate important practice operations with respect both to tasks and to settings.

2. *The Experiential Career Pattern of the Entering Professional.* This is, in a certain sense, a variation of the inventory of skills suggested in 1. above. It involves plotting the typical experiential pattern of the young graduate entering his first agency position (or of the second-year student entering an agency placement). A series of learning objectives is established to parallel temporally the natural flow of experience and expectation in the agency setting. Thus, the practitioner may first be confronted with understanding the workings and dynamics of a bureaucratic organization—the agency by which he is employed (elements of formal organization, modes of influence, communication, and decision making in a formal organization). He next may be expected to know the community in which the agency is located (methods of community survey and fact finding). Next, he may be expected to work with a committee dealing with a particular problem in the community (influence techniques in a small group, social-problem analysis).

An ordering of skills and tasks within this framework may be established deductively through the judgment of faculty or practitioners concerning what is the most usual, or by asking students entering ongoing agency placement or newly graduated students taking up first positions to keep a sequential record of experiences and expectations in their agency settings. From such materials model patterns of experience and expectation, with concomitant educational objectives, could be constructed.

3. *Conceptual Schema Concerning the Nature of Practice.* A set of learning objectives might be set up to parallel some intellectual scheme that attempts to conceptualize practice. For example, the practice text produced by the Project conceives of practice as em-

bracing activities concerned with developing services within a single agency and engaging in functions involving interorganizational planning, coordinating, and allocating. Within each of these areas of activity a series of typical practice tasks is hypothesized. The three areas of practice have in common a set of general tasks ranging from defining the problem to building structures, to formulating policy, to implementing plans. Within each of these steps there exist analytical tasks and interactional tasks. An application-skill curriculum could be fashioned easily from such a framework. The laboratory-observatory discussed in Chapter 4 is based on this scheme.

Another example of a scheme to incorporate the basic elements of practice is the one developed at Case-Western Reserve. Functional roles of all practitioners are seen as including two main types of activity: Community Problem Analysis—Policy and Program Design and Implementive Action. These are roughly analogous to the Project's analytical and interactional task areas. The school's plan then moves to Performance Task Areas of practitioners and clusters these in six general categories: (1) management of group process; (2) casing the community; (3) casing the sponsoring organization's internal and external aspects; (4) administering the organization; (5) developing professional or working relationships; (6) social-problem analysis.

While at Columbia University, Professor Slavin utilized a conceptual scheme for organizing practice skills comprising five categories: (1) engagement skills—establishing working relations, interviewing competence, etc.; (2) organizational skills—establishing structures, staffing committees, etc.; (3) planning and policy skills—policy and problem analysis, program evaluation, research and fact finding, etc.; (4) action skills—conflict management, power steering, political manipulations; (5) communication and interpretation—public relations, recording and reporting, etc.

Up to this point, our discussion has been general and suggestive. Perhaps the reader would appreciate a shift toward explication in specific terms of the guidelines that have been set down. The remaining chapters will concentrate on just such explanation and elaboration.

# 4　The Laboratory-Observatory

The proposed laboratory-observatory is recommended for the first semester of the student's career. It embraces a series of planfully structured community observational experiences and runs parallel with the related survey course, which introduces students to a range of C.O. agencies, programs, and practices. The practice text by Gurin and Perlman, *Community Organization and Social Planning,* based on the Curriculum Project's work, provides a framework for the survey course and, correspondingly, for the laboratory-observatory. The survey course might be expanded so as to include not only credit for C.O. method, but also for social-science study in complex organizations and/or community structure and process.

## I. General Description of Laboratory-Observatory

At the beginning of the term a list of projects will be selected for utilization in the laboratory. These projects will cover the range of settings that will be treated in the survey course. A possible format, using the organizational contexts around which the textbook is developed, might be as follows:

1. *Voluntary Associations*
    Two community-development projects
        Neighborhood organization
        Church group
        Block club
    Two or three social-action projects
        Alinsky-type organizations
        Welfare-rights organization
        Civil-rights group

League of Women Voters
Tenants' organization
Black-power group

2. *Direct Service Agencies*
Five or six projects involving different types of direct services, lodged in one or more agencies (selected according to accessibility and student interest):
Employment, vocational training
Family and child welfare
Hospital, clinic, other health
Recreation
Income maintenance
    public assistance
    social insurance
    pensions and compensation
Housing agency, relocation office
Adult education, remedial services
Corrections, courts, etc.

3. *Planning and Allocating Organizations*
Two private-sectoral planning
Juvenile delinquency
Aging
Mental health
Race relations, intergroup relations
One United Way (United Fund) or federation
One health and welfare council
Two or three governmental planning
Public housing
Urban renewal
Economic development
Board of education, etc.

This comprises a core of fifteen to eighteen projects and agencies covering a spectrum of types. A particular student would be assigned to study a given project or agency as his laboratory project. This would make for a seminar of a size (fifteen to eighteen students) large enough to incorporate a range of settings and still small enough to provide for a reasonable degree of exchange and discussion. This number is only suggestive; it represents perhaps an optimal upper limit.

Throughout the term the student would be making contacts in his assigned project or agency and gathering specified data that will be shared with others, as suggested and illustrated later in this chapter. While the assignments will concentrate on a given project or agency (preferably of the student's choice), he will receive on-going information (oral and written) from other students regarding their assignments. In addition, three common experiences shared by all students will be arranged in the three organizational contexts —voluntary associations, direct-service agencies, and planning and allocating organizations. In this way, every student is assured a personal experience with each of the organizational contexts.

Provision may also be made for all students to make observations and participate in special activities or events of general interest as they are undertaken by a particular project or agency or in the community at large—a mass community meeting, a fund-raising drive, etc. The student will be given an organizational *base* without being subjected to an organizational *bias*.

As an alternative, teams of two students could be assigned to each of the selected projects or agencies. In order to keep the seminar small enough for exchange, only one agency would be chosen to represent the seven basic types: community development, social action, service delivery, sectoral planning, fund or federation, council, local governmental.

The reduction in the range of settings has disadvantages, but working in pairs would probably offset these limitations (better coverage of an agency, cross validation of observations by students, mutual stimulation and learning by student pairs, fewer agencies to deal with administratively by the laboratory instructor). Utilizing either procedure, the laboratory seminar instructor might wish to capitalize on student interests by giving greater weight (more projects) to certain practice categories (such as urban planning and design, social action, etc.).

Larger schools may need to have two laboratory sections, perhaps emanating out of a single survey course. The same agencies might be used by both sections, with students pairing up from each section. If different agencies are used, then there might be sharing of information across sections to provide an even greater range of types.

There are no research data available that would suggest whether individual assignments and a wider range of agencies or paired assignments in fewer agencies would be preferable in terms of student learning.

It might be possible to focus on one or several target neighborhoods in selecting agencies. Thus, all projects and agencies included in the laboratory-observatory would be located in, or—if located outside—directing services or programs toward, these focal neighborhoods. Community contexts, patterns of interorganizational relations, etc., would be conjoint for groups of students in this way, leading perhaps to a greater coherence in the laboratory.

Each laboratory-observatory would have a faculty instructor or coordinator. (In smaller schools, of necessity, as well as in larger ones by chance, the course instructor and laboratory coordinator could be the same person.) The instructor would plan the content for the laboratory, working collaboratively with the survey-course instructor if he is a different person. The laboratory-observatory instructor would select projects for study, make initial contacts with agencies and prepare the way for student participation. Responsibility for instruction would be based entirely in the school. Agencies might be asked to appoint a contact person for the student (to provide background information, arrange appointments with other individuals, etc.), but the scope and intensity of this function would be much reduced as compared with customary field instruction.

There would be common sequential readings, lectures, or visitors for all students, as well as common sequentially assigned observations, tasks, and reports. Readings would attempt to cover basic literature in community organization using the practice text and its bibliography as a framework. While each student or pair of students would have a different base from which to observe and would be looking at various dimensions and receiving a variety of data and impressions at any given time (through visits in the neighborhood, informal discussions with staff and clients, etc.), common analytical and conceptual categories for appraising such data will be restructured and phased for all students in the laboratory.

In addition to assigned observations, students might voluntarily (as they desire and as agreed upon by the agency) take on a variety of *ad hoc* tasks of relevance to the agency, such as recruiting members, taking minutes for a meeting, visiting client homes, interpreting programs to public officials, participating in a social-action campaign, etc. The purpose of these *ad hoc* tasks is to immerse the student further in the operations of the agency and so enhance his comprehension for doing the observational assignments. These ad-

ditional tasks may satisfy the desires of some students to be more
immediately involved in action and more directly engaged in practice. At the same time, these services will provide subsidiary benefits to the agency. However, there is a danger that such assignments
will be unduly limiting and of minimal value as educational experiences. It would be important for these tasks to meet the criterion
of furthering the student's understanding of the system in which
the agency is operating, its objectives, the needs it is trying to meet,
etc. The objective for the student at this point is not centered on
the development of skills but on obtaining knowledge concerning
social needs and the ways in which they are handled by community-
organization and social-planning agencies.

The laboratory instructor should be keenly alert to take advantage of additional events or activities as they occur in the community. Should a special commission make a report or a racial
disturbance occur or a hearing be held or a voter-registration drive
be undertaken, students might observe or take a limited part (such
as testifying at the hearing) as a way of adding greater scope in
understanding community-change processes, and keeping in touch
with and getting close to significant community happenings. Such
additional activity would be examined and evaluated systematically
in terms of the cognitive framework of the lab.

As an aid to students, it is suggested that guide sheets or a loose-
leaf workbook be drawn up in connection with the assigned activities. Such a guide would draw its items in large measure from the
course outline as developed in the practice text. The workbook
might simply be an expanded list of the class sessions with space
for a check list and notes of assignments completed. It might,
however, be a full course syllabus with a more elaborate organization for recording class and field learning and observations. This
would direct the student's attention to significant factors and tie
his observations and assignments directly to the practice text in a
systematic way. Such a workbook was not produced in this project
because different schools will probably wish to emphasize different
aspects of the world of practice or draw on different theoretical
perspectives—organization theory, role theory, theory of interorganizational relations. The administration sequence at one school
of social work has developed a workbook of this type and used it
with good results. We will draw some material from this example
and develop additional guideline materials that will be useful for
schools that wish to develop such workbooks.

While the workbook will follow the course sequentially, its sub-parts would not be considered mutually exclusive either in terms of subject matter or timing. Thus, while an assignment in the eighth week may require a report on a visit to a board of directors, the student may find that the pattern of board meetings in his assigned agency requires him to schedule this in the fifth week. The seminar members would review the entire workbook at the beginning of the term so that the student will be aware of tasks and reports he is expected to complete by the end of the term. He can then schedule himself appropriately for the entire semester or year and utilize information as he obtains it. Thus, if he somewhat inadvertently discovers something significant about the staff role at midterm he might want to make a notation of this in the appropriate section of his workbook, although he is not expected to report on this subject until nearer the end of the term. The general format may be characterized as embodying flexibility within an established structure.

We assume that the laboratory may demand substantial proportions of the student's time and, hence, as a direct experimental introduction to the world of practice, it will substitute completely for the customary first-term field instruction. Depending on the weight which a school wishes to give to academic versus practice aspects of learning in the beginning period, the laboratory might entail the equivalent of one or two days of the school week. It is likely that most schools would need to make selections that will reduce the number of activities described here as possible laboratory activities. We have striven for comprehensiveness and scope, giving a framework from which appropriate elements may be chosen by the instructor and the students.

The specific activities for laboratory assignments detailed below are organized by settings and functions. The situational and problem analysis implicit in each of the following sections will need to be interpreted and adapted to the organizational context in which the student has his assignment. Some of these involve school-based projects and classroom activities; others involve the active participation of community groups and agencies and the cooperation of their leaders. Some are more appropriate to one setting than to another, but the shared experience of the seminar will expose all students to all the important information and the "common experiences" suggested at several points in the materials below will further involve all students in the same experience. The suggestions will follow this outline:

A. Community and/or neighborhood settings
B. Client populations and organizations
C. Structural and organizational aspects of agencies
D. The governing body, auspice, or sponsorship
E. The practitioner: his roles and functions
F. Interorganizational and community relations
G. Macrosystem planning and rural community work.

## A. Community and Neighborhood Setting

The student will start out by obtaining information concerning the community system in which his assigned project or agency is located. The relevant system may be a city, region, or local neighborhood. A guide sheet should be prepared by the instructor as an aid to the student in obtaining information. However, the student would not be expected to carry out a substantial community survey. The formal techniques of survey method will be covered in another course. Here some simple, basic data will be gathered and impressions recorded, in order to place the agency rather quickly in its community setting. What is expected has been characterized as casing the community. Students who are working conjointly in a target neighborhood would share this task.

Some of the factors that might be looked into include the following:

1. Characteristics of the population—use of census data, official reports, and published surveys.

2. Major problems of the community such as poverty, housing, mental illness, etc.—use of census data, agency reports, newspaper features, OEO documents, economic data, urban renewal or planning-commission documents, etc.

3. Attitudes of residents or leaders toward the community system and conception of problems—interviewing residents, agency directors, association officers, business executives, local shopkeepers, etc.

4. Physical characteristics and community climate—participation in several community events (PTA meeting, rally, city-council meeting, etc.), review of land-use maps, historical trends, walking tours, etc.

5. Services and facilities located in or serving the area—use of health and welfare council and agency service data, use of records and reports of city agencies and departments, visits to

selected agencies such as the department of public welfare, interviews with selected agency directors such as antipoverty agencies and family-service society.

6. Major institutions affecting the community system—governmental, economic, religious, welfare, etc.

7. Alternatively, the field study could take its impetus from a public problem, crisis, or controversy and focus on an issue that is current in the community or neighborhood.

Since this portion of the laboratory will extend over perhaps only a two- or three-week period, the instructor will need to be highly selective regarding the amount and kind of information requested of students. The assignment is an orientation to the environmental setting in which community-organization and social-planning functions are performed. While this external survey is proceeding, the student will be laying the groundwork in his assigned project or agency for internal observations and more systematic data gathering.

Several simple and fairly elementary books on community fact finding, pegged to the level of this particular laboratory assignment, are available as resource material for students. Included among these are Roland Warren, *Studying Your Community* (149a), Irwin Saunders, *Making Good Communities Better* (121a), and *Where It's At: A Research Guide for Community Organizing,* published by Students for a Democratic Society (149b).

During this early period in the laboratory, when the student is becoming oriented to the community and agency, the survey course will be dealing with definitional and historical aspects of community organization.

## B. Client Populations and Organizations

This portion of the laboratory will focus on those individuals or organizations that are to benefit from the actions of the assigned project or agency. Let us start with the set of laboratory activities or experiences through which the student is expected to obtain information:

1. Persons who represent an individual client and/or organizational client visit class. Students are selected to conduct each interview. Class holds discussion and critique. Alternatively a film could be used to portray different clients or problem

conditions. (Common experience indicated below may substitute here.)

2. Each student interviews a client or client organization within the assigned agency.

3. Each student interviews a client or client agency in the home or field situation.

4. The student traces the client route or course through the agency. Assume the role of the client if possible (apply for service such as public housing, accompany a client on an agency visit, engage in client-life activity—buying furniture on credit, using bus service from one part of town to another, etc.). The client might be either a consumer or member-participant in the agency.

5. The student records his experiences. Reports are duplicated and distributed to all students.

6. The class holds discussion. (Student pairs might give a critique of each other's work.)

As an example of the kinds of factors to which the student might direct his attention in undergoing these experiences, we have adapted a portion of the University of Michigan Administration Workbook referred to previously. The items listed there under "client inputs" include the following:

1. Present a profile of the clients served by this agency.
   a) Age, sex, and race
   b) Socioeconomic status
   c) Place of residence
   d) Most frequent presenting problems or concerns

2. What admission or entry criteria do clients have to meet in order to benefit from the services of the agency? How were these determined?

3. Identify and chart the different routes that clients can take in the agency, and indicate some of the major criteria used to route clients at each juncture (e.g., initial routing to major divisions in the agency, further routing to specific services, programs, or committees, movement from one unit or level to another; etc.).

4. In assigning clients to services or programs, can you differentiate subcohorts, each of which is characterized by common profile and a common service, (e.g., all clients of a particular race, social status, or problem receive a certain kind of service)?

5. Can you identify what types of clients have better chances of negotiating favorably with staff as compared to those who have little chances of doing so?

6. What other alternatives do clients have in obtaining desired services or goals?

7. To what extent is the agency dependent on clients for financial support? How are schedules of fees arrived at, how implemented?

8. To what extent is cooperation on the part of the client essential for staff to perform their tasks?

9. Can you infer from observations and other information what types of clients the agency seems to prefer? Are there community pressures that affect acceptance or rejection of certain clients?

10. Do clients in the agency have any form of representation? If so describe:

    a) The criteria used and the ways clients are recruited to such roles.

    b) The formal tasks performed.

    c) The nature of decisions and influence exerted by clients.

## COMMON EXPERIENCE

All students will jointly examine client populations in the practice context of voluntary associations. Some possible activities include the following:

(a) Visit to class by a panel of participants in a social-action program (CORE, Alinsky, etc.). Interviews of panel by students concerning their participation in the organization—roles, activities.

(b) Attendance by members of laboratory-observatory at one or several different meetings of neighborhood community-development and/or social-action meetings. Later, selected staff and members interviewed concerning member activity.

(c) Students assigned to observe and/or take part with clients of these agencies in implemental action—picketing, speaking, chairing meetings, distributing materials, etc. Clients interviewed on the scene by students who later report back to laboratory on observations and interviews. (Students should participate *with* clients if possible in selected activities.)

## C. Structural and Organizational Aspects of Agencies

This section will deal with such factors as the following:

1. Sources of financial support—supplies of funds for salaries, payments, etc.

2. Internal structure.

3. Level or scope (geographic scale—city, state, regional, national).

4. Goals, ideologies, values, programs, staffing, technologies.

5. Auspices—the people to whom staff is responsible. Governmental versus voluntary sponsorship, sectarian versus nonsectarian, racial or ethnic support and legitimation (*briefly*— this aspect will be covered more thoroughly in the next portion of the laboratory).

Information for this portion of the laboratory would be obtained from interviews with executives, interviews with staff, use of agency documents—by-laws, legislation or executive orders, annual reports, statistical reports and statements, executive or staff memos, etc.

The laboratory experiences for this section might be sequenced as follows:

1. Visit to class by an executive who would give a sample rundown on his agency. Students follow presentation with group interview for additional information.

2. Role-play-simulated interviews with different types of executives in different types of agencies. Use of tape recorder or video tape.

3. Students' interview of executive and staff member in assigned agency. Also gathering of factual information.

4. Students recording of results of interviews, observations, and survey of printed materials with regard to the organization and contextual factors specified for study. Recording to include (1) summary of specified factors (sources of financial support, internal structure, etc.), plus an organizational chart, (2) the interview process (difficulties, pressures on the executive, surprises, etc.), and (3) general impressions of the agency (atmosphere, morale, commitment, relevance, etc.).

5. Students reporting results of their study in class. All reports might be duplicated and circulated to all laboratory seminar members. Certain factors might be selected out for concentrated discussion rather than attempting to obtain full cover-

age. Alternatively, one student might give a detailed presentation on his agency, and other students indicate similarities and differences with theirs.

## D. The Governing Body, Auspice, or Sponsorship

One aspect of structure has to do with authority, power, and legitimation in the agency. Usually this resides in some decision-making body such as a private board of directors, a governmental commission, or a legislative unit.

Some areas to be investigated by students include the following:
1. To whom are the executives and staff directly responsible?
2. What authority or legitimacy lies behind the governing board—the electorate, community consensus, etc.?
3. How is authority mandated?
4. Is the governing body governmental or voluntary, sectarian or nonsectarian?
5. What interests or community segments comprise the governing body—racial, ethnic, religious, social class, geographical, etc.?
6. How does the composition of the governing body affect program and tactics?
7. How much autonomy does staff, clientele have vis-à-vis the governing board?
8. How much overlap is there between clients or members and the governing board—directly or in terms of social characterics (class, race, nationality)?
9. What is the connection between the governing body and the funding source—identical or separate?

With regard to actual operations of the board, the student might look into matters such as:
1. Location and distribution of power and influence in the board.
2. The role of the executive in regard to technical functions such as agenda preparation, minute taking, notification, etc.
3. Communication and interaction within the board.
4. Board–executive balance of influence and differentiation of function.
5. Frequency of meetings.
6. Atmosphere and quality of board meetings, etc.

The format of the lab in investigating these issues might proceed as follows:

1. Visit to class of a panel of board members. Panel of students interviews them on board matters. Follow-up discussion by seminar (common experience indicated below may substitute for 1 and 2).
2. Simulated interviews conducted by pairs of students with one another for mutual feedback.
3. Interview with chairman of board or an officer in assigned agency.
4. Attendance at a board meeting.
5. Student recording of substantive and impressionistic aspects of experience with the board.
6. Discussion within seminar on different types of auspices—emphasis on constraints and opportunities with regard to practitioner, program, clientele.

### Common Experience

All students will jointly examine the *governing* body in the practice context of direct-service agencies. Some possible activities include the following:

(a) A panel of board members from different direct-service agencies visit class. They are interviewed by class members on perception of board function and operation and perception of client needs and roles. Panel of board members and clients discuss mutual roles, relationship to program and staff, etc.

(b) Students attend a board meeting of a direct-service agency. Students could be scattered among several agencies for visitation (family-service society, settlement house, etc.) or they could go to the same board meeting. In the later case it would likely be a board of a governmental agency, where board meetings are public—like the public-welfare commission or the board of education.

(c) Students would report back observations to laboratory, based on criteria suggested by lab instructor or students. Interview by students of different board members and staff might follow the observation of the meeting. Such multiple feedback from a range of participants in the meeting would provide comprehensive observations.

## E. The Practitioner: His Roles and Functions

In this portion of the lab the emphasis would be on the tasks and activities of the C.O. practitioner in the agency. The framework and set of questions for observation will be drawn from the analytical scheme in the textbook which deals with problem-solving stages (defining the problem, building structure, formulating policy, implementing the plan and monitoring), each of which is viewed in terms of concurrent *analytical* and *interactional* tasks.

Observations would be made of a committee, study group, or action group which a C.O. practitioner in the agency staffs. Visits would be made by student(s) to approximately three successive meetings. The practitioner would be interviewed several times before and after meetings to learn of his objectives, assessment of possibilities, evalution of results, follow-up plans, major activities between meetings, etc., as well as contextual factual information on the persons involved, affected and affecting organization, etc. A sample interview schedule is reproduced in Appendix A.

The students will record in terms of the stages of problem solving involved and the kinds of tasks engaged in by the practitioner. Variations in emphasis among various settings will be discussed.

A second recording would pertain to problems of the practitioner, such as organizational constraints, ethical and value problems and dilemmas, and the relationship between professionals and nonprofessionals.

In order to get in the requisite number of observations, the student would need to begin this assignment earlier in the term to be prepared to report by this time. Again, reports would be duplicated and circulated to all students.

### COMMON EXPERIENCE

All students will jointly examine *practitioner roles and functions* in the practice context of *planning and allocating agencies*. Some possible activities include the following:

(a) Visit to class of one or more practitioners to discuss their roles in a selected problem area (housing and renewal planning, mental health planning, etc.) or a selected process (political, administrative, legislative).

(b) Visit to class of a practitioner to discuss research and fact-finding function—description of a recent project involving this function.

(c) Visit by students to research department of a welfare council or city planning commission. Observation of materials, equipment and processes. Interviews with research staff.

(d) Visit by students to a public meeting staffed by a practitioner in planning and allocating—city planning commission, city council (city manager), community mental-health board. Interview with practitioner in class before or after the meeting (or both). Student reports on observations and possible interviews.

## F. Interorganizational and Community Relations

Finally, the student might be asked to examine the assigned agency in the framework of its pattern of interorganizational and community relations.

One set of activities pertains to the character and extent of interorganizational relations. Students would be expected to interview personnel in five or six key organizations with which the assigned agency has relations of exchange or other interaction. Different agencies could be selected symbolizing different types of interorganizational relationships in terms of variables such as the type of exchange (staff, information, clients, etc.), type of interaction (cooperative or competitive), durability of interaction (permanent or *ad hoc*), formality of interaction (formal versus informal), extent of control of one agency over another (subsidiary, funding source, balance of exchange), mechanisms used (coordinating committees, newsletters, overlapping board memberships), etc. In this way, the student could in part map the network of interorganizational relations which characterizes the agency and make some assessment of the efficiency of the patterning in terms of agency goals.

Another set of activities relates to what might be referred to as the place of the agency in the community and its public-relations image. Here the student would be concerned with how the agency is viewed in the community—how well it communicates with publics of various sorts. Students might be expected to interview informants as follows:

(a) Two other relevant professional agencies.

(b) Two voluntary associations (League of Women Voters, CORE).

(c) Two political figures (mayor, political-party leader).

(d) Two community elites (businessmen, chamber-of-commerce representatives).

(e) Two client or consumer types (man in the street) not associated with the agency.

Individuals might be interviewed with regard to their knowledge of the agency, its relevancy in terms of meeting needs or dealing with problems, unmet needs or desires, how the agency might communicate better, etc.

## G. Macrosystem Planning and Rural Community Work

Because of the distance between school and site, two relevant types of settings might be difficult to cover except under special circumstances. These include state, regional, or federal planning, on the one hand, and rural community work, on the other. Thus, one or two weekends or overnight field trips might be arranged during the term. One trip might be to Washington or the state capital. One or more planning agencies might be visited. This could be coordinated with visits to the state legislature or Congress, visits to committee meetings and hearings, and interviews with state legislators and Congressmen, as well as lobbyists on opposite sides of current issues. The interviews would relate to the programs and objectives of the planning agency or agencies selected for study. The timing of the visits could be made to coincide with relevant activity in the legislative bodies or committees. The class might also engage in some predetermined lobbying for designated legislative or executive actions.

The rural aspect might include visits to an Indian reservation, migrant-worker camp, rural O.E.O. programs, etc., either singly or in combination. Where possible, visits for all or a part of the seminar might be arranged to areas emphasizing rural community work, such as Appalachia or Puerto Rico. Universities with foreign programs might arrange more extended international contacts for selected students. A consortium of Italian and American schools of social work have projected such a program following a joint conference at Brandeis and Rutgers in 1970.

## II. Summary of Final Reports

In addition to the routine feedback by seminar members to the total group, some more formalized reports would serve to summarize the experience of the students and allow their interpretations to be circulated to a wider audience both within the school and within the community. The learning experience accruing to the preparation of a report would also be valuable for the student's own development and could serve as a model for the kinds of professional reports he will be called upon to write in the future.

## A. *Summary Reports*

Students will prepare individual or group reports based on the foregoing, geared to the context of practice within which their assigned project or agency falls. Students would be expected to discuss their project or agency in terms of the factors identified with the relevant context in the practice text.

For example, voluntary associations could be analyzed in relation to the following list of factors:

(a) Existence of organizational goals and ideology.
(b) Utilization of various strategies (conflict, consensus, etc.).
(c) Sponsorship of association and degree of autonomy.
(d) Choice of targets for action.
(e) Basis for organizing and recruiting members.
(f) Characteristics of members.
(g) Internal structure and degree of formality.

Community work of direct-service agencies could be reported in terms of the following factors:

(a) Issues and problems—existence of a guiding social policy, existence of long-range planning, extent of administrative supports for planning.
(b) Community work processes—mobilization of community support for the program, interorganizational exchange, change of community resources (referral to other agency, *ad hoc* action, direct intervention).

Planning and allocating agencies could be analyzed in terms of the following factors:

(a) Geographical scope.
(b) Degree of comprehensiveness of coverage.
(c) Coordinative activities.
(d) Allocation activities.
(e) Innovation and change activities.
(f) Integration of planning with budgeting and financing.
(g) Integration of horizontal and vertical relationships.

They could also be viewed in relation to their handling of typical concerns of such agencies:

   (a) Effectiveness of means used to reach consumers.
   (b) Nature of response to client needs and wishes.
   (c) Effectiveness and appropriateness of services.
   (d) Availability of resources.

Reports from each of the three clusters of practice contexts could be given sequentially in class sessions and then discussed comparatively. Some documentation, written or taped, of this exercise might be prepared for use of future classes or sharing with community groups.

## B. *Final Report*

Each student would be expected to submit a final summary report on his assigned project or agency. Submission of the workbook with its various subsections completed sequentially might suffice for this purpose. The student could also be asked to append a concluding section that would summarize his personal experience in the project or agency together with recommendations for different audiences—the agency staff, public officials, other community agencies and groups, etc. Recommendations would include changes in policy, structure, program, staff, etc., as well as indicated legislation or needed financial support. It would also be good to have the student include a note on potential strategies, resources, and structures for achieving these recommendations.

Depending upon the nature of the relationships between school and agency, such a report might be shared with the staff of the organization. Many agencies might see such a report as a worthwhile payoff for having made themselves available for student study. This kind of objective, or at least fresh, feedback could be used by executives for evaluative purposes.

## III. Administrative and Functional Problems of Laboratory-Observatory

There are a number of administrative and functional problems associated with running a laboratory-observatory such as the one suggested here. These problems include gaining the cooperation of participating agencies, motivating students through a workable combination of involvement in action and observation, faculty time for this program, questions of coordination, the problem of more experienced students, and imposition on individuals and organizations in the community. Without minimizing these problems we will attempt to indicate possible ways in which they can be accommodated. A successful variation on the theme is also described.

### 1. *Agency Cooperation*

Agencies may be reluctant to participate in this activity on the grounds that they do not receive benefits equivalent to those produced when students are engaged in customary field instruction. Most schools that have utilized agencies in this more restricted way do not seem to have found the problem of gaining cooperation especially difficult. While agencies gain less through this procedure, they are also taxed much less than in traditional field placement. There is no requirement to provide regularly scheduled field-instruction conferences, review of records, evaluations and reports to the school, etc. The experience of the University of Michigan's administration sequence suggests that the agency needs to allot a total of fifteen to eighteen hours of staff time to this type of activity. Likewise, the agency does not need to provide office space, telephone, secretary, dictating equipment, etc. A student could manage this assignment with a table or desk provided for him in a corner of a less-used office. Experience suggests that the student should take some responsibility for negotiating the details of his arrangements in the agency. This process of negotiation will provide him with additional insights into how the organization operates.

The final report to the agency, as well as questions students ask and observations they make, will be seen by some executives as a valuable benefit for a minimal investment. Administrators may find these helpful in examining their own operations and may use them to gain support for their work from board members or from the general public.

Field agencies may be receptive to this approach because the school is thus taking over the main burden of training in the first year when students are inexperienced and unseasoned. This insures that, when agencies receive students for the more sustained practicum (customary field instruction), these students are more uniformly prepared to make productive inputs into the agency. In some instances the agencies may have first-year students in the laboratory experience and a number of second-year students engaged in practicum assignments during the same time period.

One school found that it was helped in initiating a program of observational experiences when field instructors in the department reviewed the plan beforehand and offered some response. Having approved of the procedure in principle, they were neither surprised nor hostile when approached about laboratory assignments. It has been found beneficial for the instructor rather than the student to make a first contact, possibly by telephone with a follow-up letter from the school.

### B. *Student Motivation*

Some students may find a largely observational and analytical program too limiting and thwarting of their desires to be where the action is. Several ways may be suggested to meet this need:

1. In the first place, if possible, students should select the types and even specific projects or agencies they wish to study. In this way at least a minimum base of interest and motivation is assured.

2. The laboratory instructor should attempt to involve seminar members in common experiences in significant community developments as they occur during the term. This is sound educationally in terms of the objectives of the laboratory-observatory and at the same time brings students in touch with significant events and actions.

3. The entering classes of most schools of social work include students with a wide range of preprofessional and volunteer experiences. Their assignments should be chosen to supplement and complement rather than duplicate these experiences. With this interpretation, students will recognize their need for different experiences across the full range of practice contexts.

4. In addition, channels could be provided for particularly interested students to express their desire for more active involvement in programs by actually joining at an appropriate level any ongoing agency activity. This would be optional and should not interfere or prejudice the required observational assignment.

5. Students who engage in such optional activities might use

these experiences as the basis for term papers or reports in regular academic courses or in special tutorials for which course credits might be given. One might anticipate that younger and relatively inexperienced students are more likely to desire such practice activity than are older students or those who have a background of agency experience.

## C. *Faculty Time*

The amount of faculty time required to structure and conduct a laboratory program should not be underestimated. One lab section may be the equivalent of two regular courses in terms of time and effort. However, ongoing liaison time with agencies may not require a high investment of time because the student is not engaged in ongoing practice with its attendant problems. Agency liaison will most likely involve problems of obtaining access for students to staff, clients, meetings, files, and documents, and handling occasional interpersonal difficulties.

It might be well to think of a special faculty member assigned to the laboratory and community resources area. He would be a resource person to lab instructors and other faculty analogous to the specialist in audiovisual aids. The addition of such a person with continuing responsibility for laboratory resources and community contacts might represent the personnel increment necessary to implement this plan.

Coordinating the survey course and the laboratory may present a number of problems. However, this may be dealt with structurally by coordinating parallel topical areas to be treated simultaneously. Both instructors should consult at the beginning regarding topics and timing and check with one another periodically throughout the term. Alternatively, the survey-course instructor and the lab-seminar instructor may be the same person, which would eliminate possibilities of disjunction.

Another coordinating problem has to do with the relative weight given to different subject-matter areas in the survey course and the lab-observatory. It is likely that the survey course will more quickly—perhaps by midterm—cover the main topical areas designated for examination in the lab: community-system context, client populations and organizations, structural and organizational aspects of agencies, governing boards, etc. From that time, the course would direct its attention to practice contexts and specific fields of practice.

Thus, the intellectual foundations for students carrying out their lab assignments will be presented early. In the latter part of the lab, as students report on governing bodies or staff roles, etc., the starting point might be the field of practice being covered in the survey course. Thus, if the lab is concentrating on governing boards and the survey is examining the fund and council field of practice, a student who is assigned to a local welfare council might initiate the discussion in the lab, with other students indicating contrasts and variations in the field of practice or context represented by their assignment.

## D. *Student Exemption*

In all likelihood the survey-lab course would provide new subject matter and a new analytical and comparative perspective for all students, whether experienced or not. On the other hand, should a student present himself who has a considerable amount of preprofessional experience in organizing and planning, as well as a background in community and organizational theory, such a person could be exempted from either the survey course, the lab-observatory, or all or a portion of both.

## E. *Laboratory Imposition*

The laboratory idea contains the risk of "using" agencies, clients, or neighborhoods for the benefit of students. Special care will need to be taken to see that individuals or organizations are not abused, damaged, or misused through the laboratory approach. Gaining consent of others is necessary, as is the structuring of activities to the extent possible in such a way as to yield a mutual benefit. Clients, in particular, might be paid for their participation or services. In all cases the dignity and well-being of those involved should be respected and attended to. Programs that need to be sustained should not be launched and then dropped, nor should false expectations be aroused. Ideas for specific student experiences might be elicited from agency personnel, clients, and community residents, thus minimizing the dangers of imposition.

## F. *Variations on the Theme*

The introduction this year of a complete laboratory-observatory program at the University of Michigan offered some innovations on this general scheme. The community organization practice lab concentrated on the three elements in its title: (1) the *community* as an aggregate; (2) the *organization* of a field agency; and (3) the *practice* of social work intervention in an urban setting. Three C.O. courses and one research course were coordinated with parallel laboratory sessions. The semester was divided into approximately equal thirds and the three classroom courses were offered sequentially in blocks instead of simultaneously. During the first third of the semester, the entire course on Community Theory was given, along with the laboratory experience of conducting a community survey. During the second part, the course on Organizational Theory was given coincident with lab sessions that permitted each student to make an organizational analysis of his assigned field agency. The Practice Methods course finished up the last third of the semester while in the lab each student completed a role analysis of a model practitioner at work in his field agency. The coordinated research course featured survey methodology, organizational analysis, and evaluation techniques as they were appropriate to each part of the semester. Both faculty and students found this plan useful.

# 5 Skills-Development Laboratory

The skills-development laboratory, as was suggested earlier, is designed to facilitate students' acquisition of specified professional implemental skills. Hence, the outcome is behavioral, that is, the carrying out or application of intervention techniques. "Professional skill," however, implies more than mere rote mastery of operations in a technical sense. Rather, these skills involve the application of techniques within a rational or intellectual framework, so that "how" is linked to "why" and both to bodies of knowledge and to value systems that give perspective and dignity as well as effectiveness to professional practice.

## I. Orientation to the Skills-Development Laboratory

In this chapter we will lay out a number of skill areas that are considered important for professional practice in community organization and social planning. These skill areas were selected as a result of a review of typical units in community-organization methods courses and of studies that investigated skills areas, as well as an assessment by the Project staff of some emerging salient community-organization skills based on field visits to agencies. The configuration of skill areas set down here, then, is somewhat arbitrary and unscientific—based, as it is, merely on the informed opinion of the staff. Individual schools may, with impunity, drop some of these skill areas or add others, depending on their judgment of what core competencies are required by the contemporary practitioner or the kinds of practitioners they want to produce. What we will set down here is a range of component units for a skills-development methods course and laboratory. These units may be selected out and combined at the discretion of individual schools.

Each skill area is assumed to have an intellectual foundation that places it in a professional context. Thus, running parallel to the skills-training laboratory is the methods seminar that provides the academic backdrop for the skill area involved. In the seminar, the students would be concerned with various issues: Why utilize this skill? Toward what objectives or in what value framework may this skill area be seen? Under what conditions would one employ this skill? What other actors and what technological elements are necessary to the actualization of the skill? What theoretical perspectives or intellectual schools of thought are associated with this skill area? What other skills or objectives may be associated with the carrying out of this skill? Are there phases, variations, or component subunits in applying this skill? Is it associated with personality variables? What aspects of self-discipline are required to be successful in practicing the skill? How does this skill relate to the objectives and values of community organization within the profession of social work? And so on. The laboratory, while concentrating on the "doing" of the skill, will need constantly to relate action to a set of cognitive variables such as those described.

The skill areas we list below do not possess a unitary character. Some represent processes (decision making), others suggest strategies (use of conflict), and still others embody rather delimited techniques (preparing grant proposals). Although an attempt was made, we have not been able to devise a tidy conceptual scheme for laying out these skill areas; they comprise a mixed patterning not unlike that frequently experienced in the world of practice. Strategy and technique are sometimes difficult to distinguish. Strategy usually implies a mode of action at a higher level of abstraction than technique. Nevertheless, techniques can usually be broken down further into more detail or lower levels of behavioral operation.

Skills may be imparted and experimented with in a multiplicity of different ways. In this report we will be concerned with four different media for skill development: (a) use of real situations in the community at large as well as informal and formal, traditional and nontraditional agencies and organizations in the community; (b) use of the classroom situation and its students as a group to engage in skills training exercises—such as role playing and other anticipatory techniques; (c) use of simulation games as a particular teaching medium for imparting skills; (d) use of programmed instructional devices. Accordingly, for each skill area we will consider training possibilities using each of these media. In regard to those listed under simulation games and programmed instruction, the reader is requested to refer for more detailed information to Chapters 6 and 7 respectively, which deal with these topics. With regard to community- and agency-based activity, this may be conducted by the class fairly independently or through established agencies and community groups. Thus, for example, if the purpose of the lab is to teach students how to draw up and introduce a legislative bill, students might decide on a piece of legislation they believe is necessary, draw up a bill, and attempt to have it enacted in the legislature. On the other hand by working through established community agencies and organizations they might take two approaches:

1.) Inquire of various agencies and organizations concerning whether they would like the lab to draw up any particular bill which the agency has been interested in promoting. The class would then engage in the project under the sponsorship of or in cooperation with the agency. The specific legislative action grows out of the initiative of the agency in the sense that it suggests a designated bill or legislative program it desires to see enacted.

2.) Students may decide on a piece of legislation they wish to work on. They then make inquiry of agencies interested in this area of concern as to whether they would like the student lab group to undertake this activity for them. Students are then working through existing agencies in terms of sponsorship or collaboration, but the initiative for the particular form of action has come from the lab rather than the agency. In a sense the lab is working on a contract basis with the agency: "Here is a piece of action of concern to your agency; would you like us to conduct it for you? If so, we will follow through, functioning fairly independently but on your behalf."

Activities might be conducted by the lab as a whole or by teams within the lab. Thus, the whole class might work on drawing up a particular self-selected legislative bill, or teams of students might work on different bills. Likewise, the entire class might contract with a given agency to work up legislation or teams of students might work for different agencies on a range of different bills.

While we have listed below a considerable number of skill areas, there was no attempt to be exhaustive. We may have omitted certain areas that a particular school may consider vital. Schools are encouraged to include these in the skills-development lab. On the other hand, we have drawn up a veritable smorgasbord of professional operations, more than can comfortably be consumed at one sitting or taught in one course. Units are to a greater or lesser degree practical, time limited, or controllable. From this array, each school will have to cut back selectively to a core composite of skills which it considers basic for entry into the kind of practice for which it believes it is educating. The seminar and lab courses might comprise two, four, eight, or more hours depending on the weight that a school wishes to give to them. They could be equal in credit hours to the survey and lab-observatory, but probably not less.

A number of these skills areas can be grouped functionally and logically to form clusters that might constitute the basis for course offerings in the second term or at subsequent periods in the second year. A number of potential course offerings with their component skills areas are enumerated below. These courses could be made up of a classroom section and a parallel laboratory section. Again, as with the observatory, a community-resource specialist on the faculty would be helpful in expediting this program. Suggested groupings into related clusters might include the following: *

I. Organizing Methods and Skills
   A. Management of Organizational Processes
      1. Initial organizing.
      2. Participation.
      3. Committee technology.
      4. Leadership development and training.
      5. Recruiting and training indigenous workers and volunteers.
   B. Design and Implementation of Strategies
      6. Coalitions and their formation.
      7. Bargaining.
      8. Advocate role and conflict.
      9. Broker role.
     10. Identifying and influencing the power structure.
   C. Conduct of Interpersonal Relations
     11. Interviewing.
     12. Interpersonal influence and use of self.
     13. Leading group discussion.

* We are not suggesting that the categories are mutually exclusive. For example, bargaining may take place in either organizing or planning. We have located skills under categories where we believe they receive more, not exclusive, emphasis.

II. Planning Methods and Skills
   A. Designing
      14. Fact finding and social-survey techniques.
      15. Policy analysis.
      16. Program development.
   B. Interacting
      17. Decision making.
      18. Political process.
      19. Legislative process.
      20. Administrative process.
   C. Implementing
      21. Administrative role and function.
      22. Fund raising and proposal writing.
      23. Consultation.
      24. Staff development and supervision.
      25. Promotional, educational, and public-relations techniques.

## II. Skills Areas and Correlated Activities

With the foregoing as an introduction, let us proceed to discuss the skills areas and indicate some of the correlated laboratory activities that might accompany each. These activities may take place in the community, the agency, or the classroom. Related simulation games and programmed instructions are also indicated where appropriate and feasible ones are known to exist. (The numbers after "Simulation Games" refer to the annotated descriptions that appear in Appendix B, "Community Organization Relevant Games." The titles after "Programmed Instruction" refer to the subdivisions of "Programmed Instruction Materials of Potential Use in Community Organization Education" in Appendix D—Section C.)

### 1. *Initial Organizing*

The members of the lab would be engaged in establishing a new voluntary association related to some issue or activity. In order to take into account continuity in service for the organization, it might be best to undertake this project in collaboration with some national organization that would be receptive to the idea of having a local branch or affiliate established (NAACP, American Civil Liberties Union, Welfare Rights, Cancer Society, Urban Coalition, etc.). The national office would then assume responsibility for maintaining the organization once it had been established. . . . The lab would plan a recruitment and organizational drive deciding whom to contact, how, what kinds of written materials are necessary, speaking engagements, how an initial organization meeting should be structured, etc. . . . Should organizing meetings of different groups occur in the community, groups of students might attend these on an observational basis. Evaluation of approach and recommendations would be expected. . . . The classroom could be used on a simulated basis to represent various activities along the lines suggested above.

Simulation Game: 12.

## 2. *Participation*

This unit focuses on the process of attempting to acquire broad community participation in organization activities, not necessarily in small-group activity.

Students might assist one or more agencies or organizations in attempts to recruit members or participants. For example, students could be attached to the recruitment committee of a settlement house, welfare council, welfare-mothers group, union, or political party. Or they might undertake a special project for the local OEO program aimed at increasing the extent of participation of the poor in the organization's activities and committees (including the board). Recruiting students to various university or school-of-social-work units and programs would be another possibility. In any case, there would be evaluation of approaches, outcomes and implications. Activities might include preparation of written materials, speaking before groups, speaking to individuals, talking to people in their neighborhood or home environment, etc. . . . Through simulation, the classroom could be structured to represent different types of publics and students could be assigned roles in recruiting them as members or participants in different types of activities. . . . Potential members of different kinds of organizations (including those in the university and school) could be asked to attend orientation or recruitment meetings in the lab setting. Use of one-way screens and closed circuit TV for feedback and evaluation.

### 3. *Committee Technology*

Have all students attend a particular public meeting such as an open meeting of the city council, board of education, human-relations commission, etc. Different students might take assumed roles at the meeting—minutes taking, preparation of agenda, assumed interventions and positions. The lab would reflect back on the projected and actual actions that took place. The staff worker might be interviewed in class before and after the meeting. . . . Students might be assigned to a variety of community groups for a limited period of time to carry out designated committee activities, such as minutes taking, notification, preparation of materials for meetings, physical arrangements, etc. . . . Simulated committee meetings of various kinds can be set up in the classroom with students assigned to fulfill a variety of technical staffing functions. Participants and observers can give feedback on the effectiveness of professionals' role-playing behavior. . . . Actual committee meetings in the lab setting can be arranged with evaluation following.

Programmed Instruction: COMMITTEES AND BOARDS; PARLIAMENTARY PROCEDURE.

### 4. *Leadership Development and Training*

Students might participate in various roles in organizations conducting leadership-training programs—settlement houses, OEO, adult-education groups, etc. Roles could be established in material preparation, program structure and planning, conducting discussions or lectures, etc. . . . Simulation of programs such as those suggested might be carried out in the classroom.

### 5. *Recruiting and Training Indigenous Workers and Volunteers*

Students could be assigned to assist indigenous workers or volunteers in their functions. Students might participate in various selected roles in recruitment or training programs for indigenous workers conducted by local agencies. The class might take responsibility for designing (and conducting) a training program for an agency using indigenous professionals. . . . Simulation of training sessions with indigenous professionals or volunteers could be carried on in the classroom. . . . A group of indigenous professionals or volunteers could be brought to the lab setting for one or more training sessions. One-way screen and closed-circuit TV could be used.

### 6. *Coalitions and Their Formation*

Have lab attempt to form a coalition among a number of community groups which have some similar goals but function independently. Lab might act independently or through an existing agency or community group. A coalition of white groups interested in racial justice is an example of a suitable undertaking along these lines. . . . Classroom session might include role playing of influencing individuals to participate in a coalition.

Simulation Games: 7, 6, 43.

### 7. *Bargaining*

Students participate with an agency in preparing a budget and steering it through a fund budget committee. . . . Students work with a union organizer in setting up demands and going through negotiating committee of a teacher's union or social worker's union. . . . In a welfare council, assign students to aid different agencies on opposing sides of a current issue. Arrange a conference to settle the issue. . . . Aid a welfare mother's group in negotiating with the welfare department on grievances.

Simulation Games: 45, 46, 24, 25, 8.

### 8. *Advocate Role and Conflict*

Select a conflict group that is about to engage in an action campaign. Assign students, in cooperation with the group, to a range of roles in the action. The lab activity might center on a particular event such as a peace march, protest rally, etc. . . . Make arrangements with a client organization for members of the lab to represent the group in making demands on staff or board members for welfare or governmental bureaucracies.

Simulation Games: 1, 21, 37, 10, 36.

Programmed Instruction: SOCIAL PROCESSES.

### 9. *Broker Role*

Select an agency—such as OEO—and have each student act as a broker in linking clients to broader resources. Interview clients to determine what resources are necessary. Conduct an interview (or other action) on behalf of client with resources—housing authority, mayor's office, sanitation department, welfare department, credit agencies, etc. . . . Select two groups or organizations that are in conflict over some issue. Plan an intervention strategy to resolve the issue. Have a class engage in action as broker or mediator. Different roles for different students and faculty would be determined beforehand.

### 10. *Identifying and Influencing the Power Structure*

This topic involves two subparts: (a) locating or delineating a relevant power structure; (b) designing a strategy to influence that power structure along desired lines.

The lab might select some problem or issue of interest to it. With regard to this problem or issue, the class would set out to define the operating power structure relevant to that problem (those individuals or organizations in decision-making or controlling positions with regard to resolution of the problem). Composition of the power structure would be determined through use of one or a combination of the existing methodologies—reputational, positional, behavioral. . . . Having described the power structure, the lab might design a strategy for influencing the particular group on the particular issue. Is the group open to communication or not? do vested interests exist or not? how large an area of common or public interest exists in the situation? What kind of influence or pressure, and by whom, is necessary to make an impact on the power holders? In the classroom a hypothetical plan for locating elites might be drawn up.

### 11. *Interviewing*

Students can be asked to conduct and evaluate interviews of various types in their own personal life space (friends, family, teachers, fellow students, community and agency people). . . . Students might assist at information and referral center for a delimited period of time. . . . Through a suburban action center or similar race-relations organizations, students might be asked to engage in interviews geared to changing racial attitudes of whites. (Alternatives might include interviews regarding changing health practices [smoking] or birth-control practices.) In the classroom, simulated interviews might be conducted of the three types in role-playing fashion among students regarding various subjects, in various contexts, and with opportunities to exchange roles. Clients or organizational participants from various organizations might be brought to class for interviewing purposes. Use of one-way glass or closed-circuit TV might be considered.

Simulation Game: 31.

## 12. *Interpersonal Influence and Use of Self*

Teams of two members of the lab would arrange to attend meetings of a variety of community or university groups (student council, PTA meeting, etc.). Students would have in mind a change objective through interpersonal influence. Students would team up so that an influencer and observer would attend each meeting and exchange roles at the next meeting (so that each student would be an observer and an influencer). Each student team would evaluate the interpersonal-influence strategy used, the student's self-discipline in employing it and the effect or outcome. . . . Students could be attached to organizations which attempt to change attitudes through programs of small group discussions (health agencies, civil-rights groups, mental-health associations, civic societies, etc.). Each student would be expected to conduct two small group discussions for his selected organization. Again, the notion of an influencer and observer team might be employed and the student's performance evaluated in terms of the criteria suggested above. . . . The class might be used to stimulate various types of groups and situations. Different students could be selected to influence the simulated groups in role-play fashion. Feedback from the members of the class on performance to foster self-awareness on the part of the simulated practitioner. . . . It might be possible to arrange for actual or artificially structured groups to meet in a lab setting in the classroom or behind one-way screens (similar to experiments conducted in social psychology and in the small-group dynamics field). The student practitioner would be viewed by the class, and feedback would be given concerning interpersonal influence attempts and use of self. . . . T-group and National Training Laboratory techniques might be employed, leaning heavily on interpersonal interaction experience among lab-class members as the major medium of learning. Schools desiring to employ this technique might consider utilizing the National Training Laboratory network to arrange for local consultation on methods or to employ a local NTL affiliated person to conduct this portion of the lab.

Simulation Games: 39, 31, 40, 45.

Programmed Instruction: INTERPERSONAL RELATIONS; PUBLIC RELATIONS AND COMMUNICATION.

### 13. *Leading Group Discussion*

Group discussion in this unit conveys the idea of helping a group think through a problem or issue without the practitioner influencing it in a particular direction. The role is one of enabling various opinions and points of view to emerge and for some kind of consensus to evolve from group interaction and the interplay of a variety of different points of view.

Students might be attached to various organizations that engage in programs of group discussion along the lines suggested—League of Women Voters, adult-education programs, etc. Teams of students (a discussion leader and observer) would be assigned to each meeting. Each student would be expected to perform as a discussion leader at two meetings and an observer-evaluator at two. . . . In the classroom simulation of various types of groups with various purposes and contexts might be employed with students roleplaying the practitioner. Immediate feedback on intervention would be possible. . . . Actual or composed groups could be brought into the classroom situation for intervention by selected students and observation by others (use of one-way screens, closed-circuit TV, etc.).

Simulation Games: 39, 31, 40, 45.

Programmed Instruction: COMMITTEES AND BOARDS; INTERPERSONAL RELATIONS.

### 14. *Fact Finding and Social Survey Techniques*

This skill area involves the design, implementation, and utilization of social surveys. The material might be covered in a separate methods course devoted entirely to the topic. Or it could be taught in the research sequence. Some subskills in the social-survey process might be selected out:

(a) Library research and documentation.

(b) Study design.

(c) Conducting interviews.

  (d) Questionnaire design.
  (e) Coding.
  (f) Tabulation and statistical treatment.
  (g) Preparing conclusions and recommendations.
  (h) Submitting recommendations to appropriate bodies.
  (i) Setting up sponsoring or advisory committee.

Students could be asked as a group to conduct their own neighborhood or community survey involving some set of the aforementioned skills. This could be focused on a single problem or on broad community-problem services or living patterns. . . . Alternatively, students could be assigned to various community organizations engaged in doing community or problem surveys, such as welfare councils, city-planning bodies, church denominational units, university institutes, etc. Students could be asked to engage in some limited aspects of a social survey (such as questionnnaire construction, interviewing, or coding) or in the longitudinal process of formulating and conducting a survey. . . . Practice exercises in coding, questionnaire design, analysis of data, etc., could be undertaken in the classroom. Role playing of interviews, presentation of recommendations, and setting up of an advisory committee could also be undertaken.

### 15. Policy Analysis

Contact might be made with a national planning agency, either governmental or voluntary, concerning the desire of the lab to engage in a policy analysis of some issue currently confronting the agency. (A local city or county agency could be used.) The class would undertake this analysis, determining tasks and stages necessary and distributing roles and assignments. One or more members of the lab might visit the agency from time to time for information and tentative feedback as the undertaking unfolds. A larger number of students might be involved in making a final report to agency staff upon completion of the project. The entire lab would evaluate the effectiveness of its total efforts. . . . A similar analysis could be undertaken by the lab with reference to hypothetical policy issues provided by the instructor or members of the class. This would simply constitute a practice exercise. A variation of this would be for the instructor to assign the class a project dealing with a policy issue actually studied and resolved by an agency. The lab could then compare and evaluate its effort in relation to the actual agency. Simulation Game: 38.

## 16. *Program Development*

Agencies might be contacted concerning their desire to use student assistance in program development. Working with staff, students might assume a number of roles and undertake a variety of functions related to program development. . . . Alternatively, the lab might develop a type of program of interest to its members and then attempt to make arrangements with agency willing to have it implemented. . . . Hypothetical exercises in program development might be employed in the classroom, as well as pertinent role playing, such as dealing with the resistance of older staff members to new program approaches.

## 17. *Decision Making*

Students either select or are assigned some local community problems such as housing, welfare, employment, or police-community relations. Working as a class or in subgroups, they are expected to design a plan for dealing with the problem. This may involve the collection of preliminary factual information. Certain aspects of decision making may be highlighted such as goal determination or overcoming resistance. Students may be asked to implement the plan if feasible through petitioning the mayor, presenting recommendations to appropriate bodies, or organizing an indigenous action group. . . . Students may be asked to influence one or more ongoing decision-making processes in the university or community. Direction and means of influence would have to be determined in advance. The impact on decision making of the students' input would be evaluated in the lab. . . . Simulation and role playing with regard to these issues (using real or hypothetical situations as the basis for simulation) may be carried out in the classroom.

Simulation Games: 2, 3, 36, 9, 44, 26.

Programmed Instruction: ADMINISTRATION AND MANAGEMENT; DATA PROCESSING; SYSTEMS IN EDUCATION AND TRAINING.

## 18. *Political Process*

Students might decide on some welfare objective with political implications—a fair-housing-practices law, higher welfare payments, changes in workman's-compensation practices. They would then plan a political strategy to obtain these objectives. Teams of students might speak with political-party leaders, the mayor, members of the city council, etc. . . . Students might participate in a political campaign in a variety of roles—planning strategy, passing out flyers, speaking before groups, raising funds, pressuring delegates, etc. It might be well for teams of students to work with different political parties and exchange perspectives to give an overview of the entire campaign and thus avoid accusations of partisanship. . . . Students might take part in a political drive of some type —voter registration, bond issue, housing ordinance. They could join in an existing program (League of Women Voters' registration drive) or organize a drive of their own. For example, they could design a voter-registration campaign designated to achieve a particular political impact and then offer their services in carrying this out to a given political party or civil-rights group. . . . Simulation and role playing of these situations, using actual or hypothetical circumstances, might be carried out in the classroom.

Simulation Games: 1, 12, 32, 47.

### 19. *Legislative Process*

Students attempt to influence a current legislative activity— appear at a hearing to testify, prepare a statement for a legislative commmittee, mobilize a group of influentials to take prescribed action, organize a letter-writing campaign. . . . Students decide on a piece of needed legislation not currently being acted on. Prepare a legislative draft. Attempt to have the bill introduced into the state legislature or city council (through committee chairman, local legislative representative, interested legislator, etc.). Muster community support for the bill. Students "contract" with one or more agencies to prepare legislative drafts for a bill agency desires to have enacted. Work with and through the agency to have bill introduced and acted upon. . . . Practice exercises in legislative drafting may be done as a laboratory assignment.

Simulation Games: 1, 13, 15.

Programmed Instruction: POLITICAL SCIENCE.

### 20. *Administrative Process*

*Legislative Process* and *Political Process,* above, are related activities. Students attempt to change the procedures or policies of a governmental bureau. Students may decide on a project as a class or take responsibility for promoting a change desired by a social agency or community group. . . . Students attempt to foster communication or collaboration between two or more governmental units with similar progammatic objectives but with no communication. Students can conduct activity as a class or contract with an existing social agency or community group. . . . A governmental official (city manager, city planning-commission head) might visit a class session. Attempt by students to convince him of a new approach or program. Or the situation might be role-played with different hypothesized officials with different ideologies, personalities, commitments, etc.

Simulation Games: Community Response (described in Chapter 6), 22.

Programmed Instruction: POLITICAL SCIENCE.

### 21. *Administrative Role and Functions*

Students could be assigned to assist agency executives in some selected aspects of administrative function—preparation of service statistics, evaluation of program, planning and conducting a staff meeting or a board meeting, arranging certain types of interorganization exchange, arranging community-relations programs or contacts, preparing budgets or annual reports, etc. . . . These might be simulated by role playing in the classroom.

Simulated Games: 9, 42, 38, 17.

Programmed Instruction: ADMINISTRATION AND MANAGEMENT.

### 22. *Fund Raising and Proposal Writing*

Lab members participate in various facets of a United Way campaign (or some other fund-raising group)—soliciting funds, working with a division subcommittee, taking responsibility for report meetings, etc. . . . Students prepare a grant proposal for some project or program which they believe is needed in the community. Design includes provision for the establishment of a community group or institution to maintain the program. Lab members may be involved in acquiring sponsorship of appropriate community groups or agencies for the proposal. . . . Students contact various agencies or groups to inquire about their desire to have a grant proposal written for them. The lab might select one agency for which to prepare a proposal, or teams of students or individuals might elect to perform this service for different agencies. Smaller agencies and group with limited staff and resources might welcome such attention. . . . A foundation executive might visit the classroom. Class might attempt to have him accept a hypothetical proposal they have drafted. Executive might critique the proposal and the class's approach to him. . . . A proposal-writing specialist might visit the class. Class works with him in drafting a hypothetical proposal or a real one which he is currently developing. . . . A proposal evaluator from a federal agency might visit the class. Evaluator might critique a hypothetical (or real) proposal to his agency which has been prepared by members of the class.

Programmed Instruction: PUBLIC RELATIONS AND COMMUNI-CATION.

### 23. *Consultation*

Students and faculty might constitute themselves as a consulting team on urban affairs or social-planning problems. Services would be offered to community agencies. Among responses, those would be selected which offer optimal subskill-area learning potentialities or which comprise a range of typical consultation problems. Actual fees might be charged to heighten the realism of the situation. . . . An agency director who wishes to receive consultation might be invited to the campus and the class as a whole or some group within it might offer consultation on a team basis. The class would then analyze the effectiveness of its efforts, receiving feedback from the visitor in the process. . . . Alternatively, role-playing consultation episodes of various types could be constructed and enacted, again with analysis and feedback from relevant actors.

### 24. *Staff Development and Supervision*

The lab might aid in staff-development program of an agency. The total class could participate in large organizations such as state department of welfare or mental health. The lab could prepare materials and conduct sessions on community organization and community-relations aspects of agency function and staff role. . . . Visit to class might be arranged for a staff-development specialist. Class designs a real or hypothetical training program and receives critique.

Programmed Instruction: PERSONNEL PRACTICES AND SUPER-VISION.

## 25. *Promotional, Educational, and Public Relations Techniques*

The lab might decide upon some needed program or service, or some problem condition that needs to be exposed and dramatized. The class would then conduct a community promotional campaign on the subject, using news releases, pamphlets, fact sheets, exhibits, etc. For example, the students might design an exhibit exposing inadequate housing and get it placed in some prominent public location, such as the public library or a train terminal. Instead of a class project, there might be individual or team projects. . . . Alternatively, various agencies and groups might be approached concerning their need for such a promotional program—especially smaller agencies with limited staff resources. The entire class might conduct a campaign for one agency, or teams of students could undertake programs for different agencies. . . . Practice exercises in writing news releases and fact sheets, constructing exhibits, etc., could be done in the classroom.

Simulation Game: 10.

Programmed Instruction: PUBLIC RELATIONS AND COMMUNI-CATION.

# 6 Simulation Games and Others

## Introduction

### 1. *Why Consider Simulation?*

Simulation, and particularly simulation gaming, constitutes an instructional technique that is enjoying increasingly wide use in a variety of professional and academic schools and departments. It is a tool that can find use in all parts of the social-work curriculum, and should be viewed by the reader in that light. However, because of its special relevance for the teaching of application skills, it will be discussed here mainly from that point of view.

Social workers should be interested in simulation in part because it is a new method with potential but unexplored instructional power. A recent volume (103) on educational methods states: "Simulation and games, in many forms and for many subjects, are among the most recent innovations in instructional technique." It is a technique social workers should know about if only to keep apace with developments in the allied fields. As Dawson (32) states, "Simulation is of increasing importance to social and behavioral scientists. The term appears frequently in a wide variety of social science literature and reports of social science experiments." Still, little has been written on the subject in social-work literature, and its application in teaching and research in the field has been scant. A comment made by an educator (103) about simulation and gaming in his field can be applied with even greater pertinence to social work: "The use of gamed simulation as a research and training tool continues to spread. The clientele now includes eager practitioners from political science, international relations, and psychology. Education, however, seems content to remain in the parlor, a spectator rather than player." Education has at least made a few gestures toward examining the possibilities of simulation (45). Social work, by and large, has not yet ventured into the parlor to observe what is going on.

Training is only one of a variety of uses of simulation. Dawson (32) states that simulation can be used in the following ways:

> Design—as in the construction of models of wind tunnels to test out the most efficient structure.

> Knowledge development—simulating a social process and making systematic changes in selected variables to gauge their individual effects on the total process.

> Teaching—conveying concepts and knowledge.

> Training—instruction in application operations, that is, helping students to "learn how to fill various operating roles in simulated situation."

All of these uses are relevant to our purposes, but the last point relates most directly to the domain of this report. If that part of the student's educational career that is now spent in actual practice in agencies is to be revised and shortened, some suitable substitute experiences must be provided. Experts in simulation have maintained that this technique captures many of the essential qualities of the actual operations of the real world in a more controlled or manageable context. One observer (104) states, "The trainee is able to get some feel of what he would experience in the real situation and some indication of the likely outcome of various actions and responses on his part." Discussing community-level simulations in particular, one experienced observer (95a) states:

> The most significant advantage is that gaming-simulation rapidly enhances the sophistication of the players regarding the factors at work and the relationships between the key roles in the real world. Players come to the games with imperfect concepts of community, and they leave it with shattered myths. Usually, they achieve a sense of what kind of action, when coordinated, yields what kinds of outcomes. A well-constructed game and its environment should yield more realistic mental impressions about how a large system (like a metropolis) works. It offers a low cost substitute for experience in the most responsible decision-making roles.

Through the method of simulation, then, an experience can be created for the student that incorporates some of the dimensions of actual practice, but in a context which allows the student to try himself out and develop a core of basic skills without evoking severe personal risk (to himself or others). This experience in the simulated situation can provide a stepping-stone to actual practice at a later stage in the student's educational program.

It might be well to illustrate the creation and use of simulation with a game called Community Response, both because of its clear community-organization orientation and because the underlying rationale and objectives of the game have been more clearly and and succinctly delineated than is usually the case. The simulation was developed by Michael Inbar, a sociologist from Israel who did doctoral studies at Johns Hopkins under James Coleman, a leading proponent and developer of gaming techniques. Inbar became interested in the sociology of community disasters and particularly with the capability of the community to respond quickly and efficiently so as to overcome unnecessary or extended harmful consequences of such disasters. His view was that an understanding of the natural processes of disasters and of optimizing behavior on the part of affected actors would reduce their injurious consequences.

Inbar's first step was to construct a basic model of the process or processes involved in real disaster situations, in order to "reproduce *schematically,* though accurately, the *significant* conditions and milieu in which a given social phenomenon takes place." (60) This was done through a review of the sociological literature dealing with community disasters, primarily 114 scientific field studies. Through his investigations he began to limit the area of concern to disaster which strikes only a portion of the community rather than the total community, leaving other portions capable of responding. Such catastrophes include tornadoes, fires, and limited explosions. In these types of disaster phenomena, several uniformities seem to emerge:

(a) There is little panic behavior. Amazement and daze are much more frequent than overt panic.

(b) Road and communication jams are the product of outsiders (convergence behavior), rather than of the afflicted population.

(c) Looting is uncommon in disasters, because the unafflicted have a sense of identification and solidarity toward those who have been so severely and indiscriminately victimized.

(d) The primary impact is overcome at most in a matter of hours; thus disaster behavior is limited in time scope.

(f) There is a temporary breakdown of social organization.

(g) People turn their initial attention to the well-being and rescue of family and close friends. Only after initial anxiety over loved ones is relieved are individuals able to address larger communal concerns. These role conflicts are a major factor in slowing down community reorganization.

(h) Several key agencies or formal organizations are vital to amelioration of disasters. These include:

> The department of public works—to clear the roads in order to facilitate both the approach of the rescuers and the evacuation of the victims.

> The gas, water, and electricity companies—to take care of possible broken water mains, open circuits, etc.

> The fire department whose importance is evident in the type of disasters we deal with.

> The police forces and the civil defense—to preserve order, fight against the jams, ensure priorities (ambulances), etc.

> The hospitals and Red Cross network—to provide medical help and if necessary, food and temporary shelters.

> The transportation system—to provide cars, ambulances, railroads, airports.

To operate efficiently each of these agencies needs personnel as well as material resources such as tools, gasoline, etc.

(i) Reasonably good communication is essential to dealing with disaster situations. This communication includes both intracommunity communication in the impact area and intercommunity communication. Such communication makes for an efficient allocation of available rescuers and resources, and it helps eliminate the ambiguous spread of rumor and confusion.

These points are summarized in a model of disaster behavior as follows:

> Given a community disaster, the role conflicts experienced by people are likely to give rise to individualistically-oriented behaviors. These, and the general lack of structure of the situation, lead to dysfunctional

consequences: cooperation on the community level is lowered, rumors spread, and telephone switchboards and roads tend to get jammed. Consequently, some crucial agencies may not perform properly for a variable length of time. The more and the longer this holds true, the greater the probability of destructive secondary impact consequences. Once cooperation on the community level is resumed, however, it is likely to grow quickly and the essential functions tend to be given an increasing priority over others by all the individuals (60).

This theoretic backdrop then provides the basis for constructing a specific simulation game encapsulating the dimensions of a disaster. Inbar has described the game in his own words as follows:

In its present version the game requires optimally seven to nine players. At the beginning of the game they sit together around a table on which a board is unfolded. It reproduces schematically the map of what could be a medium-sized town or an area of a large town. For instance, the map gives the location of two residential areas, a police station, a fire department, a shopping center, two hospitals, an industrial area, a city park, etc. These points are spread over the board and are connected by a network of roads which are subdivided in little squares. It takes a unit of "energy" to move from one to the other.

Each player is given a role in the simulated community. This role includes the player's location at the beginning of the game, the relatives and friends he has in the community, his job and eventually such special obligations or interests as appointments to keep or property owned.

When the game starts the players are informed that a catastrophe has occurred in an unspecified part of the town. People may have been wounded and property might have been destroyed. Each player is therefore anxious to an extent specified on the role card about the fate of the persons and things he cares for. To alleviate this anxiety, the players may try to find out what happened by listening to radio broadcasts, by telephoning to relatives, to friends or to official agencies, by asking people with whom they meet or by getting to the disaster area. In the course of these actions, the experience of the players will be that road and switchboard jams, if they occur, are a direct function of their behavior. Similarly, they will face the fact that the public agencies whose services they might require perform their functions only if the persons (players) who are in charge perform theirs. Thus the community will be without a communication network if the phone company or the police radio cars are not operated (i.e., the players are not allowed to communicate with each other and they must remove their pawn from the board—there is a state of complete blackout, except for the players who happen to meet in the streets or in a building and who are informed of the occurrence by the director of the game who centralizes all the moves on a special board). Likewise, the radio will be silent if the speaker does not broadcast, the ambulance will be pinned down if there is no gas supply, etc.

When the players gather reliable information on the location of the disaster area and on the extent of the damages, community organization becomes imperative. Indeed, some players are faced with the fact that they have relatives trapped in the disaster area. To evacuate them they must enter the impact area, and this requires the intervention of the department of public works to clear the roads, of the fire department to master the blaze, of the police station to fight road jams, etc.

If the community cannot organize itself quickly enough or efficiently enough its failure leads to the taking over by outsiders of the rescue activities, or even worse to the spread of the disaster area, which might cause damage beyond repair.

At the end of the game the players elect among themselves the three who did most for the community. Among these three, the winner is the player who was the most efficient, i.e., who accumulated the least amount of anxiety points and spent the least amount of energy points.

Once the players have played this version of the game and have gained some familiarity with the basic problems involved in a disaster they are in a position to play phase two of the game. In this phase they are allowed to engage in emergency preparation before the disaster strikes. They can duplicate some agencies and material resources as well as get trained in special tasks to increase their potential efficiency. The preparedness policy is then tested when the disaster strikes, i.e., when the basic version of the game is played once more (58).

Particular advantages of the game for community-organization teaching purposes include the use of preplanning on the part of the players to minimize the deleterious effects of the disaster, and even more, the possibility of constructing a community map, forming agencies and depicting circumstances equivalent to an actual community that students might wish to simulate in the game. On the basis of his questionnaire study of participants in the game, Inbar states that the following learning took place:

Previous planning and preparation is highly important.

The establishment of communication networks is imperative.

The performance of key personnel is necessary if public agencies are to carry out their functions.

Cooperative interorganizational and interpersonal behavior will not necessarily come about automatically, but must be initiated.

It is important not to jam roads and telephone switchboards. Calmness is essential to avoid confusion.

The basic conflict between personal loyalties and community duties can be detrimental to all.

These tests were made with subjects who were not particularly sophisticated in community-organization thinking. With a better prepared group, particularized community setting, and more refined learning objectives, the simulation might have even more relevance for community-organization practice.

This simulation is designed for six to sixteen players, takes two to six hours of playing time, and is priced at thirty dollars. The equipment is fairly complicated but has recently been redesigned for repeated use. Available from Western Publishing Company, 150 Parish Drive, Wayne, New Jersey 07470.

## 2. *Simulations and Models—the Approach Described*

In general it may be said that simulation involves a smaller or miniature representation of a large whole—in this instance, of some greater or more complex social system or process. It involves a reduction in scale and complexity of some given aspect of social reality. In this sense, it is a smaller model of a larger reality, in a form which can be manipulated and whose parts are dynamic or operating (as contrasted with static models such as pictures or diagrams). The simulation duplicates selected features of the environment so that these may be easily viewed and manipulated by students under controlled conditions.

A variety of prototypes of simulations can be cited. The Link Trainer used by the Air Force in preparing pilots is a familiar example, as well as wind tunnels for testing new airplane designs and harbor mock-ups to test the effects of the new piers or breakwaters.

The following quotation conveys the general sense of simulation as a procedure of model building:

Simulation entails the construction and manipulation of an operating model, that model being a physical or symbolic representation of all or some aspects of a social or psychological process. Simulation, for the social scientist, is the building of an operating model of an individual or group process and experimenting on this replication by manipulating its variables and their interrelationships (32).

Meier (95a) makes the interesting observation that the task of simulation is invention in reverse—that is to say, the inventor tries to create a new reality and to demonstrate that his new principle or mechanism is functional. The simulator, on the other hand, selects some human process or institution which has been functioning for some time, and attempts to capture its essential features in a smaller operating model that is also functional and that resembles the larger original. It is a process of replicating the old rather than constructing the new.

Since a model is a replication, judgment concerning the authenticity of model becomes important. Meier addresses this question as follows:

Once a working model of a portion of the real world has been constructed, some very disturbing questions arise. How does one distinguish between a good model and a poor one? The problem is very much like that of proving that a given photo is a good likeness, while others are ordinary, poor, or even worse. Scientific measures are not sufficient; therefore, a certain amount of experience judgment must eventually be introduced. The proportion of the assessment that is left to judgment when appraising a working model is much greater than for an experiment. The fundamental reason for this, of course, is that most variables are kept under control in an experiment, while no one knows, for example, how to control all the land use decisions of a metropolitan area. The crucial tests, then, are evaluations of professionals whose competence includes the phenomena that are being modeled. They are likely to know the most about the workings of the real world.

Simulations usually involve materials of various kinds and increasingly have involved machines (computers). Types include all-computer, man-computer in interaction, all-man.

The real world is the referent upon which models are constructed, and real-world practitioners are viewed as the best judges of the authenticity or validity of the model. We will have more to say on the question of authenticity at a later time.

### 3. *Definitional Problems—Simulation, Models, Simulated Games, Game Theory*

Before proceeding it would be well to untangle the interlocking strands of nomenclature involved in the subject we are pursuing. We have described simulations above as micromodels of larger or more complex social processes. Dawson (32) makes the point as follows: "Any construction of a 'model,' whether symbolic (pictorial, verbal, mathematical) or physical, might be termed a simulation." Some writers have indicated that there is little logical difference between simulations and games and that the terms are used interchangeably (116) (82). A game may be said to comprise a model with certain special features, some objective or goal, human actors, element of competition, rules of procedure, gains and losses for various actions, etc. We will discuss the special characteristics of games in the next section. As concerns game theory, this is a specialized theoretical branch of mathematics and has little direct relationship to educational gaming. Robinson (116) makes the distinction as follows:

We should note that games and simulation do not necessarily bear any relationship to game theory. The theory of games consists of mathematical assumptions about behavior under specified circumstances of conflict. Games and simulation refer to social processes that are not necessarily subject to the kinds of theorizing contained in game theory.

## 4. Simulation Games—Definition and Special Characteristics

We have suggested that games are simulations with special features such as prescribed objectives, human decision makers, rules of procedure which include payoffs of various kinds, etc. A description of business games provides a useful point of departure here. These games are seen as posing for players "the job of diagnosing a situation, setting goals and planning decisions or actions. They provide a model or set of rules for estimating the consequences of the actions that players take." (34) The authors suggest that competition is another characteristic to consider. While competition may be seen as intrinsic to business games, it is a variable to be considered in all gaming. The "cooperative-competitive" dimension is one of the key features of games according to Ohm (103). Competition may take the following forms: (a) individual-environmental interaction such as races against time or an individual competing against a computer; (b) individual-individual interaction as in two-person games; (c) within-group competition involving factions; (d) between-group interaction as in business games or international games involving separate nations. Varying degrees of cooperative interaction can be regarded within a generally competitive context. Others treat the question of competition as follows:

Although the term "game" in a technical sense implies competitive interaction (i.e. each competitor's operating results being influenced not only by its own decisions, but also by all others participating in the exercise), a growing number of games provide for competition only in the sense that each team or participant attempts to operate as efficiently as possible in a similar or identical environment (53).

Other factors cited by Ohm constitute salient characteristics of games. One is the dimension of rewards or the payoff matrix. Payoff may be viewed as feedback or evaluation response to players' actions. The basis of payoff may be measured against a predetermined standard, or standards of payoff may be evolved during the course of play. The kind of payoff is tied to learning objectives or assumptions about optimal performance in the real world. For example, in a management game, rewards may be related to a balanced development of a company's products or to development of a particularly popular product. Need studies in welfare planning contain a dimension which is similar (balanced meeting of needs versus meeting most pressing ones only).

Chance or probability is another feature specified by Ohm. The outcome is usually uncertain; thus there is usually an element of risk taking involved. Likewise gaming includes consideration of strategies for dealing with situations involving incomplete information or chance factors.

Some games base their design on the prior gathering of much real-world data (how the economy has actually operated statistically in various spheres over the past ten years). Other games are based on theoretical notions about how the world operates, and the purpose of the game is to convey these notions. The theories may be based on much or little firsthand empirical data.

Finally, games should have an atmosphere of realism about them. The degree of realism may vary considerably, depending on the context and what is to be taught.

Some games create a kind of psychological realism through a playing board and the kinds of responses players make to one another. Other games develop an elaborate procedure to foster realism. Consider, for example, the military game described below:

Operation Desk Top, as it was called, required exact realism in its exercising of the NORAD system of radar networks, air defense, and counterattack, which meant going so far as simultaneously duplicating images on radar scopes, in order to generate appropriate converging initial reports. As the operation proceeded, it eventually involved 15,000 men and officers, 268 motion picture films, 50,000 different maps and a large number of contingent factors such as simulated damage reports to be used only if the attacker reached certain specific targets, which was in a sense probabilistically determined by the reactions of the participants plus a computer program (105).

Whether simple or complex, the dimension of realism must enter into all games which attempt to mirror worldly phenomena.

## 5. *Purpose and Values of Simulated Games in Professional Education*

Simulation games are a new technique, and like all innovations are subject to mechanistic adoption in fadlike manner. As one writer has stated, "We don't know exactly what we are doing, but it sure is a lot of fun." (135) If social workers are to make use of this methodology, they ought to assess carefully what it will contribute to their learning objectives and in what way. A positive orientation to availing oneself of potentially useful tools ought well to be tempered by a skeptical appraisal of their actual utility. In this section we will attempt to spell out fairly precisely the specific ways in which simulated games may be beneficial for the tasks of social-work education. Following this, limitations will be enumerated.

Let us start with several comments by experts in the use of simulated games in business education. Greenlaw, Herron and Rawdon talk of the utility of gaming because of the complexity of practice, the difficulty of concretizing such relatively difficult and abstract terms as "planning," "executing," "coordinating" and the dilemma of the conflicting demands of "1) instructors who are forced to break subject matter down into specialized fragments in order to communicate it, and 2) students who need to experience a totality in order to fully comprehend it." (53) Here we find an expression of the classic class-field dichotomy in social-work education. Greenlaw and his colleagues feel that simulation games permit a bridging of these competing claims by incorporating some of the feel and complexity of practice in a more delimited and analytical context.

Sprague (133), who has experimented to some extent with gaming, talks about their real-life quality:

The most important feature of simulations, in my opinion, is the opportunity they provide participants to have a gut-level encounter with certain *processes* which are basic to taking part in any social system: decision-making, resource allocation, communication, and negotiation.

The participants quite literally cannot avoid making decisions. They face the reality that "no decision" has as much consequence as any other decision. They must usually decide, moreover, on the basis of incomplete information, constricted by time limits, and with only partial understanding of why their previous decisions produced the consequences they did. This seems to fit much of what we know about real-life decision making. . . .

The simulations graphically demonstrate the pitfalls of inadequate communication, the consequences of misunderstanding, the frustration of crossed messages, the ways in which the mere pressure of events can nullify intentions where face-to-face communication is impossible, and the many ways in which words may belie deeds.

Finally, simulations involve interpersonal bargaining, dealing, negotiation, and persuasion. Much of what happens in the simulation is a consequence of the individual's personal ability and style in dealing with other people, and indeed, personal characteristics of the decision-makers have been found, in research exercises, to be the key to the simulation outcomes. This, too, I think, is consistent with leadership "for real."

The other dimension, that of reducing reality to more simple and readily understandable dimensions is expressed as follows:

The real challenge is to reproduce the essential features of a city in a tiny comprehensible package. A set of maps is not enough. Years must be compressed into hours or even minutes, the number of actors must be reduced to the handful that can be accommodated in a laboratory or classroom, the physical structure must be reproduced on a table top, the historical background and law must be synopsized so that it can become familiar within days or weeks, and the interaction must remain simple enough so that it can be comprehended by a single brain. This last feature is the most difficult challenge of all (95).

Thus, the general purpose of simulation is to provide a proximate real-life practice experience but in a form which permits the major analytical or theoretical components to be more easily observable, comprehensible, manipulatable—that is to say, to make them more generally encompassable.

In addition to this most general level of purpose, several more specific purposes of simulation games have been noted by various individuals who have used this method. The Project SIMILE staff (138) has suggested most of the categories that follow:

(a) Heightened motivation and spirit of inquiry. James Coleman, a leading student of gaming, attributes heightened motivation in part to immediate feedback: "This derives from the close connection they provide between action and outcome. A player sees the consequences of his moves, and is immediately able to test them against a criterion: the moves of his opponent." The heightened-motivation idea is also promulgated by Ohm together with the following explanatory rationale:

When the actions taken in the simulation become "public" in the sense that they are brought into the instructional system level, the actions become "real" and the subsequent analysis of these actions become a reality testing process. The individual has a stake in the reality testing process since he has put forth his personal view of reality for testing against the reality of group (consensual validation) or against some externally defined criterion such as the final outcome or score of the game. If his view deviates significantly, he confronts the problem or threat of having to defend or reconstruct the framework on which his original moves or decisions were based. The extent to which the simulation and decision situations are designed to tap deeper levels of self-concept, value, and professional "face" is directly related to the motivation and involvement of play (103).

Several empirical studies have found that the motivation of students is indeed significantly increased through simulated games (13) (20) (21) (90).

(b) Simulations familiarize students with the complexity and interrelatedness of many variables in social processes.

(c) Students acquire role empathy, an appreciation of the problems and perspectives of decision makers and other community actors. "Now I know how the Secretary of State feels" or similar statements are common responses to evaluative questionnaires (14).

(d) Students acquire factual information concerning various phenomena.

(e) Students in gaming situations are obliged to develop skills in working with groups or teams of other players. Various commentators have remarked on the capacity of games for teaching interpersonal skills, such as communication, negotiation, influence, influence resistance, cooperation, etc. Meier (94) has indicated that games may be used with secondary-school students to develop a range of interpersonal skills related to organizational adaptation, the rapid forming of new organizational structures, their dissolution and their re-formation when necessary.

(f) Through their experiences in simulated situations students gain confidence regarding their ability to handle similar situations in real-life circumstances. There develops a sense of mastery over given problems or conditions which permits the student to face analogous events without undue anxiety and doubt. Says Boocock, "The legislative game data revealed a trend toward greater feelings of political efficacy." (14)

(g) As in the case of practice, simulated games force the participants to reach into their total repertoire of personal resources to deal with new situations as they arise. The SIMILE staff indicate that simulated games serve as information-retrieval devices in that they "allow students to bring into consciousness and 'process' knowledge they already have, but do not know they have." In a sense this is preparatory training for evoking a similar personal investment in real practice.

(h) Gaming leads students to a personal encounter with self which forces an examination of personal values, social philosophy, as well as general self-insight. Because of the often high and emotional interchange with an opportunity to observe concrete results of one's behavior quickly and to receive immediate feedback from others, the self becomes highly involved. Thus simulation is seen by some gaming specialists as an excellent tool for fostering self-awareness.

(i) Various games provide the opportunity and the stimulus for the participant to develop decision-making skills, either individually or in terms of group decision making. Greenlaw and his associates stress this, as this may indeed be the central learning outcome of most business simulations.

(j) The same authors (53) point out that there may be benefits in simulation in excess of those which the designer intended—that is to say, as in practice, when situations unfold, a wide range of problems and circumstances arise which make variable and multiple demands and offer a wide range of potential though unplanned learning opportunities. The point has been made in a different way as follows: Games "have provided a setting in which students cannot only be tested for their ability to *DO* things that are at least grossly related to the job of managing a real business enterprise, but in which they can also be asked to observe and analyze what others do with the same benefits they might get from a field study of a going concern. The flexibility of the technique is immense . . ." (34).

In addition to the above, with near unanimity writers on gaming have exclaimed on the immense benefits derived by the instructor in designing and conducting games. It forces the teacher to sharpen his awareness of what learning objectives he is promulgating, what variables are involved in a given social process, precisely how they relate to one another, what kinds of outcomes (quantitatively) can be expected or predicted under what given conditions for various interventions or moves. The teacher's role is shifted so that much of his time goes into the design of learning objectives and experiences, with his role with students more oriented toward that of a goad, role player, and counselor (34).

It is also pointed out that much benefit can be derived by the students if they are asked to design their own simulations, following their exposure to a prepared one, or if they are assigned the task of comparing the concepts, principles, or skills of the simulation with the real-life referent system (21).

The favorable effect on the climate of learning in the classroom has also been cited as a plus in simulation. Thus students drop their usual facades, and this subsequently leads to a more open classroom atmosphere (133).

Various writers have indicated that the simulation once designed is not a sufficient device in its own right. Inbar points out that the skill of the teacher in conducting the game was extremely important in the outcomes obtained (58).

Ohm (103) stresses the need for careful and intelligent discussion of the simulation experience with students following the run-through of the game:

The major contribution of the simulation technique may be its laboratory function of producing behavior data which is observed, measured, and recorded for subsequent analysis. The learnings intrinsic to the simulation may not be as important as the learnings based on the extrinsic analysis of the experience, and it follows that the instructional value of a post mortem analysis is dependent on the level of conceptual or theoretical development that can be applied to the data. And this, in turn, is dependent on the competency of the instructor using the simulation.

These are some of the stated or implied objectives of simulated games, or their potential peculiar strengths as teaching devices. Leaving aside for the time being, the validity of these claims, it might be well at this time to consider that simulated games may have certain built-in limitations. In the interests of achieving a balanced and objective perspective on gaming, we next look into limitations of this technique.

### 6. *Limitations of Simulation Games as Teaching Devices*

(a) One of the first and most obvious limitations of simulation games pertains to the very high expenditures of time and money necessitated in the design and development of games. It takes an estimated two years to conceptualize, design, test, and redesign a single simulation game. Robinson (116) estimates that using an already developed simulation added $650 to the cost of one political-science course. He adds, "There are 'opportunity' or 'behavioral' costs for the teachers, expenditures for forms, equipment, etc. and requirements of space."

Wolf (152a) lays out the various dimensions of cost as follows:

The cost can be analyzed into three parts. There are the first research and development costs, which will probably be borne by an institution such as ESI, or else by a commercial house which develops games for profit. Second, there are the actual production costs of the "hardware" items for the game—board, pieces, play money, or whatever is required, together with instructions for students, teachers, and any other written material that may be needed (supplementary reading, tests, and so forth). Third, there is the expenditure of time and effort by the teacher who uses the game in his class.

As a result of testing a game in a classroom and trying to obtain answers to these questions, it is likely that revisions will have to be made in the game. The revised version in turn will have to be tested out. It is necessary to go through the entire process again, because it is possible that in "improving" the game, we may inadvertently have added errors or may have made it unplayable for technical reasons. (This is not an idle fear; it has in fact happened with some games.) It is this lengthy process of testing, changing, and re-testing which makes game development costly. It should be added that in this respect, however, game development is no different than development of any new teaching materials.

(b) In addition to development costs and time investment on the part of faculty in perfecting games, resources may also be expended in actually playing games. More complex computerized games especially involve this factor:

Any game that requires a computer will involve machine time and the help at least of someone to punch input cards and run the program. A more complex game, like the Carnegie Tech Game, may draw heavily on the services of a faculty member and one or more student assistants, in addition, to help students learn the mechanics of playing the game and to keep the game running smoothly. Some special costs may be incurred in emergencies to keep a game on schedule if an umpire is sick or if a computer breaks down (11a).

(c) Another cost factor has to do with the large amounts of classroom time necessitated in playing simulation games. There is a question of the amount of payoff obtained in terms of the lengthy processes necessitated by many games. This consumes time that might be put to other use. Referring to Wolff again:

Let us turn to the expenditure of time involved in playing a game in the classroom and relate it to the utility of the game as a teaching device. It is probably fair to say that all games take relatively long to play. This is certainly true of "Empire" which takes a minimum of five classroom hours, but can take more. "Trade and Travel" which was thought to be a simple and quick game when first designed turned out to require several classroom hours also; "Adventuring" in its experimental version took a week. In general, it can be said that games take longer to play than the designers think they will, partly because the designers do not realize all the complexities they are building into their games, and partly because of the fragmentation of time that is normal in American schools (announcements, assemblies, etc.) and sometimes because of the teacher's deliberate strategy (152a).

(d) Material or hardware costs of games may also be high. Games involving computer time involve considerable expense automatically. Even a fairly simple game like Empire is estimated to cost well over twenty dollars to produce (152a).

(e) There is a problem of fitting game-based instruction into an ordinary time schedule in most learning institutions. A normal one- or two-hour period may provide only a good warm-up period for some games. Because of the dynamics of a particular game session, the time needed to obtain maximum education potential may vary considerably from class to class. In addition, there is a problem involved in getting acceptance of the gaming approach from other skeptical or conservative faculty members. The problem has been articulated as follows:

> Deans and faculty members may avoid management games because they feel that they owe their loyalty to other methods of teaching, because they doubt their ability to master the intricacies of analytic models and computer programs that are involved in games, or simply because they are too busy or too insecure to want new challenges and new problems to work on. There have been difficulties between senior and junior faculty members about credit for game experiments; and in cases where games cannot fit into the confines of a single course, some faculty members have resisted forced collaboration on teaching assignments (34).

The authors go on to suggest various ways of dealing with resistance that colleagues are likely to raise with respect to gaming.

(f) A fundamental question pertaining to gaming has to do with the validity of the replication, i.e., just how accurately does the simulated model and exercise actually approximate analogous forces in the real world. For example, in the original version of Community Response, competitive aspects of reactions of individuals in a disaster situation were given emphasis. Individuals received points for the degree to which they relieved their personal anxieties about relatives and friends located in the disaster community. The game was found to distort reality in that individuals in disaster situations seek to work cooperatively with others in dealing with community dimensions of the disaster as well as in attempting to cope with their personal problems and anxieties, especially as concern for relatives and close friends is reduced. In a later version, a person's score became a composite of how he relieved his individual anxieties as well as how he was rated by other players in terms of his communal contribution. This variation set up an interaction in the game which was closer to the way people actually behaved, as demonstrated by research. The game designer has to be constantly wary of the genuineness of this model. (See

Caplin (28) for a critique of the International Simulation, one of the best established and most used gaming procedures.)

The compromises that all games involved between realism and practicality are easy to find fault with. Even the most effective games today are only a caricature of what game designers hope to achieve (34).

(g) In addition to questions of valid replication, games may teach the wrong things in still another way. The student may develop a mechanistic approach to viewing and dealing with problems based on the structure of a particular game. He may assume that you "always do it this way," not recognizing that the richness and variability of the real world requires flexibility and adaptability which cannot always be conveyed in a simulated experience.

(h) While the simulation game has the virtue of providing the individual with a measure of self-confidences prior to the undertaking of actual practice, it may also possess the vice of fostering overconfidence. The modest student will well recognize the artificiality of the simulated procedure; other students may come to believe that they are now fully prepared to run an agency or mount a community-action campaign.

(i) Gaming appeals only to a certain segments of students. If the game is simple, bright students may lose interest, and if the game is complex, slower students may be at a loss. Some students may reject the entire concept. In some games, such as SIMSOC, certain roles are more central or significant. Players in lesser roles have tended to drop their attention. (Some of these same points may, of course, be made about any teaching device that is employed.)

(j) Games are difficult to convey from the designer to other users. Often manuals are not supplied although badly needed. The availability of various games is often passed along from one teacher to another strictly by word of mouth. Robinson (116) suggests the need for a central coordinating body which will have information on hand concerning available games. Sometimes the best way to catch on to the procedures of a game is to see it played. Robinson suggests that games and instructions for their use be put on film or video tape to facilitate their dispersion and proper use. He also states that once the general principles of game construction have been mastered they can be designed without too much difficulty. This may be a dissenting view, at least one that should not be accepted too readily.

## Evaluation of Simulation Techniques

It is not enough for a teaching method to be new or fashionable in order for it to be effective. Means need to be developed for testing and evaluating its impact on student learning. Simulation games in the past have had some enthusiastic supporters, often without an empirically based foundation for such enthusiasm. One gaming specialist (34) states the point as follows: "Most of the present support for gaming consists of intuitive judgments with little or no basis in scientifically objective evidence."

Fortunately, even though simulation games in their current use are a relatively recent teaching innovation, there is already a beginning literature that seeks to evaluate their utility. The production of such evaluative studies is perhaps explained by the interest in gaming expressed by social scientists in fields such as sociology, political science, and psychology. The potentialities for research applications of simulation have drawn these individuals into this area, and the same research orientation has led simulation designers to test their products.

The results of evaluative studies to date have been somewhat inconclusive. This may in part be attributed to the still undeveloped level of technology within the field of simulation and gaming. At any rate, findings are variable concerning the amount or type of learning that has taken place and the effectiveness of simulation over other teaching techniques for producing learning. This is indeed congruous with other research efforts, such as that of McKeachie (89) (88) which have failed to confirm the superiority of any one teaching method (including more traditional ones) over any other teaching method. Nevertheless, the capacity of simulation games to evoke student interest, motivation, and participation has been fairly well confirmed.

Robinson (116) made a careful comparison of the use of the international simulation and the case-study method in teaching foreign and international relations. He found little difference between the two in learning facts or principles. Students expressed little difference in their perceived level of interest when exposed to both teaching methodologies. However, when interest was correlated with actual behavior, such as attendance, rate of participation, and the content of a final evaluative essay, students did better in the simulation experience. Robinson concluded: "The claims we made and the expectations we had for simulation were not borne out."

Boocock and Coleman (15) have reported the results of testing several games developed at Johns Hopkins on groups of high-school students. They indicate a high level of student motivation, and only a slight tendency to do better in the acquisition or retention of factual information than was so in control groups. However, in the students engaged in simulation, there seemed to be a general effect along the lines of a greater realization of the complexity of future social situations and a greater sense of confidence in being able to cope with one's environment. The latter in particular would seem to be an important attribute to get across to social-work students in training.

A discouraging conclusion was reached by Cherryholmes in his review of six investigations of educational simulations. Cherryholmes (21) states, "Simulation does produce more student motivation and interest, but there are no consistent or statistical differences in learning, retention, critical thinking or attitude change."

Other investigators have had similar results. Miller (101) found little distinction between simulation-trained students and a control group on measures of teacher behavior in the classroom. In business education, it was found that students learned more from interactions with other players and outside management contacts than from the game itself (33).

Other studies are more strongly favorable. For example, Baker (7) found that simulation was more effective than traditional teaching methods in communicating historical facts, concepts, and attitudes to above-average junior-high-school children. Likewise, Wing reports that through simulation games students attained the same amount of learning of economic principles with considerably less investment of time (151). Another study showed that there is a definite transfer of skills from a simulated-training experience to the real-life situation. Training on a simplified task resulted in high or complete transfer to a criterion-application task (3).

After reviewing a variety of evaluative studies on simulation, two experts in simulation conclude: "We believe that the available evidence, as reviewed in this volume, justifies a general claim that simulation games are not just a refreshment from 'real' learning . . . but that games have a direct impact on intellectual learning, attitudes, and strategies, so that even brief playing sessions induce measurable effects."

Various studies have suggested factors which need to be taken into account in order to maximize the learning impact of games.

For example, Inbar's (59) findings point out that attitude and behavior of the teacher is highly significant in the outcome of gaming. Group size is also an important factor. He maintains that favorable surrounding conditions and the immediate group atmosphere surrounding the game are highly relevant.

There are implications in the Dill and Doppelt study (33), that gaming may produce a multiplier effect in other parallel-learning situations. For example, coupling a game on executive behavior with actual visits to, or assignments with, executives may have a considerable effect. Another study suggests that heterogeneous grouping of players creates a better educational outcome than homogeneous grouping (91). The degree of participation induced in players seems likewise to make a difference in derived benefits (153).

A great deal still needs to be learned about what knowledge or skill can best be imparted through games and other simulations, with what kinds of students, under what kinds of conditions. The same may be said for almost any other currently employed educational tool. Ohm's (103) comment concerning the use of simulation games in training educational administrators has relevance here for social work:

The many unsolved problems, such as the need for a taxonomy of games related to classes of outcomes, the problem of controlling or using the high involvement and motivation for desirable learning, the need for theory development and research, and the growing use and acceptance of the technique in business, government, and education here and abroad suggest that the concept of gamed instructional simulation may be in its developmental infancy. Theory and practice in educational administration may well profit from a more extensive involvement in this area.

Recognizing the limitations and uncertainties of this new educational tool, while cognizant of its employment in numerous fields and the glimmer of its potentialities, we encourage forthright experimentation with simulation and gaming in professional social-work education.

An annotated listing of available games that are relevant to community-organization practice is provided in Appendix B, and a bibliography on simulation games and other simulations is contained in Appendix C. The popularity of gaming has led to the introduction of games into the commercial market and a number of

useful ones are now available for entertainment use. We have not
attempted to list or evaluate these, but such games as Ghetto, Pollution, Blacks and Whites, Class, Group Therapy, Smog, Sensitivity,
The Cities Game, and Dirty Water, might well find a place in educational settings. Advertisements and book shops might be checked
for interesting items, their rapid proliferation precludes any complete list of games.

# 7 Programmed Instruction

Programmed instruction is a great deal better known, more firmly established, and widely used in educational endeavors than is simulation and gaming. However, programmed instruction is less oriented to field instruction, and less suitable materials are available because customarily programs are related to the acquisition of knowledge or information in specific content areas rather than to the acquisition and application of skills. This is not, however, because of any intrinsic limitation of programmed instruction for skill development. The potentialities are there and are considerable. Because of the greater public awareness of programmed instruction, our treatment of the subject here will be briefer and focused to a greater degree on problems of educational implementation.

## What Is Programmed Instruction?

Programmed instruction may be defined as a logical and controlled ordering of a learning sequence for the purposes of acquisition of knowledge by students at their own pace within their own capacity. One useful definition is stated as follows:

Programming is the process of arranging materials to be learned in a series of small steps designed to lead a student through self-instruction from what he knows to the unknown of new and more complex knowledge and principles (77).

The roots of programmed instruction may be traced back to early work in psychology and educational psychology, particularly the work of Pressey, who struck on the concept of reinforcement as a powerful education technique. Pressey (109) devised an embryonic teaching machine which could provide to students immediate feedback of their knowledge mastery. It was some thirty years later than Skinner wrote his monumental papers on teaching machines that set in motion, the whole contemporary movement of programmed instruction (129) (128). While Pressey and his associates (110) continued to stress reinforcement and the use of programmed devices for testing purposes and to supplement the work of the regular teacher, Skinner went beyond reinforcement to the basic concept of a program systematically constructed in terms of a logical series of stimulus materials and providing for autonomous self-instruction on the part of the student.

Some of the more salient characteristics of programmed instruction may be specified as follows:

(a) Clearly defined objectives: clarification of learning objectives is seen as extremely important in programmed instruction. Until this initial step is completed, no further effort ensues. A programmed instruction book has been prepared expressly on defining educational objectives (79). In addition, a guide to the classes of relevant educational objectives has been published (139). In general, objectives are expected to be specific, clear, and stated in behavioral or performance terms, that is to say, terminal behaviors or observable acts should be identified and named in order that one can determine concretely whether the learner has achieved the desired objective. In addition, it is necessary to be definite concerning significant conditions (givens and restrictions) under which the behavior will occur and the criteria of expected behavior so that the acceptable *level* of student performance is clear.

(b) Reinforcement: feedback to students of success or failure in learning. Use of feedback as reward and punishment stimuli as an impetus to learning.

(c) Small steps: division of the learning task into logical subparts which may be mastered in an incremental manner.

The content consists of concepts, information, and instructions which are encoded as units that are expository or interrogative in form, typically small in size, and often called frames. The decision rules used in presenting content, relate to the responses made by the students to expository and/or interrogative frames, the steps of the program. The decision rules are the teaching strategy (137).

(d) Individualization and autoinstruction: instruction is designed so that students may proceed at their own level under their own direction.

Programmed instruction is an innovation in the implementation of individualized or tutorial instruction. . . . In contrast with group or mass instruction, the now prevalent procedure, PI is a commitment to individualized instruction and to the facultation of individual rates of progress (137).

(e) A theoretical or conceptual design which guides construction of an instructional program. This involves the nature and size of steps, type of stimuli, etc. Programmed learning "forces the development of theoretical notions about instruction, because instructional decisions must be built into every program." (137)

Instructional programs may be of the written type that appear in printed books and pamphlets, or of the teaching-machine variety that are often computerized. Printed programs are fairly inexpensive for students to purchase and keep and are flexible in their use. Computerized programs require costly hardware and are often more difficult to design. However, they can be of more interest to students and, through network hook-ups, permit a vast number of programs on a multitude of subjects to be available to a given student or teacher at a particular time. Network systems may be university-wide, state-wide, regional, or even national. Equipment, space, and facility costs can become quite formidable in implementing such an approach.

## Some Values to Social Work Education of Programmed Instruction (149) *

### 1. *Programming as Prestructured Instruction*

This view sees programmed instruction as essentially predesigned while classroom instruction is more extemporaneously created. Clarity and precision in explicating learning objectives is forced in programmed instruction as perhaps in no other educational media. This characteristic of programmed instruction may be especially valuable in the realm of field instruction, serving as a useful counterforce to the global, diffuse way goals have previously been stated and pursued. In addition to the conscious pretesting of effectiveness in meeting objectives, "the basic assumption is that the program is to be written in large measure by the students with

* For the original draft of much of the material which follows, the authors are indebted to Henry Wallace, of Community Systems Foundation, Ann Arbor, Michigan.

whom it is to be used. Consequently, student errors are examined carefully for evidence of the program's failure to teach." (137)

## 2. *Programming as Validated Instruction*

Here programming is seen as a *process* for producing *validated* instruction (i.e. instruction which consistently produces *important* real-world behavior in students). The emphasis is on the analysis of what exactly is the behavior desired of the student and then testing and revising the program until it works smoothly and consistently. The painstaking procedures commonly used to generate programmed instruction may help to clarify these points.

(a) The programmer first probes subject-matter experts for test items and critical incidents which are believed to be important. These are called criterion frames.

(b) The criterion frames are then given to good practitioners, not-so-good practitioners, and completely untrained subjects from the student population. Only those items that discriminate between the good practitioner and others are retained.

(c) The remaining critical items are analyzed into behaviorally specific components: discriminations, decisions, productions, etc., and logically sequenced.

(d) Frame sequences consisting of rules, examples, and small test items are then constructed to train up the behaviors called for in the criterion frames.

(e) This first version is then developmentally tested. That is, the programmer sits beside individual students and probes them whenever they run into difficulty. After several rounds of tryout and revision, the program has either been successfully debugged or it is scrapped and a new design tried or else the criterion frames are reexamined.

(f) The program is now ready for field testing and evaluation against some objective measure of real-world performance.

## 3. *Programming as a Form of Educational Capital*

To the economist, programmed instruction represents a form of instructor-saving capital in the same sense that machines in factories are a form of labor-saving capital. In economic terms, programmed instruction changes the *cost structure*. It increases the fixed costs and decreases the variable costs. The following discussion will be industry oriented, because industry has given more attention to the economics of training than have academic groups.

The fixed costs are essentially the investment made in developing the program. They are the costs of ferreting out the critical behaviors which discriminate the good performer from others, the cost of analysis and design, the costs of testing and revision, and the costs of objective validation. In industry, these fixed costs may run as high as $2,000 or more per hour of instruction.

The decreased variable costs are (a) instructor teaching time (the program now does the teaching, not the instructor), (b) space (requirements for space are much more flexible when individual students interact with individual programs), (c) class size and scheduling (when individual students learn from individual programs, a class of one becomes economically feasible, as does training-as-needed; much training can be moved out of the classroom and into the field; when the application lag of new learning is decreased, there is much less forgetting), (d) student time (in industry, programming usually results in a 20–50 per cent reduction in student learning time when content is held constant).*

In short, the introduction of labor-saving capital creates what economists call economies of scale. That is, once the initial investment in capital has been made, the incremental cost of training one more student is much less than before. The net result is that, if the demand is there, many more students can be trained.

In addition to the obvious direct costs of training, industry has found several indirect cost benefits from improved instruction:

Expensive on-the-job errors are reduced.

Initial on-the-job efficiency is increased.

There are fewer drop-outs from training.

There is a lower on-the-job turnover rate.

Of all the problems involved in a new approach to teaching through programmed instruction, three stand out as being particularly important. They are selectivity, feasibility, and financeability.

*Selectivity:* deciding what to program—time and money are not available to program everything at once. In many areas programming will be virtually impossible for lack of mastery tests or because the content is changing so rapidly. Thus, it is important to allocate programming time and money so as to produce the greatest

* Note: Industry pays for student time, and as a result, finds that student time is two thirds of training costs and usually the area of greatest cost savings from programming.

return. Some objective goals here might be increasing the spread
of new knowledge, reducing student difficulties in present courses,
or physically moving training from the school to the student's residence or the field agency.

*Feasibility:* selecting and training programmers—programming
is something new. The activity content is quite different from most
present conceptions of teaching. Therefore, many good instructors
may not find programming as personally enjoyable and rewarding
as their present classroom activities, while many potentially good
programmers will not have considered teaching careers.

In addition, a new activity like programming has to compete
against the strong economic and personal satisfactions which university instructors gain from their research and service activities.

Moreover, to be a successful programmer requires several weeks
of expensive training, coaching and assistance from good programmers afterward, and about a year of slowly increasing speed and
skill. In short, it takes time and money to become good at it.

*Financeability:* regardless of how opportunistically frugal one
attempts to be, programming requires much more time per hour of
instruction than the traditional extemporaneous lecture, recitation,
and outside reading.

This time must come from other activities, and if it is significant
in quantity and quality, it must be paid for. At $2,000/hour of
instruction (a rule of thumb in industry), there are few things that
an individual school of social work could afford to program. Even
using a very "quick and dirty approach," costing only $400/hour
of instruction costs, would be prohibitive.

### 4. *Solution Strategies*

Despite the difficulties outlined above, there are three programming strategies that meet the tests of selectivity, feasibility, and
financeability. If applied in concert, they should produce a great
deal of programming activity and significantly increase both the
quantity and quality of training. They are: research-project add-
ons, faculty summer institutes, and model units.

*Research Project Add-Ons:* Sponsored research projects sometimes result in substantial increases in practice knowledge. These
results would greatly increase effectiveness in the field if they could
be quickly and easily transmitted to the overburdened practitioner.

Sponsors spend much money on many projects in hopes of adding to knowledge. It would be worth as much (if not several times more) to the sponsor to have the results of such a project spread and put into widespread use.

This is an excellent opportunity to ask for an add-on grant to program the new knowledge and distribute it through the relevant professional and agency channels.

A research add-on programming project could afford to hire people with potential as programmers, pay for their training and support them during the early stages of practice. In fact, this will probably be a necessity, because good programmers are very scarce and expensive.

*Faculty Summer Institutes:* Although most instructors do not wish to become instructional programmers, they do have a great desire to know what's happening and to be in on the action. The best way to learn what programmed instruction is all about is to do some. One-week summer institutes such as those put on by several centers are ideal for this.

At the same time, many of the interested faculty have some small content area in which they are particularly expert or which is particularly important but problematic for them. A one-week institute is about right for getting control of such topics and problems.

A model for such an institute might be the one-week institute which the University of Michigan's Center for Programmed Learning for Business recently conducted for the American Dietetics Association. Half the cost of the institute was paid for by the Public Health Service and half by the A.D.A. itself. The participants were twenty directors of Dietary Internship Programs who had been selected from a national population of sixty. For a year after the workshop, the center will provide editorial assistance to the internship directors as they complete their programs and begin new ones. CPLB will also assist the A.D.A. in establishing its own clearinghouse for published programs, including programs generated by the workshop participants.

A summer institute such as the one initiated by the A.D.A. produces several benefits:

(a) Faculty now know more about programmed instruction. They can make much more intelligent decisions about whether or not to try a published program and how to modify a colleague's program to meet their own needs.

(b) They are much better able and more likely to initiate and/or participate in programming projects such as those outlined in the research add-on strategy.

(c) After such an institute, many instructors find that many of the principles and techniques involved in programming can be applied to any instructional setting, including their own classrooms. Some find these insights the most valuable and useful products of the institute—a new and more rigorous way of thinking about instructional problems, analyzing them, and solving them.

(d) One or two instructors sometimes enjoy programming so much and find it so satisfying that they decide to become professional programmers. By the time they leave the workshop, they are planning the pursuit of federal funds and training of graduate assistants with the same vigor and intelligence that they used to pursue their research and service activities.

*Model Units:* Once the analysis of the desired behavior has been made, a considerable portion of the remaining effort is developing an instructional design.

In many cases it should be possible to develop small model programs which are relevant to broad areas of curriculum content. In other words, once an efficient general format has been perfected, different content areas can be plugged into it.

The use of model programs should greatly reduce the amount of faculty time which must be diverted from other activities. This is especially true when graduate assistants are given the models to work from and are able to program course content with only minimal assistance from a faculty subject-matter expert and/or a professional programmer.

In fact, with good models, a great deal of instructional programming can be done by students themselves. Using good models, students can construct and validate small instructional units as optional alternatives to the traditional term paper. They would probably learn as much from programming as from writing papers, and certainly the contributions to the school and posterity would be greater.

A suggested course of action for schools of social work in developing computerized programmed instruction has been proposed by Walter Ehlers as follows:

(a) Identification of the significant concepts which must be in the theory and practice courses.

(b) Submitting the concepts to the scrutiny of colleagues.

(c) Writing curricula suitable for programmed learning.

(d) Adapting the curricula to computer-based instruction and allowing for the use of additional media along with the computer.

(e) Selecting learning situations which may be simulated and which can be taught via computer-assisted instruction and related media instruction.

(f) Adequate research funds—because the development of new curricula will take a lot of time and cost a great deal of money (43).

## Implications for Social Work Practice and for Redefining Curriculum Objectives

The normal reaction to some new technology is to think of all the old tasks and activities which might be performed more effectively and efficiently using the new technology. This is necessary and desirable, but it is not enough. The ultimate and major impact of any significant new technology is that new goals and activities become possible and/or feasible.

We would be remiss if we did not point out some of the ways in which programmed instruction may change the content of the community-organization social worker's role in the field. The use of programmed instruction makes it possible to routinize and delegate tasks from the professional worker to others.

We are currently discovering that some professional tasks contain a great deal of standardized activity which might very profitably be transferred to paraprofessionals and even to clients themselves.

This is fairly obvious in the case of routine paperwork tasks, but it is also true of many tasks which have traditionally been performed face-to-face with clients and are considered to require professional expertise. Smith's program described in *Child Management* (129a) is a good example of this routinization and delegation of professional tasks, in this case from the guidance counselor and visiting teacher to the parent.

Programming requires a fairly specific behavioral analysis (a task analysis) before any teaching material is constructed. During the analysis, the task itself is often modified to make it simpler and easier. In any case, when the task has been fully described on paper, it is often decided that we now have clear-enough instruction so that almost anyone can do it, and professional expertise is not needed.

In view of these possibilities, additional course options might be considered for inclusion in community-organization curricula dealing with performance programming. In these courses about one third to one half of the time should be devoted to studying existing materials and learning principles and techniques. The rest of the time should be devoted to practicum activities in which students develop their own programs. Through this arrangement the student is equipped to educate others to carry out "professional" community-organization functions.

In addition to its use in the formal education of students in schools of social work, it has been suggested that programmed instruction may be used profitably in agencies for in-service training, by individuals for self-education to supplement academic work or make up deficiencies, and by clients to modify their behavior within the framework of professional social-work objectives.

It has been suggested by Wallace that programmed instruction's greatest impact on social work may be in continuing education of professionals and in worker-client relations (148).

As is true with other teaching approaches and educational tools, evaluation of the effectiveness of programmed instruction has produced variable and inconclusive results. In this instance, however, there has been a considerable quantity of research in the area. An excellent summary of this mass of data is as follows:

From elementary students to adult trainees, from college classrooms to Air Force installations, experiments have probed the potentialities of programmed learning. But this research is only a beginning. Much more has to come before it becomes possible to assess this new learning method adequately. . . .

In the light of the findings thus far, several tentative statements may be made about programmed learning. First of all, it *can* be effective; students have learned successfully from it. Second, programmed learning *can* reduce student error; proper analysis followed by suitable revision of the material can decrease errors even further during the learning process. Third, a learning program tends to level the differences in learning capacities among students; while all students exposed to the program may demonstrate achievement, the gain seems to be more conspicuous among the lower portion of the class distribution. This might result from both the varying time limit, which permits slower learners to progress at their own rates of speed, and the fact that any programmed sequence tends to impose a ceiling on what anyone can learn (77).

Appendix D contains selected references on programmed instruction, a directory of publishers, and a source list of relevant materials. These materials are largely content, or cognition, oriented, rather than slanted toward skill development. They are listed here, however, for information and as suggestive models.

# 8 Summary and Conclusions

Only a short summary statement will be necessary. Our discussion has covered much ground, and substantive findings and recommendations have been explicitly enunciated at various places in the body of the text.

The major recommendations of the volume will be found in Chapter 3. A thumbnail recounting of them should suffice at this point. Several guiding principles were set forth for education in application of professional skills. These include:

1. Integration of classroom teaching and application teaching.
2. Diversification of teaching techniques and learning experiences.
3. Greater direction and control by the school of the educational experience for learning application skills.
4. Greater specificity of learning objectives by the school; explicating skills to be imparted and delineating relevant tasks and experiences.
5. Some rational and ordered sequencing of learning experiences according to a prescribed plan.

Application training, we stated, includes: (a) development of specific professional skills; (b) their implementation in a holistic context; and (c) personal professional development including self-awareness and self-discipline. A format was suggested by which the first year of training gives emphasis to (a) and the second year to (b) and (c). We proposed a sequence of three curriculum stages: a laboratory-observatory, a skills-development laboratory, and a second-year practicum which would resemble the existing form of field work. The laboratories will link up directly with methods courses, thus insuring the integration of theory and practice. In the same vein, a practicum theory seminar will parallel the new field experience, linking practice reality back to academic content. To assure a rounded array of teaching methods and technologies, practical suggestions were made for the use of simulation techniques, particularly simulation gaming, programmed instruction, delimited and prestructured experiences in agencies and organizations as well as in the community-at-large, and classroom exercises and demonstrations including anticipatory practice experiences such as role playing.

As with any curriculum innovation, there is the danger that a new orthodoxy may be established, with the rigidifying and ritualizing of that which is offered tentatively and in an experimental spirit. We would like to caution against uncritical or uniform acceptance of what has been stated (perhaps sometimes, with the natural zeal of innovators, overstated). The ideas we have set forth are largely untested. Evaluation is necessary before highly optimistic or firm claims can be made. We encourage schools to build such evaluation into their curriculum planning in this area. Perhaps the proposed approach and the more customary ones could be tried concurrently in the same school with different students and the behavioral outcomes of each program systematically recorded and assessed. Some schools may wish to attempt entirely different avenues for upgrading the learning of application skill, based on particular local resources, faculty, or just better ideas.

A few practical steps in implementing these proposals would be in order. In the first place, schools may consider seriously the addition to their faculty of a specialist in community-laboratory resources. Such an individual would be responsible for making available to the school the range of opportunities in the community which could be used in a consciously planned and structured way, on both a short-term and long-term basis, to support a more rigorous application-training program. Such an individual might take responsibility for seeking out innovations in the teaching for application of practice skills.

We further recommend that the Council on Social Work Education expand its services in the use of the new media, particularly simulation and programmed instruction. Council staff should coordinate efforts to explore and engineer the new media for use in social-work education. They can perform a clearinghouse function in terms of exchange of ideas and techniques among various faculty and schools. Workshops and institutes might be sponsored to train others to use these techniques or to become designers of curriculum units employing these techniques. Such a diffusion strategy is critical because of the heavy expenditure of time and money necessary to develop any given gaming or programmed unit. Through grants and research add-on, this central staff itself might develop a series of curriculum units utilizing the new media. In addition, such staff could support efforts along these lines which are attempted by individual schools through offering consultation and working tools.

In adopting recommendations for curriculum designs in teaching practice skills proposed in this report, we urge schools to make adequate provision of time and staff. There is the need for ample lead time to plan and tool up for new operations. Allocation of a sufficient number of faculty for planning is essential. Possible increases in cost over traditional field instruction need to be investigated.

It is our view that the kind of orientation expressed in this monograph, with increased responsibility by the school for teaching professional application skills and a strengthening and concretizing of the academic or theoretical aspect of such training, will contribute to the projection of the profession into a more advanced stage of development. As we stated earlier (Chapter 3), a shift in the balance of field experience and academic-theoretical instruction toward a greater weighting of the latter would be for social work a mark of professional maturation. The Project staff hopes that our efforts will contribute to such advancement.

## APPENDIX A

# Survey Questionnaires

## *(Condensed schedules)*

### C.O. Student Questionnaire

1. School of Social Work
2. Name of student
3. Name of current field instructor
4. Sex
5. Age
6. Year in School of Social Work—First year; Second year
7. Marital Status
8. Number of Children
9. What is your current grade-point average in class work?
10. What is your current grade-point average in field work?
11. Prior to entering this school, did you have any work experience in social work or related activities?
12. Have you had *direct* work experience with any of the following: Peace Corps; VISTA; Community Action Programs, (CAP, TAP): Other OEO programs; Civil Rights Organizations; Other?

The questions below relate to your *current* field placement.

The field placement of many students often includes an assignment to more than one agency or project. These may be called secondary or satellite placements or they may be additional or alternate tasks for varying lengths of time in a laboratory or teaching center. Space is provided at each question, below, to permit two responses—one for your major placement (A) and one for a secondary placement (B). If you worked in two agencies use the (A) and (B) columns to answer for each. If you worked on two projects, (even in the same agency) use (A) and (B) for each of these. If you had an assignment (even within a single project), that involved two very different kinds of work or responsibility (for example, organizing a staff committee to develop a new program *and* recruit a client group for this program), consider these two aspects of your assignment as (A) and (B). In the space immediately below give the name of the agency, project, or program in which you had your principal assignment under (A) and your secondary assignment under (B). For the questions that follow, use the (A) and (B) columns to answer for each of your placements. If you had no secondary placement write "none" under (B) and check "No, does not apply" in the (B) column for each question.

   A. Principal Placement
   B. Secondary Placement

13. Does your field placement involve organizing people in urban neighborhood; rural U. S. area; citizen's interest or social action group not geographically based; other.

14. Does your field placement involve working with client groups to redefine goals, formulate objectives; engage in self-help activities; obtain needed goods and services; engage in social action; other.

15. Does your field placement involve working with agency staff and personnel in planning or developing new programs; implementing or staffing existing programs; research, data collection or analysis; publicity or public relations; working with Board members or volunteers; other.

16. Does your field placement involve coordinating, planning, and allocating in Welfare Councils or sectarian federations, Community Action Agency (OEO); host (non-social work) agency; national organizations, other.

17. What is the *primary* field service (setting) or problem area:
    a. Public assistance, welfare department;
    b. Employment, vocational training;
    c. Youth service, group services, recreation;
    d. Child and family services;
    e. Medical services, public health, physical handicapped;
    f. Psychiatric services, mental health, retardation;
    g. Schools and education, literacy, Head Start;
    h. Corrections, courts, prisons, probation and parole;
    i. Neighborhood development, grass-roots organization;

     j. Housing and urban renewal;

     k. Intergroup relations, civil rights, labor unions;

     l. Coordination and planning, health and welfare councils, federations;

     m. Other

18. Level of responsibility, check for (A) and (B) the answer that most closely describes your *usual* situation.

     a. Specific tasks assigned in detail and monitored closely;

     b. Specific tasks described and agreed upon, but I work pretty much on my own;

     c. Within broad policy outlines, I plan and carry out my own assignments;

     d. I am a completely free agent and have little or no limitations.

19. Significance of my assignments. Check for (A) and (B) the one that comes nearest to expressing your judgment of your placement.

     a. Extremely important to me and to the constituency with which I work;

     b. Very important to me in terms of my own interest and growth, but not too significant in its overall impact.

     c. Not very interesting to me or significant to my training but very necessary (or important) for the agency and its clientele;

     d. Most of my assignments were "busy work," not very useful to me or to anyone.

20. Was this agency or program a satisfactory field placement *for you*?

21. Which of these features is primarily responsible for your answer?

     a. The field instructor;

     b. The nature of the experience (setting, tasks, etc.);

     c. Both about equally responsible.

In the questions that follow, think of your field placement as a whole and *not* as (A) and (B) above.

22. How frequently did you have supervisory conferences with your field instructor?

23. Was group supervision (regular conferences with two or more students) used?

24. How frequently was this recording used in your supervisory conferences?

25. How important was this recording to your own learning experience?

26. Rank in order from most important (1) to least important (6), the following categories as they relate to (A) topics discussed in supervisory conferences and (B) aspects of your field experience that you found to be most useful to you.
    a. C.O. methodology—theory; practice; role; group practice; problem solving
    b. Specific job-related matters—assignments' tasks; committee, staff work
    c. Agency; setting, or field practice—mandate; jurisdiction, administration
    d. Community context of job-resources; community and interorganizational dynamics
    e. Interpersonal influence and relationships—clients; volunteers; professionals
    f. Professional growth and development use of self; record-keeping; social work values

27. From *your* point of view, what was the extent of effective integration of your field and class experience?
    a. Every effort was made to integrate class and field and they reinforced each other very well;
    b. Some efforts were made to integrate the two, but without too much success;
    c. No consistent effort appeared to be made to integrate them, but there was no serious conflict;
    d. Class and field learnings were often contradictory with resulting confusion and conflict;
    e. Other.

28. Did you find the content of your graduate courses in social and behavior sciences helpful in the context of your field placement?
    a. Serious effort was made in both class and field to integrate the two;
    b. Some attempts were made to integrate the two, to some extent they were successful;
    c. While there were some gaps, confusion, and contradiction, I managed to make a synthesis for my self;
    d. There seemed to be little or no relationship between them;
    e. Other.

29. Did you find the content of your social policy-social welfare sequence helpful in the context of your field placement?
    a. Serious effort was made in both class and field to integrate the two;
    b. Some attempts were made to integrate the two, and to some extent they were successful;
    c. While there were some gaps, confusion, and contradiction, I managed to make some synthesis for myself;
    d. There seemed to be little or no relationship between them;
    e. Other.
30. Did you find the content of your C.O. methods courses helpful in the context of your field experience?
    a. Serious effort was made in both class and field to integrate the two;
    b. Some attempts were made to integrate the two, and to some extent they were successful;
    c. While there were some gaps, confusion, and contradiction, I still managed to make some synthesis for myself;
    d. There seemed to be little or no relationship between them;
    e. Other.
31. Did you receive any stipend or financial remuneration from the agency?
32. Upon graduation, in what field of practice or science setting do you plan to work? (List as in Question 17)
33. At what level of practice would you like to engage: (A) Upon graduation. (B) At the peak of your career. Check one answer only.
    Direct practice; supervision; consultation; administration; teaching; research; undecided.
34. How firm are your post-graduate employment plans?
35. Do you have any plans for further graduate study beyond the M.S.W.?

## Agency Questionnaire

1. Name of School
2. Name of agency

3. Agency sponsorship: public; private—sectarian; private—non-sectarian; quasic-public or mixed (describe).
4. Geographical scope: rural; urban neighborhood; city or metropolitan area; state or regional; national or international.
5. Principal agency function:
   a. Provides leadership and stimulus for grass-roots organization and social action;
   b. Provides direct social services to clients (individuals and families);
   c. Provides staff services for interagency coordination, planning or allocating of resources.
6. Primary field of service (setting) or problem area:
   (See Student Questionnaire, Question 17)
7. How would you mark this agency in terms of adequacy or a c.o. placement?
   a. A good field agency placement for all c.o. students;
   b. A good field placement agency, but for special purposes or particular students;
   c. Some good features, but some not so good;
   d. Not one of our better agencies.
8. Which of these agency features is primarily responsible for your answer: the field instructor; the nature of the experience (setting, tasks, etc.); both about equally?
9. Type of field placement at this agency: individual student(s); group placement; unit placement—school-based; unit placement—agency-based; other?
10. Number of students currently placed in this agency?
11. Number of field instructors at this agency?

## School Questionnaire

1. Name of school
2. C.O. chairman
3. Is your c.o. program: (1) a one-year sequence; (2) a two-year sequence?
4. How long has your school had its present c.o. sequence?
5. Is there any standardized plan to the order or sequence of first- and second-year placements?
6. Which of these special features are included in your field instruction program: laboratory; teaching center; satellite or

other short-term placement; block placement during the school semester; summer block placement; other?

7. Have you considered such educational approaches?
8. Do you think they might be good for your school?
9. Does the school provide training instruction for the field staff as a group (meetings, seminars, workshops, institutes)?
    a. Annual or semiannual meetings with instructors;
    b. Periodic meetings during each school semester;
    c. Intensive institutes, seminars, or workshops attended by all or selected groups of instructors;
    d. Other.
10. How frequently are field instructors seen by faculty liaison or responsible school personnel: more than once a month; about once a month; about once a semester; once a year or less?
11. What efforts are being made by your school to coordinate the students' class and field experiences? (Describe briefly).
12. How effective, in general, do you feel this coordination has been?
    a. Works very well for most students in most situations;
    b. No serious problems, but lots of unanswered questions still remain;
    c. Gaps, confusions, or contradictions are evident and active plans are being promulgated to achieve better coordination;
    d. Students complain and faculty worry; but easy solutions do not seem to be forthcoming.
13. In how many agencies do you currently have c.o. placements?
14. How many field instructors do you currently use?

## Agency—Instructor Questionnaire

1. School of Social Work
2. Agency
3. Field Instructor
4. Sex
5. Age
6. Status: employed by agency; employed by school; combination (explain).
7. Instructor's academic preparation.

8. Instructor's practice concentration (method) in School of Social Work.
9. Previous experience.
10. How would you rate the adequacy of the instructor's performance: above average; about average; below average.
11. List the names of the students currently assigned to this instructor.

## Interview Guide *—Community Organization

1. Can you tell me something about the organization you work for.
2. *Probes:*
   a. What are its major activities?
   b. How is it funded?
   c. How big is it? How many people work there? How many are professionals? How many are clerks, etc.?
   d. Who do they offer service to?
   e. How is it organized? Who directs it?
3. What kind of work do you do now? What kinds of projects are you involved in? (Try to take up each project in turn.)
4. What kinds of things do you do in your work? What are you responsible for?
5. How much time do you spend on policy determination? program planning? program implementation? (Probe for degree of responsibility.)
6. How much time do you spend on interorganizational work? formal organizational contact? informal organization, association? (Probe for degree of activity.)
7. Who usually decides what areas you will work on?
8. What kinds of activities are you engaged in?
   (*Probes:* recruiting, referring, discussion, leadership, writing papers, collecting information, sampling opinion, making arrangements, preparing agenda, supervision, administration.)
9. *Projects:*
   a. When did the project begin?
   b. How much initial planning was there? Who first conceived of the idea? How long will it run?

* Prepared by Daniel Yankelovich, Inc. (The Cambridge Center for Research in the Behavioral Sciences) under contract to the Project.

    c. What major changes in direction or development have taken place?

    d. What are some of the changes?

        (*Probes:* aims curtailed, aims added, interpretation changed; growth of staff, community acceptance.)

    e. How could the project be improved?

    f. What do you consider the principal problems now faced by the program?

    g. What kinds of administrative changes could facilitate the project?

    h. What are the major limitations of the project?

        (*Probes:* finances, personnel, public policy, lack of knowledge, tested techniques, lack of planning, coordination, apathy.)

    i. If you could go back to the beginning of your association with the project, would you proceed the way you have or would you do things differently? How and why?

10. *Role Qualities:*

    a. What is your major goal, what are you trying to accomplish?

    b. What kinds of things make it tough for you to do your job? What is a help?

    c. What are you trying to influence in your work? How do you go about this? What kinds of things make it difficult to do?

    d. Can you tell me about the last time you tried to influence your boss (supervisor)? What happened?

    e. Now what about the last time you tried to influence the members of a committee you were working with? What happened? (Try to get one more example of influence)

    f. Have you had any experience with the training of non-professionals?

    g. What are your goals in regard to the outcome in dealing with the poor? (Probe for power rearrangement versus service.)

    h. What are the goals of your agency in this area?

    i. What committees are you a member of? How do you act within each?

11. *Training:*

        a. How did you learn the things that are helpful to you on your job? (Probe for: where, when, from whom, in what connection.)

        b. What kinds of experiences have been the ones that you remember most?

        c. What has been helpful that you learned in social work school? In what way has it been deficient?

        d. How would you describe the ideal kind of preparation for someone who is doing your kind of work?

        e. Suppose you were the dean of a school of social work, how would you change the curriculum in the community organization sequence?

## APPENDIX B
# Community Organization Relevant Games

Now that we have reviewed a number of background factors related to the use of simulation games for training purposes, it is appropriate to examine more specifically a range of games which might have revelance for community-organization curriculum purposes. These games will be described and their educational objectives specified wherever possible.

## 1. Legislature (4-H Game of Democracy)

This simulation was developed by James Coleman of Johns Hopkins University, where the Department of Social Relations has been engaged in a simulation gaming project funded by the Carnegie Foundation of New York. The Legislature game is actually a composite of eight different games that simulate different aspects of the legislative process. In the basic version, players act as legislators, giving speeches and bargaining with other legislators. The object is to move past those issues that are supported by their constituents and thereby insure their reelection. Issue areas include civil rights, aid to education, defense, Medicare, off-shore oil, etc. Other variations of the game involve citizens' groups and their legislative actions, the function of the floor leader, activities of legislative committees, the passage of a legislative program by the administration, and the effect of monetary factors on legislative outcomes. The games can be played by six to eleven players and take anywhere from one hour to four hours to run through. The game was produced with the cooperation of the 4-H program of the Cooperative Extension Service with the objective of teaching young people about the political process through participating in a series of simulated legislative and community meetings. The game is distributed through the National 4-H Foundation. The format and objectives of each of the game variations is indicated below:

*Game I—Legislative Session.* This variation is to be played by a set of six to ten players, each acting as a legislator and collectively acting as a legislative body deciding upon a series of public issues.

Each player is dealt a set of cards which indicate his constituents' attitudes about various issues. For example, one such card reads: "Federal aid to education—70 persons against, 30 persons for." Another reads: "Retaining military base in your constituency— 250 persons for, 50 persons against." By studying his whole set of cards, a player can tell how his district feels about the various issues and which issues are most important to them.

After an initial round of short speeches, the game alternates between (*a*) informal bargaining sessions of two or three minutes, when players may contact any other legislators and try to gain their support on issues of the greatest importance to them, and (*b*) formal sessions of the legislature, during which players bring issues to the floor, discuss them according to rules of parliamentary procedure, and vote. A legislator's success—i.e., whether or not he is reelected at the end of the game—is determined by his success in getting passed or defeated those measures his constituents most want passed or defeated (14).

In terms of its objectives, the game attempts to demonstrate the importance of bargaining, exchange, and negotiation in order for legislators best to represent the interests of their constituents and successfully be retained in office. To some degree, the game can develop skills of negotiation and exchange.

*Game II—Citizens' Action Meeting.* Each player functions as a citizen with specific age, sex, marital status, geographic residence, occupation, and race. Each has specified preferences or interests regarding the passage or defeat of various issues. Scores are based on getting things passed or defeated, plus intensity of feeling about those that were decided for or against him. Again, the idea of bargaining and exchange is highlighted, but among citizens and voluntary associations, rather than in a legislative assembly.

*Game III—Representative Democracy.* This is a combination of Games I and II. First, each player is a citizen attempting to make his preferences most strongly felt by his legislator. Second, he is a legislator in a legislative session, attempting to satisfy best the expressed preferences of his constituents.

Scores show how well each legislator has satisfied his constituents' interests and how well the legislature as a whole has satisfied the collective citizens of the society. Here again, bargaining and exchange are central in terms of learning concepts and skill development.

(Games IV to VII are all variations of Game I.)

*Game IV—A Legislator's Own Convictions.* At the end of the game each player calculates whether he is reelected. Among those who are, the overall winner is one who voted with his own convictions in the greatest number of cases. Skill in achieving a balance between personal convictions and constituent desires is central in this game. Thus, not only bargaining but ability to accommodate one's own as well as others' interest is a key learning area.

*Game V—The Power of the Floor Leader in a Legislature.* This game shows the power that exists in the chair in determining the sequence of voting on legislation. The chairman determines the order, but any item can be tabled by a majority vote. The chairman has no vote but must satisfy his constituency—therefore there are bills he wishes passed. The game can illustrate agenda building and steering the structure of content in a meeting, and accordingly develop skills along these lines.

*Game VI—Passage of a Legislative Program.* The chairman does note vote or control the order of items considered. But he can help or hinder the reelection of legislators by adding constituent votes to a legislator's score or by taking votes away. This variation shows the effect an administration can have on legislation through its role in helping to get legislators elected. To do this it must also be popular and control votes in the general populace. This game demonstrates the use of influence and pressure in affecting legislative outcomes.

*Game VII—Committee Structure in the Legislature.* Three committees are established—HEW, Interior, and Defense. Committees must vote to bring measures up on the floor. The game illustrates the notion of bargaining but uses a two-step process—the committee, then a larger assembly. Bargaining and exchange are treated in a more complex manner through the inclusion of the committee mechanism.

*Game VIII—Taxation and Public Expenditure.* Each piece of legislation has a dollar cost associated with it. Legislators lose a certain number of votes for each increase in cost, but may also lose constituent support by not enacting given legislation. Altogether, constitutents are in favor of all the bills, but if all are passed, the budget would be so high as to bring about the defeat of all legislators. Accordingly, each legislator works to hold the budget down, while attempting to pass the particular bills desired by his constituents. The game illustrates the factor of monetary constraint in legislation and program planning. Skill development involves ability to bargain and influence within financial structures and to cope with certain monetary factors.

The Game of Democracy has been available from the National 4-H Club Foundation, 7100 Connecticut Avenue, Washington, D.C. 20015. The simulation is packaged for easy commercial or educational handling. The complete game kit sells as follows: 1 to 100 kits—$1.50 each; 101 or more kits—$1.38 each. Additional worksheets are available. Also available from Western Publishing Company, 150 Parish Drive, Wayne, New Jersey 07470.

## 2. Metropolis and M.E.T.R.O.

These simulations are related to urban planning and were developed largely by Richard D. Duke with the cooperative efforts of the Tri-County Regional Planning Commission of Lansing (Michigan), Michigan State University, and the University of Michigan. Both were conceived in part as instructional tools and procedures for students of urban planning. The games allow students to develop and test actual plans, encouraging innovations in approaches. These simulations recognize that in the past there has been a conflict between urban planners and the decision makers whose sanction is necessary to execute them, the latter often criticizing the planners' product as being unrealistic, unworkable, and inflexible.

The objective of each game is to develop a plan, but one that can be revised as new developments occur rather than one that is static in the traditional manner. In the games, various interest groups, often in partial conflict, are represented by the player participants, including political functionaries, landowners, school people, and planners. Each player is given freedom of action in interpreting his role, with assistance from stereotypical prompts based on local history. He must, however, take the consequences of his decisions and actions. Since the players and enterprises are interdependent, few unilateral decisions are possible. In addition, each player has more than one role, putting him in what the authors of the game consider realistic cross pressures similar to those experienced by citizens in the multiple roles they play in society. An important result of the time-compression aspect of the game is that players are obliged to abide by decisions made earlier in time and to carry into the future the results of their current decisions.

We will present these games as they were described in a paper

area, and feedback from the computer relates both to player positions and to the growth pattern that results from the aggregate of gamed decisions. Typical decisions required of each team (different in detail and scope, as appropriate to the particular governmental unit or professional role) will be of three main types: budgets, issues, and policies.

The anticipated uses of these simulations is suggested by the authors as follows:

Skills in the use of new technologies such as urban data banks.

Skills in decision making by exposing the array of choices actually available and the beginnings of rationales for evaluating plan alternatives.

Demonstration of the complex interrelationships involved in urban affairs.

Skill in bargaining and interpersonal influence.

Skill in cross-professional collaboration.

Recognition of uncertainty as an important characteristic of the environment—thus the need to make flexible decisions.

Skill in data collection and use of analytical tools. The player can be taught institutional facts, including what facts are important.

METROPOLIS has been described in some detail in a monograph by Richard D. Duke (36) and M.E.T.R.O. in a publication of the Tri-County Regional Planning Commission (99). These documents should be studied thoroughly before a school attempts to activate these simulations or similar ones. Considerable technical skill and equipment is a requirement. It would be advisable to consult directly with Dr. Duke (School of Natural Resources and Director of Environmental Simulation Laboratory, University of Michigan, Ann Arbor, Michigan 48104).

## 3. CLUG (Cornell Land Use Game)

CLUG is another game in the city-planning area, developed by Dr. Allan G. Feldt of the Department of City and Regional Planning at Cornell University. It is an urban-systems game that involves three to fifteen players in a sequence of interdependent decisions concerning transportation, taxes, real-estate development, utilities construction, and building maintenance. The game was initially undertaken in a course in urban ecology in an attempt to provide a common conceptual framework for the presentation of various noncongruent theories. The broad range of decisions pertaining to urban land-use decisions was narrowed to a small number of attributes of cities and their surroundings that were assumed to effect urban-systems decisions. Each play of the game, accordingly, is based on a predetermined set of factors, including location and efficiency of the highway network, location of points of access to the outside world (shipping points), a particular form of real-estate taxation to support community services, a range of permissible land usages, and the location of a utility plant providing generalized municipal services to the city.

Dr. Feldt (46) describes the game as follows:

Play begins with each player in possession of a fixed amount of capital with which he may seek to buy land, construct commercial or residential properties in locations of his choice, and seek to make a profit on his investments through such activities as buying and selling land, gaining employment for his residential properties, putting his industries into operation by hiring employees, or gaining customers for his commercial service establishments from among the residential units located in the community by other players.

Given the initial parameters imposed upon a particular play of the game in the form of transportation networks, taxation policies, the location of shipping points, and the kinds of land uses allowed, most land use decisions are then based upon the degree of accessibility desired between particular forms of land use already developed during the play or anticipated land use developments which seem likely to occur in future rounds of the game. Money enters the community from the outside world through payments to industries during each round of play. It is then dispersed among the other players by means of payrolls to employees and payments by households to persons operating shopping centers for routine purchases. Money leaves the community primarily in the form of payments made to defray transportation costs, through tax payments made to support community services, and through the loss of building value due to the depreciation of buildings during each round of play. Careful planning and management by the players allows them to minimize these monetary losses to themselves and the community: *one,* through minimizing the distances between land uses which interact frequently, *two,* through prudent management of a community capital improvement program (to provide enough services to fulfill the needs of the growing community but not so much that services will be wasted on unoccupied land), and *three,* through careful juggling of renovation and construction costs on buildings already in operation. With careful management of their investment choices and wise decisions as to the location of investments, most players are able to realize an annual return of 10 to 20 per cent on their investments. Returns of even more than 20 per cent have been achieved by a very few especially prudent players and bankruptcy is a distinct possibility which has been only narrowly avoided by some.

At various times during the game, players are confronted with such decisions as whether or not to renovate their depreciated buildings or build additional roads for the community to be paid for by real estate taxes.

The game is designed for three players or three teams of players. Three men per team represent an upper limit in terms of providing more playing time than time spent in intra-team communications. Cycling time usually requires about one-half hour per round. Players familiar with the game can generate the equivalent of a medium-sized city in twenty rounds, approximately ten hours of playing time. In a personal communication the author states, "Its level of complexity is such that 4–5 hour playing sessions are desirable."

The author indicates that different players learn different things through their experience with the game. One common learning, however, has to do with the need for long-range planning and control in the development of a community. The need for coordination of activities in successful community development also becomes clear. "Thus the game certainly teaches some of the ways in which planning and controls can be used in guiding the course of community development, far beyond teaching the aspects of urban ecology that were our original interest. Further, it teaches the ways in which plans can impede growth when they tend to be too restrictive." With regard to our immediate concern in field instruction, it is interesting to note Dr. Feldt's point that "the game provides a certain amount of field experience to the participants which makes further course work in planning and related areas more significant to them." Dr. Feldt also indicates that the game produces a striking degree of involvement on the part of the players. "The game is completely engrossing. It is not at all uncommon for players scheduled to play for four hours to insist that they be allowed to continue to play for an additional four hours, often without stopping to eat."

CLUG is available from Systems Gaming Associates, 769 South Aurora Street, Ithaca, New York 14850. A basic CLUG kit may be purchased from them. A community of approximately one-half million population, which can be built in twenty to thirty rounds of play, can be constructed from the materials provided in the kit. These materials are: an erasable heavy-duty board; a set of record sheets and tax roles; rules; approximately three hundred land-use playing pieces, currency, transaction cards; assorted pins, flags, dice, and marking pencils. Kits cost $125 plus postage or shipping (each kit weighs twenty-five pounds).

A computer program to be used on time-sharing systems is at present being developed to handle the heavy bookkeeping operations required in lengthy plays of CLUG.

Systems Gaming Associates will, in addition, contract to provide consulting services for demonstrating the play of CLUG.

The rationale and a detailed description of the operations of the game can be found in "The Community Land Use Game," Ithaca, New York: Division of Urban Studies, Center for Housing and Environmental Studies, Cornell University, 1967 (mimeographed).

## 4. SIMPOLIS, a Metro-Game

SIMPOLIS is an attempt to capture some of the drama and portray some of the operational variables involved in the urban crisis. It was developed by Abt Associates, of Cambridge, Massachusetts, a private organization which has specialized in gaming and other forms of simulation design. The setting is the city of SIMPOLIS, and the aim is to communicate to participants the essence of major issues, possible responses to crisis situations, and some consequences of such crisis decisions.

The game takes place in a rectangular grid of many small groups of chairs which represent city geographic units, particularly blocks and streets. Players may circulate freely among these from their home unit. A map of the city is provided showing the geographic units and their composition in terms of social class and race. The voting power of each of these units is specified. The map also locates subway lines, parkways, bus routes, industrial sites, the airport, etc.

Players take the parts of key decision makers from government, industry, and interested citizens, of white and black races and three economic classes (lower, middle, and upper). Large numbers of individuals may participate in this simulation, reflecting the congestion and confusion of some aspects of city life. Players are given profiles which include descriptions of the role, objectives, and the votes which are controlled by the role.

The action commences with one-minute speeches by each of seven city officials enunciating their policies and relevant issues. Urban-crisis bulletins are issued intermittently, requiring immediate response from participants. Players may interact with one another in dealing with crisis—engaging in negotiations, coalition formation, protest, campaigning, and voting. Responses to one crisis may generate new crises.

Mayoral candidates emerge, announce their platforms regarding key issues, and indicate their intended administrative appointments. There is an election for mayor with all participants casting ballots by a population-weighted formula. The game is won by those units who can manage to take control of the city government.

Realism is injected into the play through profiles of key decision makers and graphic descriptions of the crisis situations. Profiles have been prepared for roles such as the mayor, traffic commissioner, representative of the NAACP (civil rights), Citizens Clean Air Association, and head of the Organized Crime Syndicate. The profile of the mayor as found in the game instructions is as follows:

You are coming to the end of your first term as the first Repocrat mayor of Simpolis in a decade. As a reform mayor, you could not help antagonizing some important conservative officials, civic leaders, and industrialists. Your present objective is to achieve sufficient public attention and immediate improvement in the seven urban crises areas. (Election is two hours away!)

Your direct administrative control covers only some of the crises areas. You have hiring and firing power over only the Police Commissioner, Traffic Commissioner, Rent Control Commissioners, and Pollution Control Commissioner. You have only some indirect influence over Borough Presidents, the City Council President, the Board of Education Chairman, the Human Rights Commissioner, and the local Poverty Program Administrator. The City Council President and Board of Education Chairman are among your principal political enemies, both being conservative Demopubs.

You must quickly develop a platform responsive to the crises in each of the seven critical areas. You must also select your appointive department heads, since you will have to announce your intended selections with your platform in the second hour of the exercise. Meanwhile, you also have many crises to deal with.

A sample crisis situation taken from the education area reads as follows:

A new elementary school has been opened in the middle of a new upper middle and middle class housing development in NW. The school is 5 blocks from an older largely Negro lower income housing project. The children in the low income housing project are assigned to another much older school also 5 blocks away. A largely Negro group of mothers and children begin a simultaneous boycott of the old school and picket of the new school. They are insisting that their children be admitted to the new school.

This simulation was still in the process of final development when last investigated by the writer. Its potential usefulness for community-organization education seems promising, but learning objectives need to be more rigorously explicated. Further information and instructions on play may be obtained from Abt Associates, 55 Wheeler Street, Cambridge, Massachusetts 02138 (Tel.: 617-492-7100).

### 5. Community Action Planning with the Poor

This is a game still in the early stages of design when last investigated by the writers. It is being developed by Dr. Clark C. Abt of Abt Associates, with the possible cooperation of O.E.O. The objective of the game is to train the staff of CAP (Community Action Program) agencies in methods of planning which includes active participation of the poor, while at the same time increasing the planning capacities of the poor in solving social problems.

In its initial form, the game calls for involvement of eleven types of community actors: unemployed workers, merchants, teachers, CAP staff, students, employed poor men, housewives, police, city officials, civil-rights leaders, and private employers. Each of these actors has a specified aim. For example, the unemployed seek jobs, merchants desire profits, police pursue order, and governmental officials look for reelection. Each actor also possesses particular resources in the community. The unemployed have time and votes, merchants hold money and influence, the police have force at their disposal, and CAP practitioners possess funds, skills, and knowledge of the power structure.

The intention of the designer was to develop the game further in terms of decision rules and win criteria through the active participation of O.E.O. staff and the local poor.

Some of the objectives of this simulation as set down by Dr. Abt include the following:

> Mutual education of CAA staff in the perceptions, preferences, priorities, and needs of the poor, and of residents in the political-economic feasibility constraints of the CAA staff.

> Quick and cheap experimentation with alternative CAA plans to predict community responses.

> Identification of innovative alternatives by the creative tensions of uninhibited group problem-solving.

> Evaluation of costs and benefits of alternative plans in human-response terms as well as in monetary terms.

> Clarification of issues and the prediction of the consequences of plans.

> Increased acceptance of CAP programs by participation of the population in the planning.

> Training of CAP staff and local residents in cooperative decision making (the human multiplier) and in coalition building (2).

These are clearly related to community-practice education. Further information may be obtained from Abt Associates, 55 Wheeler Street, Cambridge, Massachusetts.

## 6. SIMSOC

SIMSOC was created by William Gamson, professor of sociology at the University of Michigan, for use in teaching sociological and social psychological theories and principles to undergraduate students. Students participate in the formation and operation of a simulated society or community. The major theme of the game has to do with how social order is established in a communal system, and how social control and influence are exerted in the face of subgroups and other interests that are in social conflict.

The students become citizens of a society with basic resources which they can use to maintain the community, while at the same time attempting to meet their assigned and self-selected goals. Citizens live in four regions, among which they may travel at a cost. Citizens have private economic interests and social roles which represent both duties and special privileges. They may be members of different political parties that favor either central planning and coordination or decentralized decision making. Some citizens have newspapers accessible to them, others have exclusive information, others may establish a police force with powers to appropriate resources.

There is a monetary system with a basic currency called Simbucks. Basic Groups in the system include the following:

ECONORAD (Economic Advisory Group).
BASIN (Basic Industry Group).
INNOVIN (Innovative Industry Group).
POP (Party of the People).
SOP (Society Party).
HONSON (Honorary Society).
SORC (Social Research Council).
PRESS (the Newspaper).
JUDCO (Judicial Council).

Individuals may control two kinds of franchises—housing and travel. Four national indicators signify the health of the system as a whole: Food and Energy Supply, Standard of Living, Social Cohesion, and Public Commitment. Each starts at a figure of 100 at the beginning of the game and declines by 10 percent each session unless replenished by investment in public programs. The two public programs are (a) Environmental Research and Conversation and (b) Expanded Services. There is also a national broadcasting system and a police force that may be created by an individual or group of individuals. There is a cost for establishing police cadres, and while they may confiscate resources, overzealous exercise of power may result in specified units of reduction in Public Commitment or Social Cohesion. There is also a governing council to which players may be periodically elected and which has considerable latitude with respect to its manner of operation.

The author does not specify any particular way of winning the game, although a variety of possibilities exist, including the amount of money or resources accumulated by a given region or individual, being head of the governing council at the end of the game, being associated with a region that attains the highest score on national indicators, having the most efficiently governed region or the one with the widest range of participation. These various win criteria may be adopted selectively by an instructor in order to stress different learning objectives.

Dr. Gamson has set down a number of suggested written assignments for students participating in the game in order to enhance learning. These suggested learning objectives of the game are as follows:

What actions and strategies were engaged in by participants to achieve their objectives? Evaluation of effectiveness of these.

How can people and groups in a system be encouraged to contribute to the general interest even when this detracts from the pursuit of their private interest?

Under what conditions will individuals and groups hold to agreements or break them?

How much authority is necessary for system maintenance and growth? Must this be formalized, and what restraints are there on individuals with authority which prevents them from using it for selfish ends?

What factors make for regions or groups which are isolated from one another and what techniques may be used by whom to prevent such communal disunity?

What kinds of people are likely to deviate from group norms and what techniques and conditions are most likely to lead to conformity with group norms?

What features should be built into a system to create maximum or minimum freedom of action for individuals?

Under what conditions is social conflict beneficial or detrimental to a system and what techniques may be employed most efficiently to foster or manage social conflict?

What conditions and techniques can contribute to the maximum participation of individuals in the system?

How may one maximize one's influence over others in a system or minimize the influence of others?

The implications of these items for a variety of community-organization practice problems is obvious. Probably several different playings of the game would be necessary to emphasize different teaching points.

SIMSOC is designed for groups of students ranging in size from twenty-seven to sixty-two. It can be played for six to ten sessions, allowing approximately two hours per session. The game kit consists of an instructor's manual and a manual for participants, which contains the basic rules, forms used in the game, and name tags for the students. The cost is $3 plus postage for a kit. It is advisable to order a kit for each participant. Distribution has been through Campus Publishers, 711 North University Avenue, Ann Harbor, Michigan 48108. Also available through The Free Press, New York, New York; Gamson, William A. SIMSOC (*Simulated Society*), $3.95.

## 7. The Inter-Nation Simulation

This simulation is in the realm of international affairs and is one the best developed, most used, and highly researched gaming designs available. In addition, it has implications for community-organization education along the lines of interorganizational relationships, bargaining, political processes, and social roles, and the like.

The Inter-Nation Simulation is a product of the Northwestern University International Relations Program and was developed with the assistance of numerous faculty members under the overall direction of Dr. Harold Guetzkow. It was originated in 1957–58 by Guetzkow and Richard C. Snyder under sponsorship of the Carnegie Corporation and the Air Force. The simulation has been used extensively for research on international relations, as well as for teaching (55).

The Inter-Nation Simulation (INS) models an international system comprised of up to eight national entities, each under the leadership of designated decision makers who try to maintain themselves in office in the face of domestic and international pressures. The decision makers have available information on economic, military, political, and historical factors associated with their nations. They use this data to allocate basic resources for development, foreign aid and trade, defense, and for internal satisfaction of citizens in areas of consumer goods, domestic stability, and military security. Decision makers must contend with a variety of problems such as war, demands for military and economic aid, and domestic insurrection.

Teams of students are assigned to each nation included in the game (Algo, Utro, Zena, etc.). Some of the specific variables that may be manipulated include degree of personal authority, economic variables, such as ratio of consumer goods to capital goods, and military variables, such as the size of armies and the type of armaments available to them. Roles played by persons include the Head of State (Central Decision Maker), the Foreign Policy Adviser, equivalent to the foreign minister, and the Military Adviser who corresponds to the minister of defense. There is an additional role, the Domestic Opposition Leader, who is the head of the political opposition and who seeks to oust the established regime and take office. In order to stay in office, the decision makers must keep their nation secure and prosperous through satisfying the nation's Validators—those individuals and groups who influence the selection and retention of national leaders.

At the end of each period of play, approximately ninety minutes, the effects of decisions made by each national cabinet are calculated. These results thus set the groundwork for the next period of play. Participants engage in intranation meetings, fill out a series of forms, and participate in international conferences pertaining to mutual aid and other treaty agreements.

Decisional outcomes are calculated according to mathematical formulas and given exact numerical designations. Thus, there is a calculation related to the production of consumer goods versus citizen satisfaction with the subsequent standard of living. If considerable funds are expended on the military and little is invested in consumer goods, the citizens become dissatisfied. A formula indicates the level of dissatisfaction at which the Chief of State is deposed from office. Through another formula, he may lose office if the citizenry is dissatisfied with the level of the nation's security.

Included in the calculus of the game are other more subtle influences (133) such as barriers to inter-nation communication, intelligence leaks, false information, diplomatic vagueness, and interpersonal relationships among leaders of nations.

Simplified variations of the INS for teaching purposes have been developed by the Western Behavioral Science Institute at La Jolla, California, the Political Science Department of the University of Michigan, and Science Research Associates of Chicago.

The INS takes fifteen to thirty hours to run through and may include between ten and thirty-five players.

This simulation was designed to teach a wide range of concepts in the area of foreign policy and international relations. Its learning objectives for community-organization education need to be delimited and brought forward. It appears to have immediate relevancy for such matters as interorganizational relations, resource allocation, political processes, and the use of strategies such as negotiation, conflict, threat, etc.

A readily available version of the INS may be obtained through Science Research Associates, 259 East Erie Street, Chicago, Illinois 60611. Their Inter-Nations Simulations Kit is a simplified form of the original gaming procedure developed at Northwestern University, and does not require the use of computerized devices. The kit sells for $45 net; participants' manuals and an additional instructor's guide cost $1 each.

Extensive discussions of this simulation and of its uses in teaching have been written by Guetzkow.

## 8. Diplomacy

This is also a game in the field of international relations. However, the objective is clearly one that stresses conflict and exploitative relations. The game simulates conditions in Europe prior to the onset of World War I. Each player represents one of the Great Powers of Europe in 1914. The aim of the game is to gain control of Europe, which is accomplished when a player wins over a majority of the pieces on the board. Thirty-four scattered provinces on the board are designated supply centers, and each of these produces supplies sufficient to keep an army or fleet secure. A country may have only as many units as it has supply centers.

Combinations and agreements among the players may affect the course of the game a great deal. These are determined during the diplomacy period which takes place before each move. This period lasts 30 minutes before the first move, and 15 minutes before each move thereafter. These periods may end sooner if all the players agree at the time. During these periods a player may say anything he wishes. Usually the players go to another room or off to a corner in two's and three's. They try to keep the contents of their conversations secret. They may try to overhear the conversations of others. The conversations usually consist of bargaining or joint military planning, but they may include such things as exchanging information denouncing, threatening, spreading rumors, and so forth. Public announcements may be made, and documents may be written and made public or not as the players see fit. The rules do not bind a player to anything he says; deciding whom to trust as situations arise is part of the game.

Each player writes his "orders" on a slip of paper, usually keeping them secret, and these orders to the armies and fleets are exposed at once. Each player reads his orders while the others check to be sure that he is reading what he actually wrote. An illegal order simply is not followed, and the unit so ordered simply stands in its place. Orders for the first move are dated, "Spring, 1901"; for the second, "Fall, 1901"; for the third, "Spring, 1902"; and so on.

The game may be played by three to seven participants. Approximately four hours are required for a full playing.

The simulation stresses skill in the use of conflict strategies, including both the planning of a winning campaign and the outwitting of fellow players in negotiations.

A commerically packaged version of this game may be ordered through Games Research, Inc., 48 Wareham Street, Boston, Massachusetts 02118 (Tel.: 617-426-3625). It sells for $7.95.

## 9. The Carnegie Tech Management Game

The Carnegie Tech Management Game is one of the most intricately complex, well known, and widely used of all simulation games. Work on the simulation was begun in 1957 at the Graduate School of Industrial Management at Carnegie Tech, with the participation of men such as William R. Dill, then associate dean, and Kalman J. Cohen, Mangement Game administrator and professor of economics and industrial administration. It was the first management game to be used in a graduate business school and was a precursor of what was to be a widespread movement in business education.

Because of its strong business orientation, it may not be a serious possibility for schools of social work. However, it is suggested as a model of simulation gaming that may be adapted, and worthwhile literature regarding it is readily available.

The game attempts to reflect the multifarious problems involved in running a typical industrial enterprise—in this instance, the packaged detergent industry. Students take part in three competing companies, each of which is made up of seven to ten players with various executive roles. It is a highly complicated game that requires some 100 to 300 decisions during each simulated month of play. Anywhere from two to three hours are consumed in each set of decisions, and it takes thirty to fifty months to bring into effect the long-range planning outcomes involved in the game. Playing time can extend over months of curriculum time or be compressed into some twenty-four hours.

The simulation was modeled on selected actual workings of the market in this industry and is based on a tremendous mass of statistical data gathered over time from the field. Thus, decisions made by players set into motion a wide range of economic and organizational consequences that are similar to those actually brought about by similar decisions within the industry. The game is entirely computerized, which permits rapid feedback to participants of a great variety of effects of different decisions and actions.

At the beginning of the game players obtain charts and sheets that contain basic information concerning the background of their companies. Team decisions pertain to the amount of money and resources applied to such business areas as production, research, marketing, etc. There are four regional outlets available for marketing up to three products which are manufactured from seven raw materials. The computer, programmed with a number of cause-and-effect formulas, caculates consequences, issues reports, and sets the framework for decisions in the next quarter of activity.

As an example of the richness of detail in the game, production men at the beginning of play and at numerous intervals receive information concerning raw materials necessary for each product, lead times required for raw-material orders, space necessary for storage of raw materials and for finished products, productivity predictions for workers for each product, wage rates, hiring and firing costs, costs for storage of excess inventory, changes in costs for various raw materials, shipping costs and time from factory to warehouse, costs of storage at district warehouses.

This simulation was designed not so much to develop or impart specific skills as to create the climate and conditions intrinsic to the actual operations and management of a business firm. It was intended to place the students in a real management environment with its many complexities (including competition and uncertainty) but in a controlled context and with vivid and rapid feedback of operational decisions.

Some more specific management capabilities that the game engenders have been enumerated by the authors (24) as follows:

An ability to abstract, organize and use information from a complex and diffuse environment;

An ability to forecast and plan;

An ability to combine the role of generalist and specialist;

An ability to work effectively with other people.

This simulation appears to have only limited utility for community-organization education in social work, perhaps in certain areas of administration and fiscal management and planning. It is suggestive, however, of a methodology of game design that may be adopted with profit to the environment of social-welfare organizational activity.

(The field of business seems to be ideal for the utilization of simulation-game models, in that the factor of competition among individuals and collectivities, which is intrinsic to games, is also basic to the business world. Outcome of competition in the business world, in addition, can be easily quantified in dollars-and-cents terms and readily transfered to the simulated situation.)

The Carnegie Tech Game may be obtained through the Graduate School of Industrial Administration, Carnegie Institute of Technology, Schenley Park, Pittsburgh, Pennsylvania 15213. Tapes include card listings for the game, starting conditions, and a period of standard history decisions. There is also available an appended marketing-analysis training exercise.

Further descriptive material concerning this game may be found in the Cohen reference above as well as in several other sources (53) (25) (23).

An impressive array of simulation games have been developed in the field of business and management education and training over the last ten years by universities, the American Management Association, and individual business and industrial concerns. Greenlaw and his associates (53) list and describe eighty-nine of these. They cover a wide range of subject matter: level of management, type of product, number and diversity of products, roles of participants, type of information provided for decisions, etc. (2). In overall design the key features of these simulations appear to be quite similar, based on the model of the Carnegie game. We will not discuss these games further here, but will rather refer the reader to the Greenlaw volume which is the most comprehensive and intelligent treatment of the subject that we are aware of. The reader may be interested in looking into one other game, the Executive Action Simulation by Lowell Herron (57), because it is readily available for use through a commerically distributed publication, and it incorporates some of the complex decisional affects of the Carnegie Game without the necessity of computer technology.

## 10. The Propaganda Game

This game is designed to reveal to players the techniques used in certain mass-communications operations to distort the thinking processes of people. The game is based on the book *Thinking Straighter,* by George Henry Moulds, professor of philosophy at Kent State University. It was developed in gaming form by Robert W. Allen and Lorne Greene. Mr. Allen is currently director of the Nova Academic Games Project at the Nova Schools in Fort Lauderdale, Florida.

Examples of the use of various propaganda techniques are expressed on cards, and the winner of the game is the player who correctly identifies the greatest number of examples according to the technique categories developed by the authors. Techniques included the following:

> Techniques of self-deception: prejudice, academic detachment, drawing the line, rationalization, wishful thinking, etc.

> Techniques of language: emotional terms, metaphor and simile, emphasis, vagueness, ambiguity, etc.

> Techniques of irrelevance: appearance, manner, degrees and titles, status, technical jargon, slogans, etc.

> Techniques of exploitation: appeal to pity, appeal to flattery, appeal to ridicule, appeal to prestige, bargain appeal, folksy appeal, join-the-bandwagon appeal, etc.

> Techniques of form: concurrency, *post hoc,* selected instances, faulty analogy, division, non sequitur, etc.

> Techniques of maneuver: diversion, *ad hominem,* leading question, complex question, attacking a straw man, victory by definition, etc.

The game may be played by two to four players, or in another form by an equal number of players and a reader. Equipment includes a clear-thinking chart and technique cards with a prediction dial.

While the game is intended to unmask distorted communications, it can also be used to examine different means of influencing target groups through employing different kinds of communications. As the authors say in their instruction booklet, "Propaganda . . . can be employed to move persons to acts of warmth and kindness. It is important, therefore, that we consider a person's motives for using a propaganda technique, as well as understanding that a technique has been used."

The Propaganda Game was designed originally with Grades 5-12 in mind. The simulation aspects are minimal, marking it more as a game than a simulation game. It is available from the Marct Company, Box 1392, Fort Lauderdale, Florida 33302, or from Wff'n Proof, New Haven, Connecticut 06501. The cost is $5.50, including postage and handling charges. A film on use of the game can be ordered from Academic Games, Nova Schools, Fort Lauderdale, Florida.

### 11. Credibility Gap

Two professors of English at the University of Massachusetts, Dr. Arnold Silver and Dr. John C. Weston, have concocted a game similar to Propaganda, but with a contemporary political twist and a touch or two of ironic humor. This game is named Creditability Gap and deals with simulated untruthful govermental officials and wary citizens. The objective of the game is to make people more sensitive and discerning in responding to communications from political leaders.

The game is described as follows in *The New York Times* (102):

The game is played with dice, a Liberty Bell token for each player, a deck of "Citizen's Cards," from which the player is dealt an opening hand and from which he draws each round, and another deck of cards called the "Adiministration Pack of Lies."

By throwing dice, the players proceed around a three-ring track, marked off in squares and printed in red and white on a blue board. The goal is to reach the center of the maze, where there waits the "Big Wheel" and his "Truth Vault."

Players start circling the track at the "Washington Airport," pro-

gressing over 96 squares according to the roll of the dice and instructions in the two sets of cards.

As the players move forward they acquire "truth trophies" for un-
covering political lies in 36 categories.

The value of each trophy depends on the gravity of the lie uncovered.
An "artful ambiguity" and a "diversionary anecdote," for example,
are worth one point apiece, while an "indignant evasion" and "impas-
sioned doubletalk" rate two points, a "strategic deception" three and
an "escalating lie" four.

If a player holds the right combination of cards when he lands on
a square with a telephone or mail box he can call or write the "Big
Wheel," thus gaining access to the top cards in the "Pack of Lies" and
earning trophies according to the card's numerical value.

There are perils in the "Pack of Lies," however. A player might draw
an Administration "snow job" card and have to give up two trophies.
(All players start the game with two trophies, on the assumption that
everybody must be aware of at least two Adminstration fibs even before the truth hunt begins.)

Although a winning strategy depends mostly on the use of cards
drawn and discarded, fortune can suddenly change through penalities,
which get tougher as the player nears the "Truth Vault."

For example, a player who has moved smartly ahead by way of such
a square as "anonymous leak" and collected three trophies by landing
in "State Department Archives" might strand himself in a "statistical
cobweb" and have to yield two trophies.

The first player to gain 20 trophies wins the game, which can be
played by up to four persons.

The game takes between thirty and ninety minutes to complete
and may be played by two, three, or four, individually or in teams.
It sells for $5.95 (plus 55 cents for shipping charges) and is avail-
able from Amherst Game Company, Box 5, South Pleasant Street,
Amherst, Massachusetts 01002.

In addition to the simulation games described above, we will
make reference to several others in more abbreviated form, largely
because our information concerning them is less complete. In most
instances these are less known and used gaming procedures or are
early versions in the process of being more fully perfected. In other
cases relevance to community-organzation pratice is more remote.

## 12. Plans

This is a simulation of the role of pressure groups in the United
States. It was adapted from a Systems Development Corporation

Manual TM-WD-19, which was written by R. Boguslaw, R. Davis, and E. Glick. This simulation was developed by the staff of Project SIMILE, the Western Behavioral Sciences Institute, La Jolla, California 92037.

## 13. Napoli

This is a simulation of selected aspects of the legislative process. It was created by and is available through the staff of Project SIMILE at the Western Behavioral Science Institute, La Jolla, California.

## 14. Economic System

This simulation, developed by James S. Coleman and Robert Harris of Johns Hopkins, deals with interrelationships in the competitive economic system. In the game, mine workers, manufacturers, workers, and farmers produce and consume goods while attempting to make a profit and maintain a high standard of living. In addition to teaching principles of economics, learnings may be derived concerning interorganizational relations and the interplay of different interest groups. The game is packaged for commerical distribution. It can be played with seven to thirteen participants, and takes two to three hours to play. It may be ordered through Western Publishing Company, 150 Parish Drive, Wayne, New Jersey 07470.

## 15. Sitte

This is a simulation developed by Hall Sprague to illustrate the operations of pressure groups in the urban situation. It deals with problems and options of a typical city. Five interest groups, representing business, education, government, the disenfranchised, and humanists, contend with one another over ways to make their city better while differing in basic orientation and method. Further information is available through Dr. Hall Sprague of Project SIMILE, Western Behavioral Science Institute, La Jolla, California.

## 16. Slumlord

A game involving the interplay of housing tenants and landlords. Being developed by Abt Associates, Cambridge, Massachusetts.

## 17. Sepex

A game which involves forty school superintendents coordinating their activities in the interests of better educational development. Being developed by Abt Associates, Cambridge, Massachusetts.

## 18. Urban

Problems of urban transportation are explored with reference to factors such as housing, schools, and employment. Being developed by Abt Associates, Cambridge, Massachusetts 02138.

## 19. Neighborhood

Problems of land acquisition and use are dealt with. Being developed by Abt Associates, Cambridge, Massachusetts.

## 20. LUGS

This is a land use game designed for the training of urban planners. For information contact John L. Taylor, Department of Town and Regional Planning, the University of Sheffield, Sheffield S10 2TN, Great Britain.

## 21. Revolutionary Conflict

This is a simulation of internal revolutionary conflict, under circumstances in which the number of possible gains available to each side is not fixed. The simulation might be useful for an understanding of conflict strategies and social-action approaches. A discussion of the simulation may be found in Holly J. Kinley, "Development of Strategies in Simulation of Internal Revolutionary Conflict," *American Behavioral Scientist*, 10:5–9 (1966).

## 22. Simulation of American Government

The student is expected to perform many of the functions carried out by governmental officials. The objective is to help the student obtain an understanding of the procedures and interactions which occur in the American governmental system. Available through

Dale M. Garvey, Kansas State Teachers College, Division of Social Sciences, Emporia, Kansas 66801.

## 23. Negotiation Game

This simulation attempts to demonstrate some of the conditions and actions encountered in professional bargaining and negotiations in the field of education. For further information see John J. Horvat, "Feedback in the Negotiations Games," AERA Symposium: *Feedback in Simulation Techniques*, February 18, 1967.

## 24. A Game of Educational Influence: School Boards and Teachers

This is a partially developed game involving differences in policy orientations between teachers and school-board members. Three school-board members and three teachers play the game in a bargaining and influence meeting. Players represent constituencies, and there is an exchange of "influence chips" which represent a player's power to shape decisions. The effects of pressure groups, including civil-rights activists, council of churches, chamber of commerce, and labor council, are also taken into account. Information is available from Sue B. Etter or Professor Frederick L. Goodman, School of Education, University of Michigan, Ann Arbor, Michigan 48105.

## 25. Labor versus Management

A simulation of bargaining in the trade-union field. For information see J. D. Gearon, "Labor vs. Management: A Simulation Game," *Social Education*, October, 1966, pp. 421–22.

## 26. Interracial Simulation

Students participate in a process of attempting to integrate a racially mixed community of six different neighborhoods. Information may be obtained from David Yount and Paul De Kock, El Capitan High School, Lakeside, California 92040.

## 27. The Ghetto Game

The Ghetto Game simulates the pressures that the urban poor live under and the choices that face them as they seek to improve their life situation. It is a game of mobility in this particular socioeconomic group.

Each player is given a personal profile of his educational, family, and economic situation, together with the number of hour points he has available to play with each round. There are ten rounds in the game. In each round the player allocates his hours among several alternatives: work, school, hustling, passing time, welfare, and neighborhood improvement. Hours invested in these activites yield different degrees of satisfaction. The aim of the player is to maximize his satisfaction.

The game teaches that improving one's economic situation demands a wise and strategic use of time. It illustrates the fact that an early investment in education pays off throughout life. However, it also makes clear that there are great barriers to completing one's education in ghetto schools: inadequate staff and materials, family responsibilities, and emotional pressures that distract and discourage one from study.

The players learn that the condition of their neighborhood affects all of them, whether or not they are concerned about it. They find out that they can improve neighborhood conditions by investing effort in community action.

They experience vicariously the economic pressures that drive people to engage in illegal activities despite the risk involved, that cause people to choose to be on welfare, that motivate people to defer present gratification for a greater future reward. It deals with the ways in which having children affects one's economic situation and the special problems that working mothers have.

As he plays the game, the player has the experience of planning the life strategies for a poor person and meeting with the discouragement, frustrations, and occasional good luck that are the common lot of the poor.

The game is designed for ten players, but as few as six or seven can play. A four-round game can be played in one hour, a ten-round game in two hours.

Available through Western Publishing Company, 150 Parish Drive, Wayne, New Jersey 07470. Anticipated cost is $12 to $15.

## 28. Inter-City Competition

This is a game that deals with problems of community growth and development. It is described in Robert F. Edwards and Dorothy E. Francis, "Intercity Competition, the Community Growth Game," *General Systems*, 8:183–208, 1963.

## 29. The Counselor Game

This game has to do with the way in which a counselor invests his time within a school situation. It draws on some of the methods of business games, but criteria units for success relate to blocks of time rather than dollars. Feedback is given to the players regarding responses to their use of time by the school administration, the community, and students. Information may be obtained from Dr. Garry Walz, Educational Research and Information Center, University of Michigan, Ann Arbor, Michigan 48105.

## 30. Coin Game

This is a game dealing with insurgency and counterinsurgency and was developed by Dr. Clark G. Abt and Dr. Morton Gordon at Abt Associates, Cambridge, Massachusetts.

## 31. Counseling-Information Game

This is designed to model any situation in which one group of people is responsible for improving the performance of another group by providing them with information. The information exchanged in the game concerns a simple game of logic which is played by those who assume the roles of students or information-system users. Several teams of counselors compete—and cooperate—in an effort to improve the performance of those actually playing the logic game.

A rather wide array of problems are imbedded in the situation, ranging from those caused by too much or too little redundancy in the messages exchanged to those which stem from a failure to perceive the need for an evolving organizational structure within a team as members of the team gain skill and insight relative to the particular tasks they are performing.

A minimum of three hours is required, and a day-long session, involving considerable discussion of the problems encountered and their implications, may be the most desirable format for utilizing the game. Anywhere from sixteen to fifty players may participate at one time.

The game was developed by Professor Frederick L. Goodman of the School of Education, University of Michigan. Further details in *Educational Researcher: Newsletter of the American Educational Research Association*, Supplement 1967, p. 15.

## 32. Precinct Level Campaign Model

Electorial canvassing strategies may be explored through use of this computerized simulation. Information may be obtained through Professor Gerald Kramer of the University of Rochester.

## 33. Tracts

A sociopolitical simulation illustrating controversy over land use in a simulated core-city area. In Tracts, each student assumes the role of a member of a special-interest group, such as planning commission, urban-housing development, industry, and private land development. Each sector seeks to control the fate of sixteen city blocks through influence, incentive coalitions, and capital. Entire classroom may play. Cost $28.50. Information may be obtained from Instructional Simulations, Inc., Box 212, Newport, Minnesota 55055.

## 34. Campaign

A simulation dealing with the election of state legislators within a two party system. Issues, campaign tactics, news coverage, vote switching, and party workers are all factors affecting the candidates' actions and responses. Information may be obtained from Instructional Simulations, Inc., Box 212, Newport, Minnesota 55055.

## 35. Order

An opportunity to apply, or learn when to apply, rules of order for effective committee or group work. Based on Robert's Rules of Order, Order requires astute management of resolutions and people to maintain purpose and direction. Cost $48. Information may be obtained from Instructional Simulations, Inc., Box 212, Newport, Minnesota 55055.

(Most of the games that follow are basically research models or rather abstract in theoretical orientation. They are suggestive of possibilities rather than practical vehicles available for use in teaching application skills.)

## 36. Temper

Strategic decision making is the major process focused on in this simulation. It was developed by Dr. Clark C. Abt, Dr. Morton Gordon, and Mr. James Hodder of the Raytheon Company. Information may be obtained through Abt Associates, Cambridge, Massachusetts.

## 37. Political-Military Gaming Exercise

This game deals with political decision making and policy planning. It was developed by Professor Lincoln Bloomfield of M.I.T., from whom further information may be obtained.

## 38. National Policy Formation

This is a simulation of conflict among pressure groups with regard to policy issues. It was developed by Drs. Robert Boguslaw, Robert Davis, and E. B. Glick of the Systems Development Corporation, of Falls Church, California, and is available through that organization.

## 39. Conformity Status Characteristics

This is a computerized simulation of the persuasion process in small groups. It could be potentially utilized in gaming form. It is being developed by Professor Bernard Cohen of Stanford University, to whom request for further information should be addressed.

## 40. Homunculus

This is a computerized model of interpersonal relations with gaming potentials. It was developed by Dr. John T. and Jeanne E.

Gullahorn of the Systems Development Corporation, Santa Monica, California. See *Homunculus: A Simulation of Social Interaction,* Michigan State University, East Lansing, Michigan, 1962.

### 41. San Francisco Community Renewal Project Model

This is a computerized model dealing with land use and development. It was developed by the Arthur D. Little Company in order to predict and evaluate the composition, quantity, quality, cost, and demand for housing in the San Francisco area. The effects of various proposed policy actions may be traced through use of a computer program. Drs. Cyril C. Herman and Ira M. Robinson of A. D. Little, Inc., were the chief designers.

### 42. Crisiscom

Various aspects of affect in the decision maker's perception are highlighted in this computerized game. It is being developed by Professor Ithiel Pool of M.I.T.

### 43. Three-Person Coalition Game

This game focuses on bargaining and coalition formation. It is being developed by Professor William Riker of the University of Rochester. See William H. Riker and Richard C. Niemi, "Anonymity and Rationality in the Essential Three Person Game," *Human Relations,* 17:131–41, 1964.

### 44. Leviathan

This is a game using computerized methods to explore aspects of decision making in an organization. For information contact Dr. Sidney Rome, Systems Development Corporation, Santa Monica, California.

### 45. Two Person Non-Verbal Bargaining

Bargaining processes are explored in this game, with an emphasis on blocks to communication. Information may be obtained from Professor Thomas Schelling of Harvard University.

## 46. Territories Game

Bargaining tactics and communication are the subject of attention in this computerized game. Contact Dr. Gerald Shure, Systems Development Corporation, Santa Monica, California.

## 47. Pittsburgh Urban Renewal Model

This is a simulation of social and economic aspects of urban development in the Pittsburgh area. It attempts to simulate the entire metropolitan area, showing effects of decisions and interrelationships among such factors as employment flows, residential and commerical patterns of movement, and industrial growth. This simulation was designed by Dr. Wilbur Steger of the CONSAD Research Corporation, Pittsburgh, Pennsylvania.

This simulation centers around a mock election in the hypothetical community of Woodbury. Information is given to participants concerning the characteristics of each of the nine wards making up the area. Players represent various roles operative in political campaigns such as candidates, representatives, pressure-group activists, newspaper reporters, etc. Umpires evaluate the outcomes and effectiveness of various moves aimed at winning the campaign.

A description of this simulation can be found in "Woodbury Political Simulation: An Introduction to the Woodbury Political Simulation," from Professor Marshall H. Withed, Department of History and Political Science, Rensselaer Polytechnic Institute, Troy, New York 12181.

## APPENDIX C

# Source List—Simulation Games and Others

### I. General References on Simulations and Gaming

Abt, Clark C., "Heuristic Games for Secondary Schools." Cambridge, Mass.: Abt Associates, 1965 (mimeographed report).

————, "The Rediscovery of Exploratory Play, Problem-Solving and Heuristic Gaming as a More Serious Form of Education." Paper presented at the Lake Arrowhead Conference on Innovation in Education, December, 1965.

————, *Games for Learning.* Occasional Paper No. 7. Cambridge, Mass.: The Social Studies Curriculum Program, 1966.

————, *Serious Games,* New York: The Viking Press, 1970.

Bogdanoff, E., *et al. Simulation: An Introduction to a New Technology,* TM-499, Santa Monica, Calif.: Systems Development Corporation, March, 1960.

Boocock, Sarane E., and E. O. Schild, eds., *Simulation Games in Learning.* Beverly Hills, California: Sage Publications, 1968.

Caillois, Roger, *Man, Play, and Games.* New York: The Free Press, 1961.

Gagne, Robert M. "Simulators," in R. Glaser, ed., *Training Research and Education,* Science Editions, New York: John Wiley and Sons, Inc., 1965.

Geisler, M. A., *Integration of Modeling and Simulation in Organizational Studies.* Santa Monica, Calif.: The RAND Corporation, P-1634, Mandill, 1959.

Greenlaw, P. S., Herron, L. W., and R. H. Rawdon, *Business Simulation.* Englewood Cliffs, N. J.: Prentice-Hall, 1962.

Guetzkow, H. W., ed., *Simulation in Social Sciences: Readings.* Englewood Cliffs, N. J.: Prentice-Hall, 1962.

"Instructional Simulation Newsletter," *Teaching Research,* Oregon State System of Higher Education, Monmouth, Ore. 97361.

"Instructional Simulation: A Research Development and Dissemination Activity," *Teaching Research,* Oregon State System of Higher Education, Monmouth, Ore., 97361.

Malcolm, D. G., ed., *Report of System Simulation Symposium.* Baltimore: Waverly Press, Inc., 1957.

Project SIMILE, *Occasional Newsletter about Uses of Simulations and Games for Education and Training,* Nos. 1–3, September, 1965–April, 1966. Western Behavioral Sciences Institute, La Jolla, Calif.

Rapoport, Anatol, *Fights, Games and Debates.* Ann Arbor: University of Michigan Press, 1960.

Robinson, James A., "Simulation and Games," in Peter H. Rossi and Bruce J. Biddle, eds., *The New Media and Education.* Chicago: Aldine Publishing Company, 1966, pp. 85–123.

## II. *Business—Management—Economics*

Cohen, K. J., and Eric Rhenman, "The Role of Management Games in Education and Research." *Management Science,* 7:131–66 (1961).

Craft, C. J., *et al. Management Games.* New York: Reinhold, 1961.

Dill, William R. *et al. Proceedings of the Conference on Business Games.* New Orleans: School of Business Adminstration, Tulane University, 1961.

Greenlaw, P. S., *et al. Business Simulation.* Englewood Cliffs, N. J.: Prentice-Hall, 1962.

*Proceedings of the National Symposium on Management Games.* Lawrence, Kans.: Center for Research in Business, University of Kansas, May, 1959.

Rawdon, Richard H. Bureau of Industrial Relations, *Learning Management Skill from Simulation Gaming.* Ann Arbor, Mich.: University of Michigan, 1960.

Shubik, Martin, "Simulation of Industry and Firm," *American Economic Review* Vol. L:908–19 (1960).

*Simulation and Gaming: A Symposium.* American Management Association, Report No. 5, 1961.

Vance, Stanley, *Management Decision Simulation.* New York: McGraw-Hill, Inc., 1960.

## III. *Education: Teachers and Educational Administrators*

Cogswell, J. F., et al. *New Solutions to Implementing Instructional Media Through Analysis and Simulations of School Organization.* Technical Memorandum TM-1809, Santa Monica, Calif.: Systems Development Corporation, 1964.

Cruickshank, Donald R., *The Longacre School: A Simulated Lab-*

*oratory for the Study of Teaching.* Knoxville: University of Tennessee, College of Education, (mimeographed) n.d.

Culbertson, Jack, *Simulation in Administrative Training.* Columbus, Ohio: University Council for Educational Administration, 1960.

Fattu, N. A. and S. Elam (eds.), *Simulation Model for Education, Fourth Annual Phi Delta Kappa Symposium on Educational Design.* Bloomington, Ind.: School of Education, University of Indiana, 1965.

Forbes, John, "Operational Gaming and Decision Simulation." *Journal of Educational Measurement,* 2:15–18 (1965).

Hemphill, J. K., Griffiths, D. E., and N. Frederiksen, *Administrative Performance and Personality: a Study of the Principal in a Simulated Elementary School.* New York: Bureau of Publications, Teachers College, Columbia University, 1962.

Twelker, Paul A., "The Teaching Research Automated Classroom (TRAC): A Facility for Innovative Change." *The Journal of the Association for Programmed Learning,* in press. (Also available as a mimeographed paper from *Teaching Research,* Oregon State System of Higher Education, Monmouth, Ore. 97361.)

University Council for Education Administration, *Simulation in Administrative Trainees.* Columbus, Ohio: University Council for Educational Administration, 1960.

Vlcek, C., "Classroom Simulation in Teacher Education," *Audiovisual Instruction,* February, 1966.

Wynn, Richard, "Simulation: Terrible Reality in the Preparation of School Administrators." *Phi Delta Kappan,* 46:17–173 (1964.)

## IV. *Political Science—International Relations*

Bloomfield, Lincoln P., "Political Gaming," *U. S. Naval Institute Proceedings,* 86:57–64 (September, 1960).

Coher, Bernard C., "Political Gaming in the Classroom," *Journal of Politics,* 24:367–381 (1962).

Goldhamer, H., and Speier, H., "Some Observations on Political Gaming,"*World Politics,* 12:71–83 (October, 1959).

Guetzkow, H., Alger, C. F., Brody, R. A., Noel, R. C., and R. C. Snyder, *Simulation in International Relations: Developments for Research and Teaching.* Englewood Cliffs, N.J.: Prentice-Hall, 1963.

## V. *City Planning and Urban Development*

Duke, Richard D., *Gaming Simulation in Urban Research*. East Lansing, Mich.: Institute for Community Development, Michigan State University, 1964.

Feldt, Allan G., "Operational Gaming in Planning Education," *Journal of the American Institute of Planners*, 22:17–23 (January, 1966).

Grundstein, Nathan, "Computer Simulation of a Community for Gaming." Paper presented at the Denver Meeting of the American Association for the Advancement of Science, 1961.

Meier, Richard L., "Game, Procedure in the Simulation of Cities," in Leonard J. Duhl, ed., *The Urban Condition: People and Policy in the Metropolis*. New York: Basic Books, 1963, pp. 248–354.

## VI. *Other Fields*

Beaird, James H., and Standish, John T., *Audio Simulation in Counselor Training*. Final report, Title VII, Project No. 1245, NDEA of 1958, Grant No. 7–47–0000–235, December 1964.

Bellman, Richard, Friend, Merril B., and Kurland, Leonard, "Simulation of the Initial Psychiatric Interview." *Behavioral Science*, 11:389–399 (1966).

Berkun, M. M., "Psychological and Physiological Criteria for Stress Simulation Research." Paper read at 3rd Annual Symposium, Human Factors Society of Los Angeles, June, 1963.

Braithwaite, R. B., *Theory of Games as a Tool for the Moral Philosopher*. Cambridge: Cambridge University Press, 1955, 1964.

Brotman, L. and J. Minker, Computer Simulation of a Complex Communication System. (Abstract) Jorsa, 5, February, 1957.

Foster, R. J., and J. Danielian, *An Analysis of Human Relations Training and Its Implications for Overseas Performance*. Technical Report 66–15, Human Resources Research Office, George Washington University, Alexandria, Va., August, 1966.

Flagle, C. D., "Simulation Techniques," in C. C. Flagle, *et al.* eds., *Operations Research and Systems Engineering*. Baltimore: Johns Hopkins Press, 1960.

Kahn, H. and I. Mann, *War Gaming*. Santa Monica, Calif.: The RAND Corporation, P–1167, July 30, 1957.

Loughary, John W., Friesen, Deloss, and Robert Hurst Autocoun,

"A Computer-Based Automated Counseling Simulation System." *Personnel and Guidance Journal,* 45:6015 (Summer, 1966).

McKnight, A., and James and Harold G. Hunter, *An Experimental Evaluation of Driver Simulator for Safety Training,* Human Resources Research Office, George Washington University, Alexandria, Va., June, 1966.

Meier, Richard L., "Explorations in the Realm of Organization Theory. IV: The Simulation of Social Organizations,"*Behavioral Science,* 6: 232–48 (1961).

Rowan, T. C. "Simulation in Air Force System Training," in D. G. Malcolm, ed., *Report of System Simulation Symposium,* Baltimore: Waverly Press, Inc., 1958.

VII. *Bibliographies of Simulation and Gaming Materials*

Cruickshank, Donald R., "Related Readings on Simulation—A Bibliography." Knoxville, Tenn.: College of Education, University of Tennessee, mimeographed, n. d.

Deacon, A. R. L., Jr., *Selected References on Simulation and Games,* (processed). Saranac Lake, N. Y.: American Management Association Academy, April 1960.

Garvey, Sale M., and Sancha K., *Simulation, Role Playing and Sociodrama in the Social Studies: with an Annotated Bibliography.* The Emporia State Research Studies. Emporia, Kans. Kansas State Teachers College, December, 1967.

Harman, Harry H., "Simulation: A Survey," in *Proceedings of the Western Joint Computer Conference.* Los Angeles, Calif., July 1–9, 1961. (First printed as System Development Corporation paper, Report No. SP 260, July, 1961).

Hartman, John J., *Annotated Bibliography on Simulation in the Social Sciences.* Ames, Iowa: Agriculture and Home Economics Experimental Station, Iowa State University, 1966.

Hickok, W. H., *A Bibliography of Research Studies on Games and Simulations.* Portland, Ore.: Northwest Regional Education Laboratory, March, 1967.

"Instructional Uses of Simulation: A Selected Bibliography." *Teaching Research,* Oregon State System of Higher Education, Monmouth, Ore. In cooperation with Northwest Regional Educational Laboratory, Portland, Ore., September, 1967.

Malcolm, Donald G., "Bibliography on the Use of Simulation in Management Analysis." *Operations Research,* 8:169–177

(1960). This bibliography of system-simulation items represents a fair sampling of simulation literature up to 1960.

McClintock, Charles G., and David M. Messick, "Empirical Approaches to Game Theory and Bargaining: A Bibliography," in Ludwig von Bertalanffy and Anatol Rapoport, eds., *General Systems: Yearbook of the Society for General Systems Research.* 11:229–238 (1966).

Pitts, Forrest R., *Varieties of Simulation: A Review and Bibliography.* Bulletin No. 4, Bibliography Series. Philadelphia: Regional Science Research Institute, University of Pennsylvania, 1968.

Rapoport, A., and Carol Orwant, "Experimental Games: A Review." *Behavioral Science,* 7:1–37 (January, 1962).

Riley, Vera, and J. P. Young, *Bibliography on War Gaming* (processed). Baltimore: The Johns Hopkins University, April 1957.

Roecklein, J. E., *Simulation of Organizations: An Annotated Bibliography.* Alexandria, Va.: Human Resources Research Office, Division No. 4, George Washington University, Infantry, March, 1967.

Scott, E., *Simulation of Social Processes. A preliminary report of a survey of current research in the behavioral sciences.* Santa Monica, Calif.: Systems Development Corporation, TM–435, 1959, p. 15.

Shubik, Martin, "Bibliography on Simulation, Gaming, Artificial Intelligence, and Allied Topics," *Journal of American Statistical Association,* 55:736–751 (December 1960).

Tansey, P. J., and Derick Unwir, *Simulation Gaming in Education, Training and Business.* Coleraine, Northern Ireland: Education Center, New University of Ulster, July, 1969.

Thomas, L. Jean, ed., *A bibliography of reports issued by the behavioral sciences laboratory: Engineering Psychology, Simulation Techniques.* Wright-Patterson Air Force Base, Ohio: 657th Aerospace Medical Research Laboratories, Behavioral Sciences Laboratory, 1962.

Werner, Roland and Joan T., *Bibliography of Simulations: Social Systems and Education.* La Jolla, Calif.: Western Behavioral Science Institute, 1969.

VIII. *Centers of Activity in Simulation and Gaming*

Abt Associates, Inc., 55 Wheeler Street, Cambridge, Massachusetts
02138. Tel. (617) 491-8850. Dr. Clark C. Abt. This is a private
organization involved in simulation, gaming, systems analysis,
and model making. It has developed at least fifteen simulation
games for various organizations, addressed to a variety of age
groupings, from elementary to graduate students.

Board of Cooperative Educational Services in Northern Westches-
ter (BOCES). Center for Educational Services and Research,
845 Fox Meadow Road, Yorktown Heights, New York 10598.
Tel. (914) 245-7031. Dr. Richard L. Wing. Concentration on
computerized games oriented toward individual instruction in the
public schools. This is a special project funded in part by the
Office of Education and private grants.

Carnegie Institute of Technology, Graduate School of Industrial
Administration, Pittsburgh, Pennsylvania 15213. Tel. (412)
621-2600. A sizable faculty group has been involved in the
creation and continuing development of the Carnegie Tech Management Game. Expertise is available in designing highly complex, computerized gaming simulations.

Commission on Educational Media, Association for Supervision
and Curriculum Development, National Education Association,
Washington, D. C. The commission explores new teaching techniques. It sponsored a conference Simulation, Stimulation for
Learning, April, 1968, San Diego, California. Papers were presented on various aspects of and approaches to simulation in
the instructional setting.

Environmental Simulation Lab, School of Landscape Architecture,
University of Michigan, Ann Arbor, Michigan 48104. Tel. (313)
763-0258. Dr. Richard Duke. This project aims at the use of
simulation and gaming for the purpose of urban planning and
design. The lab is employed for the training of graduate students
in urban planning as well as for research into urban processes.

Johns Hopkins University, Department of Social Relations, Charles
and 34th Street, Baltimore, Maryland 21218. Tel. (301) 467-
3300. Dr. James S. Coleman. Some ten games have been or are
being developed by this project. It has received funding from the
Carnegie Foundation of New York. Emphasis is on noncom-
puterized simulation games related to social processes. The Staff

has organized a nonprofit corporation named Academic Games Associates to aid in making games available.

Northwestern University International Relations Program, Department of Political Science, Northwestern University, Evanston, Illinois 60201. Tel. (312) 492-3741. Dr. Harold Guetzkow. A considerable number of faculty members developed and have continued to work on the Inter-Nation Simulation. The group has had considerable experience in the use of simulated games for the purpose of teaching international relations and doing research international relations processes.

Nova Academic Games Project, Nova Schools and Nova University, Fort Lauderdale, Florida 33314. Tel. (305) 587-6660. Robert W. Allan. This project has utilized simulated games extensively in a basic academic program. The Nova Academic Olympics has attracted participants from various parts of the country. Films and other materials promoting and illustrating the use of simulation games have been produced by the project staff. Ford Foundation support aids the program. The project uses existing games and has developed additional ones of its own.

Project SIMILE, Western Behavioral Sciences Institute, 1121 Terrey Pines Road, La Jolla, California 92037. Tel. (714) 459-3811. Dr. Hall Sprague. This project was founded through initial funding from the Kettering Foundation for the specific purpose of developing simulation games and other simulations for teaching purposes. It serves in part as a coodinating agency for those involved in the field and activity promotes the use of simulations by teachers through workshops, newsletters, and the like. The project has also designed some half-dozen simulation games for junior high through adult age levels.

Science Research Associates, 259 East Erie Street, Chicago, Illinois 60611. Tel. (321) 944-7552. Miss Michele Del Genie. An organization which distributes simulation games, programmed-instruction materials, and other educational tools.

Simulmatics Corporation, 16 East 41st Street, New York, New York 10017. Tel. (212) 246-4022. An organization specializing in the fabrication and distribution of simulation games.

The Social Studies Curriculum Program, Educational Services, 15 Mifflin Street, Cambridge, Massachusetts 02138. Tel. (617) 868-5800. Dr. Lawrence. The purpose of the Social Studies Curriculum Program is to enhance the teaching of social studies in the public schools through the use of new approaches and new media. In developing units of study in the social-studies area, games and other simulations are being drawn upon and created. Social Studies Curriculum Study Center, 1809 Chicago Avenue, Evanston, Illinois 60201. Dr. Cleo Cherryholmes. This project is developing simulations for use in social-studies curricula.

Systems Development Corporation, Santa Barbara, California 93102. This organization has focused on systems analysis and training methods for use in Air Force Operations. Extensive use has been made of simulations and gaming for training purposes. See William R. Goodman, "The Systems Development Corporation and Systems Training," *The American Psychologist,* 1:524–28 (August, 1957).

Systems Gaming Associates, 769 South Aurora Street, Ithaca, New York 14850. Mr. Anthony Bruce Dotson. This organization focuses on simulation gaming in the area of urban planning, and has chiefly been involved in the distribution of CLUG (Cornell Land Use Game). It offers consultation in gaming techniques.

Teaching Research, a division of the Oregon State System of Higher Education, Oregon College of Education, Monmouth, Oregon 97361. Tel. (503) 838-1220. Dr. Paul A. Twelker. This project has focused on the development of a range of simulation techniques for the training of teachers, and has conducted evaluative studies of effectiveness. Several bulletins and reports have been issued and a newsletter has been instituted. In the summer of 1968, the Project, in cooperation with the Office of Education, conducted a four-week institute entitled: Simulation in College Instruction: Institute in Educational Media for College and University Faculty Personnel. Proceedings are expected.

# Source List—Programmed Instruction

## A. Selected References on Programmed Instruction

GENERAL

Campbell, Ina, *Teaching Machines and Programmed Learning: A Bibliography*. New York: Teaching Materials Corp., 1961.

Galanter, Eugene, ed., *Automatic Teaching: The State of the Art*. New York: John Wiley and Sons, 1959.

Lumsdaine, A. A., and R. Glaser, eds., *Teaching Machines and Programmed Learning: A Source Book*. Washington, D. C.: National Education Association, 1960.

Lysaught, Jerome P., and Clarence M. Williams, *A Guide to Programmed Instruction*. New York: John Wiley and Sons, 1963.

Parnes, Sidney J., *Programming Creative Behavior*. USOE Title VII Project No. 5–0716. Buffalo, N. Y.: State University of New York, 1966.

Rubia, Eugene D., *Bibliography of Published Self-Instructional Programs in Health Sciences,* Ann Arbor, Mich.: Center for Research on Learning and Teaching, University of Michigan, 1967.

Stolurow, Lawrence M., "Programmed Instruction and Teaching Machines" in Peter H. Rossi and Bruce J. Biddle, eds., *The New Media and Education*. Chicago: Aldine Publishing Company, 1966, pp. 124–76.

SOCIAL WORK

Bertcher, Harvey, "Skill Instruction for Social Work." Paper presented at Field Instructor's Meeting, University of Michigan, Ann Arbor, Mich., May 17, 1967.

Ehlers, Walter H., "Computer Assisted Instruction." Paper presented at Annual Program Meeting, Council on Social Work Education, Minneapolis, January 24, 1968.

Polak, Edward, "Sequential Specification of Learning Tasks and Teaching Foci in Group Work Field Instruction—Preliminary

Draft." Paper presented at Field Instructor's Meeting, University of Michigan, Ann Arbor, Mich., May 17, 1967.

Thomas, Edwin J., and Roger M. Lind, "Programmed Instruction as Potentially Useful in Social Work Education: An Annotated Bibliography." *Social Work Education Reporter*, 15: 22–27 (March, 1967).

Wallace, Henry J., "Programmed Instruction and Social Work: An Analysis of Problems and Possibilities." Ann Arbor, Mich.: Community Systems Foundation, January, 1968.

## B. Directory of Publishers of Programmed Instruction Materials

ADDISON: Addison-Wesley Publishing Company, Inc., Reading, Mass. 08167.

ALLYN: Allyn and Bacon Inc., 150 Tremont Street, Boston, Mass. 02116.

AJN: American Journal of Nursing, P.I. Reprints, 10 Columbus Circle, New York, N. Y. 10019.

AMA: American Management Association, Inc., 135 West 50th Street, New York, N. Y. 10020.

ANN ARBOR: Ann Arbor Publishers, 610 Forest, Ann Arbor, Mich. 48104.

APPLETON: Appleton-Century Crofts, 440 Park Avenue South, New York, N. Y. 10016.

ARGYLE: Argyle Publishing Corporation, 200 Madison Avenue, New York, N. Y. 10016.

ASSOCIATION: Association Press, 291 Broadway, New York, N. Y. 10007.

BEHAVIORAL: Behavioral Research Laboratories, Ladera Professional Center, Box 577, Palo Alto, Calif.

COLUMBIA U: Coulmbia University, Teachers College, Bureau of Publications, 525 West 120th Street, New York, N. Y.

CORONET: Coronet Learning Programs, Coronet Instructional Films, 65 East South Water Street, Chicago, Ill. 60601.

DOUBLEDAY: Doubleday & Company, Inc., 501 Franklin Avenue, Garden City, N. Y. 10017.

ETC: Education and Training Consultants Company, 979 Teakwood Road, Los Angeles, Calif. 90049.

ED SYSTEMS: Educational Systems Development, 31270 Stephenson Highway, P. O. Box 457, Royal Oak, Mich. 48068.

FEARON: Fearon Publishers, Inc., 2165 Park Boulevard, Palo Alto, Calif. 94306.

FOLLETT: Follett Publishing Company, 1010 West Washington Boulevard, Chicago, Ill. 60607.

GINN: Ginn and Company, Statler Building, Boston, Mass. 02117.

GRAFLEX: Graflex, Inc., 3750 Monroe Avenue, Rochester, N. Y. 14603.

HARCOURT: Harcourt, Brace & World, Inc., 757 Third Avenue, New York, N. Y. 10017.

HARPER: Harper & Row, Publishers, Inc., 49 East 33rd Street, New York, N. Y. 10016.

HEATH: D. C. Heath and Company, 285 Columbus Avenue, Boston, Mass. 02116.

HOUGHTON: Houghton Mifflin Company, 110 Tremont Street, Boston, Mass. 02107.

HUMAN: Human Development Institute, 1299 W. Peachtree Street, N. E., Alanta, Ga. 30309.

IES: International Educational Services, Inc., Division of International Textbook Co., Dept. 852A, Scranton, Pa. 18515.

IRWIN: Richard D. Irwin, Inc., 1818 Ridge Road, Homewood, Ill. 60430.

LEARNING: Learning Inc., 131 East Sixth Avenue, Scottsdale, Ariz. 85215.

McGRAW: McGraw-Hill Book Co., 330 W. 42nd Street, New York, N. Y. 10036.

MACMILLAN: The Macmillan Company, 866 Third Avenue, New York, N. Y. 10022.

MAYNARD: Maynard Research Council, 718 Wallace Avenue, Pittsburgh, Pa. 15221.

NCR: National Cash Register, Marketing Services, Dayton, Ohio 45409.

PRENTICE: Prentice-Hall, Inc., Englewood Cliffs, N. J. 07632.

PROG LEARN: Programmed Learning of London Limited, 111 Mount Plesant Avenue, London, Ontario, Can.

RESOURCES: Resources Development Corporation, 2736 Grand River Avenue, East Lansing, Mich. 48823.

SCOTT: Scott, Foresman and Company, 1900 East Lake Avenue, Glenview, Ill. 60025.

VIDEOSONIC: Videosonic Systems Division, Unitutor Texts, Hughes Aircraft Co., P.O. Box 3310, Fullerton, Calif. 92634.

WADSWORTH: Wadsworth Publishing Company Inc., Ralston Park, Belmont, Calif. 94002.
WILEY: John Wiley & Sons, Inc., 605 Third Avenue, New York, N. Y. 10016.

### C. Programmed Instruction Materials of Potential Use in Community Organization Education *

ADMINISTRATION AND MANAGEMENT

*The Act of Delegating.* N. Gardner and J. Davis (DOUBLEDAY). 126 pp. $3.95. Guide to the sensible distribution of work. For efficient use of employee's and manager's time and potential.

*Business Administration: An Introductory Management Approach.* A. Weimer (IRWIN). 125 pp., supplement; $7.95 text. Programmed supplement to chapter "Decision Help from Linear Programming Game Theory & Related Areas" included with text N/C. Text not programmed.

*Effective Executive Practices.* N. Gardner (DOUBLEDAY). 364 pp. $4.95. Successful practices in problems of time, authority, decisions, planning, management contracts and functions. Index

*How to Be a Good Executive.* (IES). Part I, $4.95; the organized mind, executive development, drive. Part II, $4.95; handling people, executive responsibility.

*Objective Decision Making Program.* (MAYNARD). $100. Solving complex problems through use of matrix algebra and linear programming procedures.

*Principles of Management: A Program for Self-Instruction.* L. Kazmier (McGRAW). 320 pp., $2.95 soft, $4.95 cloth ed. For management development courses or in addition to other texts. Instructor's manual.

*Programmed Organization and Management Principles.* H. H. Albers and L. Schoer (WILEY). 115 pp. $2.95. Involves the student with decision-making problems in a variety of business and industrial contexts.

COMMITTEES AND BOARDS

*Step by Step in Better Board and Committee Work.* R. Sorenson and W. C. Tuck (ASSOCIATION). 119 pp. $3.

* From Carl A. Hendershot, *Programmed Learning: A Bibliography of Programs and Presentation Devices,* Bay City, Mich., Carl A. Hendershot, n.d.

DATA PROCESSING

*Basic Computer Programming.* T. Scott (DOUBLEDAY). 492 pp. $5.95. A nontechnical introduction to basic operating principles of digital computers and guide to techniques of programming. Index, self-tests.

*Computer Programming Techniques.* T. Scott (DOUBLEDAY). 664 pp. $7.95. Follows above volume. Subroutines, editing, debugging, floating decimal arithmetic, etc. The most widely used machine languages. Both volumes can be of use to those who only need to identify problems for computer solution. Index.

*Fundamentals of Processing Data Electronically* (NCR). 4 hrs.; 22 pp.; $2. Introductory overview of data processing. Not oriented to any specific equipment. Four volumes.

*A Programmed Introduction of PERT: Program Evaluation and Review Technique—Federal Electric* (WILEY). 145 pp. Bus.-Ind. $3.95. For project planning. PERT diagrams and associated work-flow charts.

ECONOMICS

*The American Economics System.* R. Attiyeh, K. Lumsden and S. Weiner (BEHAVIORAL). Set of seven texts and supplement: *Capitalism, Communism and Socialism,* $2.40; *The Federal Reserve System and Its Effect on Money and Banking,* $2.40; *The Free Enterprise System,* $2.40; *The Gross National Product,* $2.40; *International Trade,* $2.40; *The Problems of Economic Stability and Growth,* $2.40; *Taxes and Government Spending,* $2.40. The set of seven is $8.95. Basic concepts of economics applied to current economic problems. For each volume: test booklet, 54 cents, teacher's manual, 75 cents. Specimen sets include text, tests, manual.

*Student Guide for Economics and the Modern World,* 2nd ed. L. Abbott, J. Brown and S. Parry (HARCOURT). 240 pp. $3.25. Spring 1967. To complement the text. Programmed units in key theoretical chapters.

*Student's Manual to Accompany Modern Economics.* L. Tarshis (HOUGHTON). 350 pp. Intro. Econ. $3.95 est. Manual by G. Winston and F. S. O'Brien. Approx. 108 pp. Programmed. January, 1967.

*U.S. Monetary Policy.* P. Park and L. Lidwell (ED. SYSTEMS). An introduction. 3–6 hrs.; 69 frames; $2. Objectives and execution of policies, Federal Reserve Banks, instruments of monetary policy.

HEALTH

*Health, Health Problems, and Health Agencies.* Jensen, Poindexter and DuBois (ED. SYSTEMS). 3–6 hrs.; 170 frames; $2. January, 1967.

INSTRUCTIONAL TECHNIQUES

*Analysis as a Process.* L. Silvern (ETC). 15 min. 44 frames. $36. Steps in analyzing. Stimulus-response situations. 44 color 35-mm. slides plus a 15-minute tape.

*Designing Instructional Systems.* L. Silvern (ETC). Sound-slide presentations for group instruction.

*Fundamentals of Teaching Machine and Programmed Learning Systems.* L. Silvern (ETC). $33.

INTERPERSONAL RELATIONS

*Business and Industrial Relationship Improvement Program* (HUMAN). 600 frames. Bus. Ind. $19.50. Interpersonal relationships for the management team developed through structured and nonstructured interaction with others. Two or more persons required. Part 1, two persons working together; Part 2, six to sixteen persons participating.

*General Relationship Improvement Program* (HUMAN). 600 frames. $19.50. For leadership training to civic organizations; religious groups; professional work such as business administration, nursing, mental hygiene; psychology courses. Interaction of two participants in conversation, role playing, directed and nondirected discussions. Oriented to facilitate change in one's relationships with others.

LAW

*Practical Law.* W. Lehman (DOUBLEDAY). 414 pp. $4.95. Everyday legal matters. Sales, insurance contracts, mortgages, leases, deeds. Index, glossary of terms, discussion of federal and state court systems.

MEDICAL-NURSING

*Fundamentals of Nutrition II.* Aids of Diagnosis. M. M. Seedor (COLUMBIA U.). 336 pp. $4. Basic Patient Care: A Programmed Introduction to Nursing Fundamentals. Anderson (SAUNDERS). 10 hrs.; 234 pp. $3.75. Post-tests, checklists, illustrations, index.

Reprints of articles published in *The American Journal of Nursing* (AJN). "Anxiety Recognition and Intervention," 55 cents, 10 copies $4.50, 25 copies $10.50. "Intravenous Infusion of Vasopressors," 55 cents, 50 copies $19., 100 copies $35. "Ward Management for Quality Patient Care" 55 cents, 50 copies $19, 100 copies $35.

PARLIAMENTARY PROCEDURE
*How to Conduct Meetings: A Programmed Instruction Manual on Parliamentary Procedure.* Wiksell (HARPER). 6 hrs. 500 frames; $2.50.
*Parliamentary Procedure.* J. Gray and R. Rea (SCOTT). 780 frames. $2. For more efficient use of Robert's Rules of Order (Revised), copy required for references.
*Parliamentary Procedure.* W. Lehman (DOUBLEDAY). 347 pp. $4.95. Rules, motions, points of order, appeal, organizations, officers' duties. Index, dictionary of terms, actions, and procedures.

PERSONNEL PRACTICES AND SUPERVISION
*How to Improve Your Supervisory Training Skills.* J. Blyth and M. Alter (ARGYLE). 3¼ hrs.; 262 frames; $9.75. Putting effective techniques to use.
*Introduction to Basic Supervision of People.* R. J. Burby (ADDISON). 175 pp. $4.95. Basic principles of supervision. Skills and guidelines for supervisors.
*Prime VII: Effective Interviewing for the Supervisor* (AMA). 15 hrs.; 859 frames; $27. Nondirective approach; employment, appraisal, and disciplinary interviewing.
*Prime VIII: On-the-Job Training* (AMA). 14 hrs.; 1,055 frames; $27. For first-time managers. Determining training needs and guidelines.

POLITICAL SCIENCE
*The American Constitution.* G. Leinwand (DOUBLEDAY). 396 pp.; $5.95. History, purpose, and function. Checks and balances, powers and procedures in American democracy. Index, glossary.
*American Government.* S. B. Rosenhack (BEHAVIORAL). Vol. I, 870 frames, $3.67; Vol. II, 119 frames, $3.67. The federal sys-

tem, division of powers and responsibilities. Lawmaking, branches of government, political behavior. For each book: tests, 48 cents; manual, 56 cents.

*The Bill of Rights* (CORONET). 15–30 min. 301 frames; $1.50.

*Every Four Years: A Programmed Text on the Presidential Electoral System.* V. Penn, Teaching Systems Corp. (ALLYN). 201 frames. $1.08. Emphasis on the growth and development of the electoral system. Teacher's manual with tests and historical notes.

*How a Bill Becomes Law* (GINN). 612 frames. $1.08. Federal legislation.

*How a Bill Becomes Law.* F. Newman (MACMILLAN). 574 frames; $3.48, $1.04. Mechanics, aspects, and influences of lawmaking in the U. S. Congress, including committee hearings, filibusters, lobbying, etc. Reviews. Teacher's manual $1.44.

*An Introduction to American Government.* Rosenhack #6520 (ADDISON). 966 frames; $4.60. Instructor's manual with tests #6521, $1.30. The basic structure and functions of the Federal Government.

*The Members of Congress* (LEARNING); United States Constitution. P. McCloskey, Jr. (BEHAVIORAL). 923 frames; 25 cents and $2.87. Includes historical setting up of the constitution, formation of the state governments, branches of Federal Government, Bill of Rights. Tests, 41 cents; manual, 53 cents.

*Our Federal Constitution.* Hanshaw, Gothsall, Thompson and Rogers (PRENTICE). $2.76. The fundamental principles and their application as shown through direct quotations from the Constitution.

*The United States Constitution.* McCloskey #4550 (ADDISON). 923 frames; $3.60. Instructor's manual with tests #4551, $1.15. Understanding the language of the Constitution, its historical precedents and interpretations.

PROGRAMMED LEARNING

*Fundamentals of Teaching Machine and Programmed Learning Systems.* L. C. Silvern (ETC). 40.1 hrs.; 1752 steps; $33 complete. No device required. Administrative Factors Guide (110 pp.) describing tryout and validation data; $4.50. Has three wire-bound volumes and plastic folio with sliding mask.

*Good Frames and Bad: A Grammar of Frame Writing.* S. Markle (WILEY). 278 frames; $4.95. For those writing or selecting units of programmed instruction. Basic instruction and experience in frame construction. Instructor's manual available.

*A Guide to Evaluating Self-Instructional Programs.* Jacobs, Maier and Stolurow (HOLT). The "How-To's" of Programming (VIDEOSONIC). $950. A self-instructional audiovisual workshop course in the methods and techniques of producing audiovisual programs. Orientation, analyses, script writing, photographing, narration, recording, finalization. On film in 7 programs. Use of VIDEOSONIC Model 102BR machine included.

*Preparing Instructional Objectives.* R. Mager (FEARON). 62 *pp.;* $1.75. A programmed approach to the preparation of objectives for programmed and other instructional materials.

*Programmed Learning: A Practicum.* Rummler, Smith, Brethower, Market and Schrader (ANN ARBOR). 1 hr.; 54 frames; $5. For writers of programmed instruction. Also suitable for those supervising the use of programs or seeking effective techniques for conventional instruction.

PSYCHOLOGY AND GUIDANCE

*Improving Communication in Marriage* (HUMAN). 500 frames; $14.50.

*An Overview of Psychology.* J. Waxler, A. P. Osanyi (ED. SYSTEMS). 3–8 hrs.; 106 frames; $2.25. General psychology, areas of specialization.

PUBLIC RELATIONS AND COMMUNICATION

*An Auto-Instructional Text in Correct Writing.* Everett, Dumas and Wall (HEATH). 402 pp.; $4. Diagnostic test, vocabulary building, exercises in correct writing and applying rules learned. Suitable for high-school business.

*Effective Writing.* K. Smith and J. Stapleford (DOUBLEDAY). 481 pp.; $5.95. Writing clear, forceful prose, including subject-verb agreement, pronoun reference, and arrangement of ideas. Index.

*How to Listen and Read Effectively* (ARGYLE). $9.75. To be published.

*How to Say What You Mean* (AMA). 5 hrs.; 386 frames; $15. For clear expression. Tested on supervisors, chief clerks, stenographers, clerks, correspondents. Spiral-bound manual, tests, vinyl mask.

*How to Write Effective Reports.* Federal Electric Corp. #2045

(ADDISON). 310 pp.; $6.95. Rules for readable, interesting, and correct reporting. Instructor's manual #2047.

*Improving Your Written Communications.* S. Parry (ARGYLE). 4¾ hrs.; 318 frames; $9.75. For all levels of managemet. Writing letters, memos, reports.

*The Memorandum.* J. Ball (RESOURCES). 2 hrs.; 145 frames; $1.25.

*Prime V: Basic Skills in Communication* (AMA). 20 hrs.; 1,094 frames; $27. Using words effectively, interpreting statements, generalizations, accurate and persuasive communications.

*A Program for Effective Writing.* J. Reid and R. Shurter (APPLETON). 252 pp.; $3.90. Practical application of writing principles. For class work or homework with class instruction.

*Public Relations* (IES). Part 1, "The Why and Where of Public Relations"; 399 frames; $4.95. You and public relations, business and public attitudes toward PR, costs. Part 2, "The What and How of Public Relations"; 321 frames. $4.95. Techniques and policies, trade and customer relations.

SOCIAL PROCESSES

*Basic Sociological Concepts.* Abell, Dent, and Lyon (PROG. LEARN). 2 hrs.; 174 frames; $1.25.

*The Environments of Modern Society.* T. Tollefson, L. Blatch and D. Fiems (ED. SYSTEMS). 2–6 hrs.; 164 frames; $2.00. Urbanization, suburbanization.

*Social Behavior: A Program for Self-Instruction* (McGRAW). 459 pp.; $4.95 est.

*Social Conflicts in Modern Society.* Blatch, Tollefson, Feims and Meuser (ED. SYSTEMS). 3–6 hrs.; 104 frames; $2. Intergroup conflicts, prejudice.

*The Social Process Framework.* M. Tondow, M. Orten and V. V. Arnspiger (FOLLETT). 733 frames; $3.20. Values to improve ability to make decisions, for personal development.

*Social Stratification in Modern Society.* Blatch, Tollefson, Carolyn and Meuser (ED. SYSTEMS). 2–6 hrs.; 163 frames; $2.00. Roles, types, systems, U. S.

STATISTICS

*Descriptive Statistics: A Programmed Textbook.* L. Gotkin and L. Goldstein (WILEY). Vol. 1, 858 frames; $3.95. Contains "fast tract" for review. Teacher's manual is available. From sampling through measures of dispersion. Worksheets and problems included. Normal curve, correlation, regression.

*Descriptive Statistics.* H. Alexander and R. Smith (HEATH). 15–20 hrs.; 114 pp.; $2.55. Elementary statistics. Auxiliary to the lecture or as basic text. Test and index.

*Introduction to Probability (65004).* A. Gratian (GRAFLEX). 1–2 hrs.; 216 frames; $1. Reading level 7.5. Probability ($P = f/n$) and multiplication principle. Permutations and factorial notation. Teacher's manual.

*Probability: A Programmed Workbook.* ENTELEK Incorporated #4866 (ADDISON). 958 frames; $4.95. To accompany texts on probability by Mosteller-Rourke-Thomas (mastery of symbolic language as used in the textbook).

*Programmed Introduction to Statistics.* F. Elzey (WADSWORTH). 376 pp.; $5.25. A basic or supplementary text. Suggested for nonmath-oriented, social-science and psychology courses. Elementary statistics; analysis of variance, interpreting statistical tests, computations. Prerequisite: minimum basic algebra. Glossary and tables for reference.

*Statistical Concepts: A Basic Programme.* Amos, Brown and Mink (HARPER). 263 frames; $1.75. For general educational psychology, introduction to behavioral science.

*Statistical Concepts: A Program for Self-Instruction.* C. McCollough and L. Van Atta (McGRAW). 1,200 frames; $3.95 soft; $5.95 cloth. Teacher's manual.

*Statistics: A Unit for Introductory Psychology.* Kinchla #3690 (ADDISON). 1,614 frames; $5.25. Logic of statistical inference and statistical description of data, variables, distributions. Teacher's manual with tests #3691.

SYSTEMS IN EDUCATION AND TRAINING

*Analysis as a Process.* L. C. Silvern (ETC). 15 min.; 44 frames; $36. 44 color 35-mm. slides; 15-min. prerecorded tape, workbook; instructs how to analyze objects, actions, and information.

*Basic Analysis.* L. C. Silvern (ETC). 19.7 hrs.; 623 frames; $39.50. All devices and equipment supplied. Has Administrative Factors Guide (72 pp.) describing tryout and validation data, $2.80. Has one wirebound text, plastic folio with sliding mask, two reels of 8-mm. color film, viewer with lamp and batteries, one reel ¼-in. prerecorded magnetic tape, one kit of physical objects.

210 A New Look at Field Instruction

*Model Concept and Simulation.* L. C. Silvern (ETC). 29 min.; 52
frames; $42. 52 color 35-mm. slides; 29-min. prerecorded tape;
presents synthesis of simulation process in flow-chart form.
*Systems Engineering of Learning—The Training System.* L. C. Silvern and D. G. Perrin (ETC). 46 min.; 108 optical frames; $40.
Black-and-white filmstrip (35-mm.) with accompanying prerecorded magnetic tape, 3.75 ips, monophonic. Instructs system
conceptualizations using flow-chart model techniques, describes
methods of system analysis and synthesis.
*Systems Using Feedback.* L. C. Silvern (ETC). 22 min.; 35 frames;
$30. 85 color 35-mm. slides, 22-min. prerecorded tape; concept
of feedback, step by step.

SOME ADDITIONAL PROGRAMS OF RELEVANCE TO SOCIAL WORK
Bertcher, Harvey and Frank F. Maple. "Group Composition: An
Instructional Program," Ann Arbor, Michigan: The University
of Michigan, School of Social Work, September, 1967.
Bertcher, Harvey and Sheldon Rose. "Establishing a Contract with
the Group," Ann Arbor, Michigan: The University of Michigan,
School of Social Work, in process.
Kamp, Martin and John Starkweather. "The Electronic Computer
as an Interviewer," Sacramento: State of California, Department
of Mental Hygiene, Bureau of Research, July 1965.
Silverberg, Dana, James Brink, and Roger Lind. "Social Work
Interviewing Program-experimental," Ann Arbor, Michigan: The
University of Michigan, School of Social Work, October 1966.
Starkweather, J. M. Kamp and A. Monto. "Psychiatric Interview
Simulation by Computer," *Methods of Information in Medicine,*
6:15–23, 1967.
Thomas, Edwin and Ronald Feldman. *Concepts of Role Theory:
An Introduction Through Programmed Instruction and Pro-
grammed Case Analysis.* Ann Arbor, Michigan: Campus Pub-
lishers, 1964.

# List of References

1. Edith Abbott, *Social Welfare and Professional Education,* (Chicago: University of Chicago Press, 1942), p. 59.
2. Clark C. Abt, "Simulation Games for Community Action Planning with the Poor," Cambridge, Mass., Abt Associates, n.d. (mimeographed).
3. Jack A. Adams, "Some Considerations: the Design and Use of Dynamic Flight Simulators," in Howard Guetzkow, ed., *Simulation in Social Science: Readings,* (Englewood Cliffs, N. J.: Prentice-Hall, 1962), pp. 29–47.
4. G. Lester Anderson, "Professional Education: Present Status and Continuing Problems," in *Education for the Professions* (Chicago: National Society for the Study of Education, 1962), p. 18.
5. G. Lester Anderson and Merton W. Ertell, "Extra-Institutional Forces Affecting Professional Education," in *Education for the Professions,* (Chicago: National Society for the Study of Education, 1962), p. 235.
6. Herbert H. Aptekar, "Supervision and the Development of Professional Responsibility: An Application of Systems Theory." Paper presented for field instructors, Wurzweiler School of Social Work, Yeshiva University, April 29, 1965 (mimeographed).
7. Eugene H. Baker, "A Pre-Civil War Simulation for Teaching American History," in Sarane S. Boocock and E. O. Schild, *Simulation Games in Learning* (Beverly Hills, Calif.: Sage Publications, 1968), pp. 135–43.
8. Albert Bandura and Richard H. Walters, "Social Learning and Personality Development," in Leonard Krasner and Leonard P. Ullman, eds., *Research in Behavior Modification,* (New York: Holt, Rinehart and Winston, 1965).
8a. Robert L. Barker and Thomas L. Briggs, *Differential Use of*

*Social Work Manpower* (New York: National Association of Social Workers, 1968), pp. 160–68.

9. Mildred C. Berry, "Field Work Training in Community Organization," in *The Community Organization Method in Social Work Education* (New York: Council on Social Work Education, 1959), pp. 72–73, 80–81.

10. Howard Becker and James Carper, "The Development of Identification with an Occupation," *American Journal of Sociology,* 61:289–98 (1956).

11. Bernard Berelson, *Graduate Education in the United States,* Carnegie Series in American Education (New York: McGraw-Hill Book Company Inc., 1960).

12. Lloyd Blanch, *Education for the Professions* (Washington, D. C.: Government Printing Office, 1955).

12a. Benjamin S. Bloom, ed., *Taxonomy of Educational Objectives Handbook I: Cognitive Domains* (New York: Longmans, Green & Co., 1956).

13. Werner W. Boehm, *Objectives of the Social Work Curriculum of the Future* (New York: Council on Social Work Education, 1959), Chapter IX, p. 36.

14. Sarane S. Boocock, "An Experimental Study of Learning Effects of Two Games with Simulated Environments," *American Behavioral Scientist,* 10:8–17 (1966).

15. ——— and James S. Coleman, "Games with Simulated Environments in Learning," *Sociology of Education,* 39:215–236 (1966).

15a. ——— and E. O. Schild, *Simulation Games in Learning* (Beverly Hills, Calif.: Sage Publications, 1968).

16. John S. Brubacher, "The Evolution of Professional Education," in *Education for the Professions* (Chicago: National Society for the Study of Education, 1962), pp. 63, 65.

17. Eveline M. Burns, "Tomorrow's Social Needs and Social Work Education," *Journal of Education for Social Work,* 2:10–20 (Spring, 1966).

18. Mary E. Burns, "Historical Development of the Process of Casework Supervision." Dissertation. University of Chicago, August, 1958.

19. A. M. Carr-Saunders and P. A. Wilson, *The Professions* (Oxford: Clarendon Press, 1933).

20. Cleo H. Cherryholmes, "Developments in Simulation of International Relations for High School Teaching." Unpublished master's thesis, Kansas State Teachers College, 1963.

21. ———, "Some Current Research on Effectiveness of Educational Simulations: Implications for Alternative Strategies," *American Behavioral Scientist,* 10:4–7 (1966).

21a. *Closing the Gap in Social Work Manpower* (Washington, D. C.: U. S. Department of Health, Education and Welfare, 1965).

22. Morris L. Cogan, "Toward a Definition of Profession," *Harvard Educational Review,* 23:33–50 (Winter, 1953).

23. K. J. Cohen, et al., "The Carnegie Tech Management Game," *Journal of Business,* 33:303–321 (1960).

24. ———, "The Carnegie Tech Management Game," in Harold Guetzkow, ed., *Simulation in Social Science: Readings,* (Englewood Cliffs, N. J.: Prentice-Hall, 1962), pp. 104–23.

25. ———, *The Carnegie Tech Management Game: An Experiment in Business Education* (Homewood, Ill.: Richard D. Irwin, 1964).

26. James Coleman, et al., *Adolescent Society* (New York: The Free Press, 1961), p. 324.

27. "Community Organization Curriculum Development Project: Progress Report and Project Plans," Council on Social Work Education, February 18, 1966 (mimeographed).

28. W. D. Caplin, "Inter-Nation Simulation and Contemporary Theories of International Relations," *American Political Science Review,* 60: 562–78 (1966).

29. Lela B. Costin, "Values in Social Work Education: A Study," *Social Service Review,* 38:271–80, September, 1964, p. 276.

30. "Curriculum Plan for the Two Year Community Work Program." School of Social Service Administration, University of Chicago, May, 1966 (mimeographed).

31. Bess Dana, "The Role of National Agencies in Stimulating the Improvement and Expansion of Field Instruction Resources," in *Field Instruction in Graduate Social Work Education: Old Problems and New Proposals* (New York: Council on Social Work Education, 1966), pp. 63, 64.

32. Richard E. Dawson, "Simulation in the Social Sciences," in Harold Guetzkow, ed., *Simulation in Social Science: Readings,* (Englewood Cliffs, N. J.: Prentice-Hall, 1962), p. 1.

33. William R. Dill and Neil Doppelt, "The Acquisition of Experience in a Complex Management Game," *Management Science,* 10(1), 30–46, 1963. (Reprinted in "Simulation Models for Education," Fourth Annual Phi Delta Kappa Symposium on Educational Research. Bloomington, Ill.: Phi Delta Kappa, pp. 71–103, 1965.)

34. William R. Dill, James R. Jackson, and James W. Sweeney, *Proceedings of the Conference on Business Games* (New Orleans: Tulane University, 1962), p. 16.

35. William R. Dill, et al., *Tulane University Conference on Business Games,* (New Orleans: Tulane University, 1961), p. 13.

36. Richard D. Duke, *Gaming Simulation in Urban Design* (Lansing, Mich.: Institute for Community Development and Services, 1964).

38. Minna Green Duncan, "An Experiment in Applying New Methods in Field Work," *Social Casework,* 44:185–92 (April, 1963).

39. Arthur Dunham, *Community Welfare Organization* (New York: Thomas Y. Crowell Co., 1958).

40. ————, *Types of Jobs in Community Organization* (Columbia, Mo.: Department of Regional and Community Affairs, School of Social and Community Services, 1960).

41. "Editorial Notes: The Agency's Responsibility for Field Instruction," *Social Casework,* 44:210 (April, 1963).

42. *Education for the Professions.* Sixty-first Yearbook. (Chicago: National Society for the Study of Education, 1962).

42a. "Education: Its Contribution to the Manpower Equation," Arnulf M. Pins, in *Manpower in Social Welfare: Research Perspectives,* Edward E. Schwartz, ed. (New York: National Association of Social Workers, 1966), pp. 108–42.

43. Walter H. Ehlers, "Computer Assisted Instruction in Social Work." Paper delivered at the Annual Program Meeting, Council on Social Work Education, Minneapolis, January, 1968.

44. Elizabeth Elmer, "Mental Health Emphasis in Casework Field Instruction," *Social Work,* 7:77–83 (July, 1962).

45. Nicholas A. Fater and Stanley Elam, eds., *Simulation Models for Education* (Bloomington, Ind.: Phi Delta Kappa, 1965).

45a. Fedele Fauri, "Achieving the Great Society, the Contribution of Social Work Education." Paper, Annual Meeting, Council on Social Work Education, January, 1966.

46. Allan G. Feldt, "Operational Gaming in Planning Education," *Journal of the American Institute of Planners,* 22:17–23 (January, 1966), p. 19.

47. *Field Instruction in Graduate Social Work Education: Old Problems and New Proposals* (New York: Council on Social Work Education, 1966).

48. Abraham Flexner, "Is Social Work a Profession?" *Proceedings of the National Conference of Charities and Correction* (Chicago: The Hildmann Printing Company, 1915), pp. 576–90.

49. David G. Gil, "Social Work Teams," *Child Welfare,* October, 1965, pp. 442–46.

50. Ruth Gilpin, "Concurrence in the Block Plan of Social Work Education." University of Pennsylvania, Dissertation. June, 1960.

51. Deborah Golden, Arnulf Pins, and Wyatt C. Jones, *Students in Schools of Social Work: A Study of Characteristics and Factors Affecting Career Choice and Practice Concentration* (New York: Council on Social Work Education, 1971).

52. William J. Goode, "Encroachment, Charlatanism, and the Emerging Profession: Psychology, Sociology and Medicine," *American Sociological Review,* 15:903 (December, 1960).

53. Paul S. Greenlaw, Lowell W. Herron, and Richard H. Rawdon, *Business Simulation in Industrial and University Education* (Englewood Cliffs, N. J.: Prentice-Hall, 1962).

54. "Training for Policy-Making Roles through Organizational Simulation," in *Proceedings,* 14th Annual Conference, American Society of Training Directors, May, 1958.

55. Harold H. Guetzkow, et al., *Simulation in International Relations: Developments for Research and Teaching* (Englewood Cliffs, N. J.: Prentice-Hall, 1963).

56. Mark P. Hale, "The Parameters of Agency-School Social Work Educational Planning," *Journal of Social Work Education,* 2:32–40 (Spring, 1966).

57. Lowell W. Herron, *Executive Action Simulation* (Englewood Cliffs, N. J.: Prentice-Hall, 1960).

57a. Margaret E. Hoffman, "Experiment in Block Field Placement—the Block Plan at West Virginia University, 1946–48." West Virginia University School of Social Work (mimeographed).

58. Michael Inbar, "The Differential Impact of a Game Simulating a Community Disaster," *American Behavioral Scientist,* 10:18–27 (1966).

59. ———, "Individual and Group Effects on Language and Learning in a Game Simulating a Community Disaster," in Sarane S. Boocock and E. O. Schild, eds., *Simulation Games in Learning* (Beverly Hills, Calif.: Sage Publications, 1968), pp. 169–70.

60. ———, "The Theoretical Background of the Community Response Game." Ann Arbor, Mich.: University of Michigan, n.d. (mimeographed).

60a. Betty Lacy Jones, ed., *Current Patterns in Field Instruction in Graduate Social Work Education* (New York: Council on Social Work Education, 1969).

61. Wyatt C. Jones with Jack Rothman, "Community Organization Field Instructions: Report of an Informal Survey." Community Organization Curriculum Development Project (New York: Council on Social Work Education, November, 1966), mimeographed.

62. Jadwiga Judd, et al., "Group Supervision: A Vehicle for Professional Development," *Social Work,* 7:96–102 (January, 1962).

63. Alfred Kadushin, "Interview Observations as a Teaching Device," *Social Casework,* 37:334–41 (1956).

64. Katherine A. Kendall, "Education for Social Work," *Social Work Yearbook* (New York: Columbia University Press, 1954), p. 172.

65. John C. Kidneigh, "History of American Social Work," in *The Encyclopedia of Social Work* (New York: National Association of Social Workers, 1965), p. 15.

66. Walter L. Kindelsperger, "Responsible Entry into the Profession—Some Current Issues," *Journal of Education for Social Work,* 2:41–50 (Spring, 1966).

67. ———, and Helen Cassidy, *Social Work Training Centers: Tentative Analysis of the Structure and Learning Environment* (New Orleans: School of Social Work, Tulane University, 1966).

68. Richard L. Kozelka, "Business—the Emerging Profession," in *Education for the Professions* (Chicago: National Society for the Study of Education, 1962), pp. 168–89.

69. Dorothy Lange, "Four Processes of Field Instruction in Casework: The Field Instructor's Contribution to Instructor-Student Interaction in Second Year Field Work," *Social Service Review,* 37:263–73 (September, 1963).

70. Armand Lauffer, "A New Breed of Social Activists Comes to Social Work: Comparison of Community Organization Students with Their Peers in Casework and Group Work," *Journal of Education for Social Work,* 7:41–51 (Winter 1971).

71. Mary Lewis, Dorothy Howerton, and Walter L. Kindelsperger, *An Experimental Design for First-Year Field Instruction* (New Orleans: School of Social Work, Tulane University, 1962).

72. Gertrude Leyendecker, "A Family Agency Reviews Its Educational Program," *Social Casework,* 44:210 (April, 1963).

73. Ronald Lippitt, et al., *The Dynamics of Planned Change* (New York: Harcourt, Brace, 1958).

74. Eugene Litwak and Henry J. Meyer, "The School and the Family: Linking Organizations and External Groups," in Paul F. Lazersfeld, et al., eds., *The Uses of Sociology* (New York: Basic Books, 1967).

75. Harry L. Lurie, *The Community Organization Method in Social Work Education* (New York: Council on Social Work Education, 1959).

76. Kenneth S. Lynn, ed., "The Professions," *Daedalus,* Vol. 94 (Fall, 1963).

77. Jerome P. Lysought and Clarence M. Williams, *A Guide to Programmed Instruction* (New York: John Wiley and Sons, 1963), p. 2.

78. Robert H. MacRae, "Community Organization," in *The Community Organization Method in Social Work Education* (New York: Council on Social Work Education, 1959), p. 173.

79. Robert F. Mager, *Preparing Instructional Objectives* (Palo Alto, Calif.: Fearon Publishers, Inc., 1962).

80. Rachel B. Marks, "Education for Social Work," in *The Encyclopedia of Social Work* (New York: National Association of Social Workers, 1965), p. 281.

80a. Margaret Matson, *Field Experience in Undergraduate Programs in Social Welfare,* (New York: Council on Social Work Education, 1967).

81. T. R. McConnell, G. Lester Anderson, and Pauline Hunter, "The University and Professional Education," in *Education for the Professions* (Chicago: Society for the Study of Education, 1962), pp. 254–78.

82. John McDonald and Franc Ricciardi, "The Business Decision Game," *Fortune,* Vol. LVII, No. 3 (1958), pp. 140–214.

83. William J. McGlothlin, *Patterns of Professional Education* (New York: G. P. Putnam's Sons, 1960), pp. 52, 213–34.

84. ———, *The Professional Schools* (New York: The Center for Applied Research in Education, 1964), p. 104.

85. Earl J. McGrath, *The Graduate School and the Decline of Liberal Education* (New York: Teachers College, Columbia University, 1959).

86. ———, "The Ideal Education for the Professional Man," in *Education for the Professions* (Chicago: Society for the Study of Education, 1962), pp. 281–301.

87. Rita A. McGuire, "Field Instruction in Social Group Work." Dissertation, Columbia University, January, 1963.

88. Wilbert J. McKeachie, "Research on Teaching at the College and University Level," in N. L. Gage, ed., *Handbook of Research on Teaching* (Chicago: Rand McNally & Co., 1963), pp. 118–72.

89. ———, "Students Groups and Teaching Methods," *The American Psychologists,* 13:580–84 (1958).

90. James L. McKenny and William R. Dill, "Influences on Learning of Simulation Games," *American Behavioral Scientist,* 10:26–32 (1966).

91. ———, "Variations in Administrative Techniques in Two Business Games," in Sarane S. Boocock and E. O. Schild, eds., *Simulation Games in Learning* (Beverly Hills, Calif.: Sage Publications, 1968), pp. 217–31.

92. C. F. McNeil and Robert B. Lefferts, "A Point of View about Community Organization for Social Welfare," in *The Community Organization Method in Social Work Education* (New York: Council on Social Work Education, 1959), pp. 205–06.

93. Elizabeth G. Meier, *The History of the New York School of Social Work* (New York: Columbia University Press, 1954), pp. 35, 40.

94. Richard L. Meier, "Explorations in the Realm of Organization Theory IV: The Simulation of Social Organization," *Behavioral Science,* 6:232–48 (July, 1961).

95. ———, "Gaming Procedure in the Simulation of Cities," *The Urban Condition* (New York: Basic Books, 1963), p. 358.

95a. ———, "Introduction," in Richard D. Duke, *Gaming Simulation in Urban Research* (East Lansing, Mich.: Michigan State University Press, 1964), p. iii.

96. Eleanor Merrifield, "Changing Patterns and Programs in Field Instruction," *Social Service Review,* 37:274–82 (September, 1963).

97. Robert K. Merton, *Social Theory and Social Structure* (New York: The Free Press, 1957).

98. ———, et al., *The Student Physician* (Cambridge, Mass.: Harvard University Press, 1957).

99. *METRO, A Gaming Simulation: Toward a New Science of Urban Planning* (Lansing, Mich.: Tri-County Regional Planning Commission, January, 1966).

100. George E. Miller, "Medicine," in *Education for the Professions* (Chicago: National Society for the Study of Education, 1962), p. 112.

101. Gerald W. Miller, "An Attempt to Determine Certain Effects of Laboratory Classroom Simulation Training on Selected Dimensions of Teacher Behavior." Unpublished doctoral dissertation, University of Oregon, August, 1967.

102. *New York Times,* November 26, 1967, p. 134.

103. Robert E. Ohm, "Gamed Instructional Simulation: An Exploratory Model," *Educational Administration Quarterly,* April, 1966, p. 110.

104. Guy H. Orcutt, "Simulation of Economic Systems," *The American Economic Review,* Vol. L, No. 5 (1960), p. 895.

105. Michael Parkis, "Center of Learning and Teaching," University of Michigan (mimeographed), p. 5.

106. "A Plan for Field Instruction" School of Social Work, University of Michigan, February 21, 1966, (mimeographed).

107. George Plutchok, "Supervision in Group-Service Agencies: Its Universality and Particularity." Dissertation, University of Pennsylvania, May, 1963.

108. Mildred Pratt, "Faculty-Student Manual—Community Laboratory" (Pittsburgh: Graduate School of Social Work, University of Pittsburgh, 1965–1966).

109. S. L. Pressey, "A Simple Apparatus Which Gives Tests and Scores—and Teaching," *School and Society,* 23:373–76 (1926).

110. ————, "Development and Appraisal of Devices Providing Immediate Automatic Scoring of Objective Tests and Concomitant Self-Instruction," *Journal of Psychology,* 29:417–47 (1950).

110a. "Proposed Community Organization Field Instruction Program," Berkeley, Calif.: University of California (mimeographed), 1967.

111. Eva Schindler-Raiman, "Community Organization: Selected Aspects of Practice." Ph.D. dissertation, University of Southern California, June, 1962.

112. Jeanette Regensburg, "A Report of Exploratory Project in Field Instruction," in *Field Instruction in Graduate Social Work Education: Old Problems and New Proposals* (New York: Council on Social Work Education, 1966), pp. 23–56.

113. *Regional Planning for Social Work Education* (Nashville, Tenn.: Vanderbilt University and Scarritt and Peabody Colleges, 1948).

114. Bertha C. Reynolds, *Learning and Teaching in the Practice of Social Work* (New York: Farrar and Rinehart, 1942).

115. Mary E. Richmond, "The Need for a Training School in Applied Philanthropy," *NCCC Proceedings,* 1897, pp. 181–88.

115a. Lilian Ripple, ed. *Innovations in Teaching Social Work Practice,* (New York: Council on Social Work Education, (1970).

116. James A. Robinson, "Simulation and Games," in Peter H. Rossi and Bruce J. Biddle, eds., *The New Media and Education* (Chicago: Aldine Publishing Co., 1966), p. 86.

117. Alex Rosen, "A Social Work Practitioner to Meet New Challenges," in *The Social Welfare Forum* (New York: Columbia University Press, 1965), pp. 224–37.

118. Hans Rosenhaupt, *Graduate Students' Experience at Columbia University* (New York: Columbia University Press, 1958).

119. Peter H. Rossi and Bruce J. Biddle, eds., *The New Media and Education* (Chicago: Aldine Publishing Company, 1966).

120. Beulah Rothman, "Process of Socialization to the Profession of Social Work." Dissertation, Columbia University, June, 1963.

120a. Jack Rothman, "Education for Professional Application: A Study of Field Instruction in Community Organization." Community Organization Curriculum Development Project, Council on Social Work Education, August, 1966 (mimeographed).

121. Francis J. Ryan and Donald R. Bardill, "Joint Interviewing by Field Instructor and Student," *Social Casework,* 45:471–74 (October, 1964).

121a. Irwin T. Sanders, *Making Good Communities Better* (Lexington, Ky.: University of Kentucky Press, KP107, rev. 1953).

122. Margaret S. Schubert, "Curriculum Policy Dilemmas in Field Instruction," *Journal of Social Work Education,* 1:35–46 (Fall, 1965).

122a. ———, *Field Instruction in Social Casework* (Chicago: University of Chicago Press, 1963).

123. Meyer Schwartz, "Professional Training for Community

Work." Annual Program Meeting, Council on Social Work Education, January, 1959 (mimeographed).

124. Thomas Sherrard, "Curriculum Development Studies and Manpower Needs—Some Implications for Curriculum Building." National Conference on Social Welfare, May 25, 1965 (mimeographed).

125. Everett C. Shimp, "The Case for A Curriculum in Community Organization for Social Welfare," in Harry L. Lurie, ed., *The Community Organization Method in Social Work Education* (New York: Council on Social Work Education, 1959), pp. 231–45.

126. Frances Shively, "An Analysis of the Construct 'Relationship' as It Is Used in Social Work." Dissertation, Washington University (St. Louis), June, 1961.

127. Mildred Sikkema, "A Proposal for an Innovation in Field Learning and Teaching," in *Field Instruction in Graduate Social Work Education: Old Problems and New Proposals,* (New York: Council on Social Work Education, 1966), pp. 1–22.

128. B. F. Skinner, "The Science of Learning and the Art of Teaching," *Harvard Educational Review,* 24:86–97, 1954. Also in A. A. Lumsdrive and R. Glaser, eds., *Teaching Machines and Programmed Learning: A Source Book* (Washington: National Educational Association, 1960).

129. ———, "Teaching Machines," *Science,* 128:969–77 (1958).

129a. Judith M. and Donald E. P. Smith, *Child Management: A Program for Parents* (Ann Arbor, Mich.: Ann Arbor Publishers, 1967).

130. Elliot Dunlap Smith, ed., *Education for Professional Responsibility* (Pittsburgh: Carnegie Press, 1948).

130a. "Social Welfare Administration and Policy: Practice Skill Training." University of Michigan, School of Social Work, Fall, 1967 (mimeographed).

131. "Social Change Through Social Welfare and the Law," in *The Social Welfare Forum, 1965* (New York: Columbia University Press, 1965).

132. Mary Louise Somers and Paul Gitlin, "Innovations in Field

Instruction in Social Group Work," *Journal of Education for Social Work Education,* 2:52–58 (Spring, 1966).

133. Hall T. Sprague, "Using Simulations to Teach International Relations," Project SIMILE, Western Behavioral Sciences Institute, La Jolla, Calif., n.d.

134. *Statistics on Social Work Education, 1954, 1963* (New York: Council on Social Work Education).

135. Jack D. Steele, "How Valuable Is Simulation as a Teaching Tool," in *Simulations and Gaming: A Symposium.* AMA Management Report no. 55 (New York: American Management Association, 1961), pp. 27–37.

136. Bernice Stephens, "An Experiment: A Brief Field Experience in Social Welfare Planning and Social Action for Casework Students," *Social Work Education Reporter,* March, 1966, pp. 24–25.

137. Lawrence M. Stolurow, "Programmed Instruction and Teaching Machines," in Peter H. Rossi and Bruce J. Biddle, eds., *The New Media and Education* (Chicago: Aldine Publishing Company, 1966), p. 143.

138. "A Study of Educational Uses of Simulation." Western Behavioral Science Institute, La Jolla, Calif., February, 1966 (mimeographed).

140. B. Richard Teare, Jr., "Engineering," in *Education for the Professions* (Chicago: National Society for the Study of Education, 1962), pp. 120–39.

141. Edwin Thomas and Roger M. Lind, "Programmed Instruction as Potentially Useful in Social Work Education: An Annotated Bibliography," *Social Work Education Reporter,* 15:22–27 (March, 1967).

142. Charlotte Towle, "The Place of Help in Supervision," *Social Service Review,* 37:403–15 (December, 1963).

143. ———, *The Learner in Education for the Professions* (Chicago: The University of Chicago Press, 1954).

144. *Training for Social Work: Third International Survey* (New York: United Nations, Department of Economic and Social Affairs, 1958), p. 108.

145. *Training for Social Work: Fourth International Survey* (New York: United Nations, Department of Economic and Social Affairs, 1964).

224                                        **A New Look at Field Instruction**

146. John Turner, "Urban League Business—an Approach to Action." Paper presented at the 1966 Conference of the Urban League, Philadelphia, Pennsylvania, July 31–August 4, 1966.

147. Barbara K. Varley, "Socialization in Social Work Education: A Study of the Value Areas of Change and Non-Change During Social Work Training." Dissertation, Western Reserve University, September, 1962.

148. Henry J. Wallace, "Programmed Instruction and Social Work: An Analysis of Problems and Possibilities," *Social Work Education Reporter,* March, 1967.

149. ———, "Programmed Instruction and Social Work," Ann Arbor, Mich., Community Systems Foundation, January, 1968.

149a. Roland L. Warren, *Studying Your Community* (New York: The Free Press, 1965).

149b. *Where It's At,* Radical Education Project (San Francisco: The Movement Press, 1967).

150. Margaret Williamson, *Supervision—New Patterns and Processes* (New York: Association Press, 1961).

151. Richard L. Wing, "Two Computer-Based Economics Games for Sixth Graders," in Sarane S. Boocock and E. O. Schild, eds., *Simulation Games in Learning* (Beverly Hills, Calif.: Sage Publications, 1968) pp. 155–65.

152. Ernest F. Witte, *Realities of Staffing Social Welfare Programs, The Social Welfare Forum* (New York: Columbia University Press, 1963), pp. 178–94.

152a. Peter Wolff, *The Game of Empire.* Occasional Paper, No. 9, The Social Studies Curriculum Program, Cambridge, Mass. 1966.

153. Gerald Zaltman, "Degree of Participation and Learning in a Consumer Economics Game," in Sarane S. Boocock and E. O. Schild, eds., *Simulation Games in Learning* (Beverly Hills, Calif.: Sage Publications, 1968).